CAN DO

Campbell Newman and
the Challenge of Reform

CAN DO

CAMPBELL NEWMAN AND THE CHALLENGE OF REFORM

Gavin King

Connor Court Publishing

Connor Court Publishing Pty Ltd

Copyright © Gavin King 2015

ALL RIGHTS RESERVED. This book contains material protected under International and Federal Copyright Laws and Treaties. Any unauthorised reprint or use of this material is prohibited. No part of this book may be reproduced or transmitted in any form or by any means, electronic or mechanical, including photocopying, recording, or by any information storage and retrieval system without express written permission from the publisher.

PO Box 224W
Ballarat VIC 3350
sales@connorcourt.com
www.connorcourt.com

ISBN: 9781925138658 (pbk)

Cover design by Aaron Coshaw

Cover photo by Dominika Lis

Printed in Australia

Contents

Preface	vii
1. The Die is Cast	1
2. Newcomers	21
3. What It Takes	48
4. Top Job for an Outsider	86
5. King of a Divided Castle	112
6. Outcomes	145
7. The Cost of Victory	168
8. Policy Versus Politics – Part One	196
9. Policy Versus Politics – Part Two	218
10. A New Journey	270
Epilogue – Reform: A Call to Arms	284
Author's Acknowledgements	322
Appendix: Campbell Newman's Key Achievements in Public Office	324
References	327

Preface

One of my favourite anecdotes about Campbell Newman is the one told by some of his former backbenchers. The maxim many of them lived by during their term as the Government of Queensland goes something like:

> What's worse than getting a call from Campbell Newman at 7:30 in the morning?
>
> Seeing three missed calls from Campbell at 7:45am.

It says much about the sharp respect he commanded among those who worked with and for him, whether it was his time as an army officer, business manager, Lord Mayor or Premier. You had to be on your game with Campbell. He demands very high standards of his staff and colleagues, almost as high as the bar he sets for himself.

Another reflection on Campbell I particularly agree with is a phrase originally coined to describe Tony Abbott, who was deposed as Prime Minister just days before this book hit the printing presses. Marketing and election campaign veteran Toby Ralph wrote that "if you want to hate Abbott, you'd best not meet him". Having worked with him on the 2004 campaign for Brisbane Lord Mayor and observed him from afar, Ralph believes the same theory applies to Campbell. Like so many figures in the public realm, the private side of Campbell Newman is worlds apart from the perception his enemies and many in the broader community formed of him via the media, the unions and various vested interest groups.

If I had to sum up the chasm between the private reality and the public perception of Campbell Newman, I'd turn to a most unlikely source in Jenny Macklin. Her description of Kevin Rudd's personality in her interview for the ABC television series *The Killing Season* was short and perfect. When asked to describe the dichotomy of Rudd's personality – the opposite and equal forces of his relentless drive and his compassion – Macklin simply shrugs and sums him up with the three-word phrase: "People are complex". She could've been talking about so many political leaders throughout history. She could have been talking about the Campbell Newman I came to know and write about it in this book.

Throughout the process of interviewing and writing about him, I sought out those who had worked with him or known him on a personal level. The perceptions of armchair critics and the broad-stroke observations from those who had fleeting interactions with him are not featured in this book. All too often in today's society the very people who are paid to shape the public's view of a political leader – the journalists, press galleries, commentators, union leaders and academics – have had little if any qualitative exposure to the elected official they're espousing a view on. In contemporary public life, we tend to skate over the complexity of our leaders and believe the sound bites, the tweets, the internet memes and the cheap headlines fed to us every minute of every day.

Some of the people I spoke to for this book had mixed and often negative views about Campbell, but most who had more than a cursory experience of his company praised and admired him. My experience and opinion of him has evolved since working as an Assistant Minister and Member of Parliament in his LNP Government between 2012 and 2015. Increasingly I found him to be an engaging and caustically funny bloke, a fan of Monty Python who can break out into a word-for-word rap rendition of one of his favourite songs, Eminem's "Lose Yourself". He is fast-paced, whip smart and sharper than a tack, as you would expect from an engineer with an MBA who consulted to multi-national firms before making the transition to leader of Australia's largest council and, ultimately, Premier of Queensland. He is genuinely concerned and interested in people's well-being and their health. Spend more than 10 minutes with him in one sitting and you're likely to experience a combination of all of the above.

On occasion, he can also be frustrating to deal with, sometimes dismissive or abrupt. As his long-term colleague and friend Ben Myers says: some people have high EQs, the measure of emotional intelligence, and Campbell isn't one of them. When faced with a problem or difficult situation, the high EQ politician gives platitudes and hugs. Campbell gives solutions and action plans. Instead of endearing himself to the person he's helping and making it look good for the cameras, Campbell's busy making a list.

First and foremost Campbell Newman is a family man: the son of two parents he loved deeply and, in terms of his father, misses terribly after he was taken too soon; the protective and loving father of two girls and, perhaps most tellingly, the devoted, loyal and affectionate husband to Lisa.

He's also a leader, and a complex one. He was a conviction politician, and he paid the price at the ballot box after one term in government. The ups and downs of that three-year term, his fascinating family history, as well as his varied careers in the army, the private sector, and politics are all explored in this book. If nothing else, this is a yarn about a bloke who sacrificed a lot and gave his best to get things done.

While his time as Premier of Queensland was brief, his tenure altered the course of politics in ways both overt and subtle. By the time he lost the 2015 election, unions were revitalised and emboldened, election campaigns were dirtier and more personal, politicians had retreated into a timid shadow of the profession's former self, and the reform agenda had stalled. The changes he enacted and lessons he learned provide important topics for debate. The challenge of reform and the nature of government, service delivery and economic growth are explored in the final section of this book.

I hope you enjoy it and debate it, as much as I did writing it.

Gavin King

1

The Die Is Cast

Early 2011

Campbell Newman sits in an elevated row of pews looking down on a funeral service, a slow burn of frustration with the Queensland Government playing on his mind. The temperature is already 30C on this muggy Wednesday morning of 2 February 2011. The atmosphere is even more oppressive inside the high-spired Albert Street Uniting Church in Brisbane's CBD. Campbell, the 47-year-old Lord Mayor of Brisbane, takes off his dark suit jacket to cope with the heat. It's so hot the lacquer of the pews becomes sticky and stains the back of his white business shirt.

Flanked on both sides by two of his closest confidantes in Mark Brodie and Ben Myers, Campbell reflects on his life and career and his future. He tells himself it's now or never. The state Labor Government is no longer listening to local councils on a range of issues across Queensland. His working relationship with Premier Anna Bligh is almost untenable, bordering on poisonous. They've been at each other's throats for years now.

The situation on his side of politics is also unravelling, at least behind the scenes. With an election looming, the Liberal National Party is struggling to make any inroads to power with John-Paul Langbroek as Opposition Leader. Despite all of the Government's follies, another Labor win in the upcoming election is increasingly on the cards. The LNP hierarchy is nervous. They fear the party is headed for a rerun of the election loss in 2009. Back then, when LNP leader Lawrence Springborg took on Premier Anna Bligh, polling showed the newly merged conservative party was a chance of winning government against the embattled Labor incumbent.

Now, the latest polling is showing up similar trends. But while the published polls show the LNP is the front-runner, it is by no means a convincing lead. Friction between Langbroek's office and LNP headquarters is increasing, with personalities in both camps clashing. Broader concerns within the party are mounting about Langbroek's small target, softly-softly approach. Talk about the need for a replacement within LNP circles is heating up.

Familiar call to service

Unbeknownst to either LNP headquarters or Langbroek's office, Campbell is reaching his own conclusion on state political matters as the funeral carries on below him. Through a mix of circumstance and chance, Campbell is experiencing a familiar call to arms. A funeral had previously served as an agent of change in his life. It was a process of reflection and remembrance at his father Kevin Newman's funeral service more than a decade earlier in July 1999 that first led him into politics. As the then Prime Minister John Howard delivered the eulogy, Campbell was in the front row of pews, weighing up his own mortality. It was then he first realised he wanted more than a financially successful business career.

This latest pivotal moment inside the Brisbane church is a continuation of his family's trajectory into public service. For decades, the Newmans had served; in the army, for the community, around the Cabinet table of federal governments. Kevin Newman had taken an enormous leap of faith in the late 1970s to leave a distinguished army career and make a run at a safe Labor seat in Tasmania. He won in a landslide.

On this muggy morning in Brisbane in 2011, some 35 years after his father's career gamble paid off, Campbell decides it's time for him to roll the dice too. The stakes now are much higher than the odds faced by his father. True to form and character, Campbell is going to crash through or crash in the biggest game of chance he had ever taken.

A complex plan

In the solemn surrounds of this heritage-listed church on Albert St, a strategic, highly complex plan unfolds in his head. Like so many challenges and projects he had managed in the past, Campbell checks off a mental list. He is, after all, a man with three decades of experience across three different careers. First he was a military engineer, then a logistics and management consultant in the private sector, and now he's a capital city Lord Mayor delivering billions of dollars' worth of road and traffic infrastructure.

The first step of his plan is possibly the easiest to make. He will resign from the high-profile position of Brisbane Lord Mayor, the largest Local Government authority in the Southern Hemisphere. Campbell had enjoyed seven years of popularity and success. He is Can Do Campbell, and for a time the most senior Liberal Party politician in Australia following the downfall of the Howard Government in 2007. With the next council election due in around 12 months – a campaign he is expected to win in a landslide – his decision to stand down would be a tectonic shock, but something he had already discussed with his wife Lisa.

As this plan rapidly develops in his mind, the second move is more audacious and fraught with complexity and risk. Almost simultaneously with his resignation as Lord Mayor, he would make one of the boldest political moves Australia had ever seen. Campbell is going to making a run as the next Premier of Queensland from outside the Parliament. It would be a personal and professional risk of exceptional magnitude.

While he made this decisive call as he sat reflecting on his future during that funeral service on 2 February, he was driven to this fork in the road of his career by the harrowing events of the past few weeks.

The politics of flooding

Campbell had long highlighted the failings of successive state Labor Governments to keep pace with the water storage and flood mitigation infrastructure Brisbane's high population growth demanded. Numerous reports and recommendations over the years exposed the need for action, particularly in the Brisbane River and Bremer River catchments. But the reports were all rejected and dismissed by successive Labor Governments, and very little was ever done. Similarly, the previous Labor Lord Mayor and Council had shirked their responsibilities on this issue.

With the storm season approaching in late 2010, Campbell had publicly warned of "raging torrents" and the grave threat to thousands of local properties. His dire predictions were brushed aside as unnecessary scare-mongering. About four weeks after issuing his warning, Campbell's predictions of dangerous flooding came true. The waters began rising in low-lying suburbs on the morning of 11 January. By that afternoon, Brisbane River had broken its banks. More than 2100 streets in 94 suburbs across the city were evacuated. When the river peaked on 13 January, an estimated 15,000 homes and businesses and 160 roads had been inundated. More than half of the city's ferry terminals were severely damaged or in some cases swept away. In the first four days following the floods, more than 32,000 tonnes of debris was trucked out of affected suburbs, the equivalent of two months' worth of rubbish typically collected in Brisbane.

The city is still cleaning up the aftermath of the most destructive floods in a generation when Campbell exits the church and steps onto Albert St on this bright and humid morning of 2 February. To a degree, he is still smarting from the earlier criticism over his storm warnings. But Campbell doesn't want vindication. Instead, he wants the Government to take action to avoid such widespread destruction in the future.

Journalist Piers Akerman, writing in *The Daily Telegraph* in the days after the floods, noted:

> Despite warnings by scientific and engineering experts in 1999, successive Labor-dominated Brisbane councils and Queensland Labor Governments worked to reject and bury recommendations for sweeping changes in planning, emergency relief and transparency when true flood levels for Brisbane were revealed in the aftermath of the record 1974 floods.[1]

With an eye on Anna Bligh's resurgence in the polls and how it might propel Labor to victory at the next state election, Campbell believes Queenslanders deserve to know that more could, and should, have been done.

On a political level, LNP president Bruce McIver knows Campbell's leadership throughout the disaster would provide the circuit-breaker the LNP needed to curb Bligh's renaissance. But McIver isn't too hopeful Campbell will make the switch. As recently as 22 January, the Lord Mayor had ruled out the move to state politics in an interview with *The Australian*:

> Mr Newman's strong performance since Brisbane flooded last week reignited hopes among some conservatives that he could be drafted to state politics to buttress the Liberal National Party. But he put paid to that, affirming that he would stay put in City Hall. 'I've committed to do another term in this city. I'm standing for election in March next year'.[2]

Contrary to popular theories, the recognition Campbell received for his work during the floods plays a minor role in his unprecedented leap to the state arena. While his elevated profile and leadership during the floods made the move more viable than ever, his resentment at the Labor Government's policy failures over recent years is the most powerful motivating factor behind his plan.

Campbell dislikes hypocrisy above most other personal qualities of politicians, and Bligh's enthusiastic embrace of the community in the wake of the natural disaster is exasperating. Bligh and her Government had failed to act on flood mitigation. They had scoffed at his predictions of a flood disaster just a couple of months earlier. The hypocrisy on the issue of flooding is just the latest in a litany of let downs, lies and railroading behaviour by Queensland Labor Governments. Campbell believes the Labor Party's focus had shifted from delivering good governance in the interest of Queenslanders to a win-at-all-costs mentality. They had become hell-bent on staying in power for power's sake.

The Bligh Government's treatment of Councils is another personal grievance. Bligh, in particular, seems utterly resistant to any devolution of power that would allow Local Government authorities to make decisions impacting their own communities and constituencies. The Bligh Government's centralised 'we know best' attitude towards local Councils had angered Mayors across the state. For Campbell, the Government's nonsensical demands on the Brisbane City Council in the wake of the floods became the last straw.

In the days after the floods hit Brisbane, the river was still running a vivid shade of tawny mud. Tonnes of "tar-like sludge"[3] had been dumped on hundreds of streets across the city, and the Council proposed to collect it and deposit it back in the river, the quickest and most practical way to deal with the mess. The putrid sludge was lying on the bottom of the river before the flooding rains came. Putting it back there was cost-effective and logical. Regardless of Council's argument, the Bligh Government refused to grant the necessary permits to carry out the plan, leading to significant delays and extra costs for the city's ratepayers. This type of circuitous, top-down decision-making that had become so common under the Bligh Government infuriated Campbell.

Another issue involving water also fuels his simmering anger and motivates him to make the decision to run for Premier. It began in 2007 just a month after Bligh assumed the top job from Peter Beattie. Bligh had inherited an increasingly bitter fight over water assets. The state wanted control of the council's water infrastructure, a takeover the Mayors of south-east Queensland strongly resisted. The fight got ugly and played out in a very public way. The councils called it "the great water swindle" while Bligh used Parliamentary privilege to hit back. She singled out Campbell for special attack:

> The truth is that Campbell Newman cannot tell the truth. He is a man whose word means nothing. He is dishonest and he has lied about every page of the report.[4]

While Campbell and Beattie had maintained a respectful working relationship, Bligh's confrontational approach as Premier put them on a permanent war footing.

It's time for change in Queensland

To cap off Campbell's growing resentment of the Bligh Government, he despairs at the billion dollar Queensland Health payroll debacle and the ingrained reluctance to cut red tape for small business to help them kickstart the state's stalled economy.

With an election due at any point in the next 12 months, the final tipping point is Bligh's unexpected resurgence. Her opportunistic performance during the floods was so convincing many on the conservative side of politics fear Labor could fall over the line at the next election. External events had intervened to reverse Bligh's fortunes. She was lucky to still be in the top job by the time the floods arrived in early January; internal plotting to replace her with the then Attorney-General Cameron Dick had been afoot since late 2010.

On 8 January 2011, just days before the floods hit Brisbane, 67 percent of people surveyed in a Newspoll were dissatisfied with her performance as Premier. Labor's primary vote had crashed to a new low of 26 percent. Bligh was a dead Premier walking. Her standing was so shaky the LNP under the leadership of John-Paul Langbroek was coasting, hoping to win the next election by default with a small target, low-risk strategy.

As the flood waters rose, Bligh's leadership was saved from the brink of a leadership coup with her stirring "We are Queenslanders" speech on 13 February rallying the broken spirit of a state. With its war cry of "We're the ones that they knock down, and we get up again" the sentiment in her speech becomes emblematic of her own political recovery. By the time the memorial service at the Albert St Uniting Church is being held, Bligh's popularity is soaring. Campbell could almost see the cogs of a snap election gearing up in Bligh's mind.

Unwittingly, Bligh's popularity is about to skyrocket even further with her handling of Cyclone Yasi. The Category 5 powerhouse of a storm makes landfall in North Queensland on 3 February, the day after the funeral at the Albert St church. Campbell can't sit by and watch Labor fall over the line on the back of Bligh's break-out performance during the natural disasters.

At this time, his concern about a snap election and his slow-burning anger at Labor's woeful record is merging with the chorus of supporters calling on him to step up and run for Premier. As bad Labor Governments kept winning elections, their pleas had grown louder and more persistent. Business people and grassroots LNP members urged him to do it. Brisbane residents came up to him in

At a Brisbane Festival function with Anna Bligh in 2006

Campbell accepts a donation for the Brisbane flood appeal at a function on 12 February 2011 where he first spoke to Tim Nicholls about his plan to run for Premier. Credit: *The Epoch Times*

the streets and implored him to run for the top job. Bligh's revival suddenly supercharged their overtures to Campbell. Queensland needs a Can Do Premier, they beseeched, a man of action to grab the reins of government and get the state back on track.

A deal with Lisa

Up to this point of his career, Campbell had both resisted and rejected their intermittent advances. He was always adverse to the prospect of a long career in politics, vowing to bow out when he had achieved what he wanted for Brisbane. But his long-standing refusal to make the switch to state politics actually stemmed from a promise he had made to Lisa, his best friend and wife of more than 20 years. They had consulted at length and mutually agreed on every life and career decision they had ever made.

Midway through 2010, more than six months before Campbell's ultimate decision to run for Premier, they had decided their life in politics would soon end. Indeed, before the Brisbane floods turned their lives upside down, they had agreed they would leave City Hall in late 2011, possibly October. After nearly seven years as the Lord Mayor and Lady Mayoress of Brisbane, they had decided it was time to move on and hand over the job to someone else. They wanted to step out of the public spotlight, get their lives back and pursue various business interests. Together they planned to orchestrate a smooth transition and handover to a new Lord Mayor before exiting graciously and on their own terms ahead of the March 2012 council elections.

Perhaps it is no accident then that Campbell makes up his mind to run for Premier without any input from Lisa. When he makes that decision while sitting inside the church, Lisa is just a block away sorting through paperwork at her desk at the temporary council headquarters at Roy Harvey House on Ann St, the temporary base for council operations while the ambitious $210 million refurbishment of historic City Hall is underway. Lisa expects her husband to arrive back from the funeral at any moment. The afternoon is supposed to provide a rare chance for them to spend time together, albeit briefly. They had barely seen each other for weeks, ever since returning home from a New Year family holiday in the Girraween National Park, south-west of Brisbane, on 9 January. The floods had hit within 48 hours of their return home. Campbell and Lisa were thrust into the non-stop recovery effort with little respite for a full two weeks. There were periods of nearly 24 hours at a time when they did not see each other.

If Lisa had been at the funeral with her husband on this February morning, perhaps his internal deliberations to run for Premier may not have crystallised into a decision. As it had in the past, her presence would have tempered his decision-making process. Never before had he made a life-changing resolution with such far-reaching implications for their family without Lisa's input. Once before, when Campbell had his epiphany at the funeral of his father, Lisa was by his side. On the plane back home to Brisbane following that heart-breaking service in Canberra, Campbell told Lisa he wanted to serve in public office. Within three years of his father's death, Campbell would launch an audacious bid to become the Lord Mayor of Brisbane, at the urging of Lisa.

This time it's different. As the memorial service at the Albert St Uniting Church concludes around 11am, and mourners file outside into the steamy mid-morning light, Campbell turns to Ben Myers and Mark Brodie. He asks them to walk back with him to his office on Ann St. He wants to have a chat. When he arrives there, he bounds past the desk where Lisa is working and gives her a cursory glance on his way into his office. Myers and Brodie are trying to keep up just behind him. Lisa hears the click of the lock on his door, an unusual occurrence. She assumes something big is going down, probably related to the ongoing flood recovery efforts. Nevertheless, Lisa notes her husband's demeanor, a certain look in his eye. She can't recall the last time he had locked his office door.

You're crazy

Inside his office, Campbell asks Myers and Brodie to take a seat. He tells them matter-of-factly about his plan to become Premier. Myers and Brodie are well aware of the many advances over the years beckoning Campbell to make the jump to state politics. But they had no clue he had just made up his mind while sitting beside them at the funeral, or how serious he is about it. When Campbell asks for feedback, Myers replies:

> I think you're crazy. I think you're under-estimating how crazy the LNP organisation is, and how dysfunctional the whole state sphere is.[5]

Despite counseling against the move, Myers and Brodie agree to start making covert inquiries as to how it might happen. Senior party leaders and current state LNP MPs had to be sounded out. Would the party room of 34 MPs support an unelected figurehead leading them from outside the Parliament? A challenge to depose current Opposition Leader John-Paul Langbroek and his deputy Lawrence Springborg needs to be plotted and executed. How could Campbell's emissaries possibly do the numbers without alerting the wider world to the plan? What role will the LNP party executive play? Logistical questions also needed answering: how would he derive an income after quitting the Mayoralty and how would his leadership interact with the official Opposition Leader's position inside the Parliament? Crucially, a suitable electorate for him to contest at the next election must also be found, again in extreme confidence.

They speak to Campbell's trusted principal media adviser on Council, Kylie Lindsay, who agrees to join the team if her boss follows through with the plan. Myers and Brodie meet with McIver and his LNP vice-president Gary Spence, as does Campbell a week later. That was the moment McIver realised Campbell was serious about a tilt at state politics. The party president commissions statewide polling to gauge Campbell's appeal outside Brisbane.

Another critical piece of the puzzle is the urgent need to find a successor to replace him as Lord Mayor. Campbell holds the role of Lord Mayor in great esteem. He wants the transition done with respect for the people of Brisbane while maintaining the conservative's hold over the position. Any replacement would need to be a natural and seamless fit, at very short notice. Long-serving deputy Graham Quirk is the obvious choice. The timing of this political chess move is absolutely crucial to the grand plan. According to the Local Government Act, a Mayoral resignation made more than 12 months before the next council election would spark a by-election. Campbell knows this would potentially throw the Council into disarray. From this moment on he cannot allow his decision to become public knowledge for at least another seven weeks.

Of all the machinations and maneuverings unfolding at this point, Lisa does not learn of her husband's monumental decision for at least another three weeks after the funeral at the Albert St church. The damage to their marriage lasts for months. Lisa reflected:

> That was what made me so incensed. I was available to discuss it with him when he was first telling Ben and Mark. I was right outside that door.

While Lisa continues to be "blissfully unaware", as she later described it, the circle of people who come to know of Campbell's decision is widening by the day. Clandestine meetings and discrete phone calls increase in frequency. At different junctures, senior LNP figures tried to secure him the safe Brisbane seat of Moggill, held by former Liberal leader Bruce Flegg. Some of the approaches to

Flegg, most notably by LNP treasurer Barry O'Sullivan, would later spark an investigation by the Crime and Misconduct Commission into allegations of inducements. Nothing untoward was found and the CMC investigation later cleared those involved.[6]

The LNP Member for Buderim Steve Dickson calls Myers with an idea to draft Campbell into the state arena, weeks after that train had left the station. Myers spies value in Campbell being able to eyeball a sitting MP and shadow minister, and sets up a weekend meeting between Dickson and Campbell at a park at Beerburrum in the Glasshouse Mountains. Campbell gets the positive response from Dickson he is looking for.

A week later on 12 February, Campbell and Lisa attend the Brisbane Lunar New Year and Lantern Multicultural Festival on the oval at McGregor State School. On this sweltering Brisbane day, they are in the front row under a marquee a few seats away from Tim Nicholls, the LNP Member for Clayfield and Shadow Treasurer. Opposition Leader John-Paul Langbroek is also there, but he departs before the event finishes to attend another function. The then Multicultural Affairs Minister Annastacia Palaszczuk is also there, seated next to Lisa. When the traditional lion dance is complete and official proceedings are wrapping up, Campbell asks Tim Nicholls for a moment to talk.

Nicholls is a former solicitor and Brisbane councillor who worked alongside Campbell for two years before winning the seat of Clayfield at the 2006 state election. He is cognisant of the desire to draft the Lord Mayor into State Parliament, and the pair had mused on the possibility at different times in the past. But today, Campbell is more resolute than ever before. Under the speckled shade of a suite of mango trees on the far side of the school oval, Campbell asks Nicholls for his thoughts. Does Nicholls want him to make the unprecedented and risky leap to join the state team? As a key Liberal powerbroker, Nicholls is critical to the success of the plan. Tellingly, Nicholls would have to give up on his own leadership ambitions, for now. At one critical point of this lengthy discussion, Nicholls points his finger at Campbell and taps him in the chest, saying: "You have' to want to do it in here. You've got to do it for the right reasons. You've got to believe it."[7]

Nicholls knows the popular Lord Mayor is the right person for the job, but wants to know Campbell is committed to the job at hand. Nicholls asks for some time to mull it over and two days later, in a brief phone, he gives Campbell the green light.

The final pieces of this remarkable political puzzle are almost in place. Lisa is the last hurdle.

What the hell do you mean 'Premier'?

Early on the morning of Friday, 18 March, Lisa is busy preparing for the day ahead, organising their daughters for school and university while working through her own to-do list. The household is too busy for much conversation. Campbell is ready earlier than usual and about to rush out the front door. He casually mentions to Lisa from a nearby room:

> You might see something in the media later today. There might be some speculation about me running for Premier. I've been thinking about it. I'm considering doing it.

Lisa stops what she's doing in the kitchen. A rush of fear and panic overcomes her. Before he makes it out the door, Lisa rushes up the stairs to grab hold of him, and asks: "What the hell do you mean 'Premier'?"

Lisa is fuming. She sensed this moment coming, but had no clear indication it was about to happen so quickly. Despite all of their plans to exit politics, Lisa knows their life will not be the same again. Lisa later said:

> I was blissfully unaware of it. I had no time. I literally had

it burst upon me that Friday. Cam was a ball of fire, like he normally is, he was firing on all cylinders, and he was racing out the front door to a waiting car there to pick him up. I just remember this dreadful feeling that morning when he sprung it on me. I still can feel it, in the pit of my stomach.[8]

At 6pm that night, Channel 9's veteran political reporter Spencer Jolly breaks the story: "I can reveal that major moves are being made within the LNP to dump the Opposition Leader John-Paul Langbroek and replace him with Brisbane's Lord Mayor Campbell Newman."

With those words, every phone in the house bursts into song and continues well past midnight. Facing a media onslaught, Campbell refuses to publicly confirm or deny the Channel 9 story. The media ambush him the following morning at one of his regular 'Lord Mayor Listens' mobile office booths outside a local shopping centre. He declines to comment. He can't comment. The jigsaw puzzle is not yet complete.

The following day, Sunday, 20 March, the LNP's campaign director James McGrath takes part in the 10km Twilight Run at the University of Queensland. Without taking time to change clothes and refresh, McGrath drives over to the Newman residence on a mission. Clutching the latest polling commissioned by McIver, McGrath is there to convince Campbell once and for all that he should run for state politics. McGrath doesn't know Campbell had made up his mind weeks earlier. The only thing left to tell the LNP was the seat he had chosen to stand in. McGrath later recalled:

> We're sitting in the loungeroom and I'm talking about polling and how the campaign's tracking and then all of a sudden Campbell tells me he's going to run in Ashgrove. I had a look of pure terror on my face. I couldn't believe it. Campbell says 'I can see you're really excited about that'. I wasn't excited. I was so shocked I couldn't speak! I was swearing and screaming profusely in my head. But on the outside, the calm, professional campaign director in me says

'that would be interesting Campbell, that certainly would be a challenge'. But this was the big issue, and people forget about it. There were no other options. We had no other seat for him. Aaron Dillaway was already pre-selected in Ashgrove and he deserves immense credit for stepping aside for Campbell. If Aaron hadn't done the right thing by the party, I don't know what we would've done.[9]

This complex shuffling of political thrones is hurtling forward at a rapid rate. At about 2pm on Monday, 21 March, a meeting is hastily arranged for that same night between Campbell, Tim Nicholls and senior LNP Parliamentarian Jeff Seeney. Later that evening the gather on the back deck of Nicholls' traditional Queenslander home in Hendra in Brisbane's inner north-east. It is the first time Campbell discusses his plan with Seeney. Over a few beers, the trio work through every possible political and logistical scenario. They devise plans to manage the fallout of dumping Langbroek and Springborg and count and recount the numbers within the LNP caucus. They speak to LNP president Bruce McIver and other key party leaders and agree to make Seeney the Opposition Leader inside the Parliament, acting as a "general manager of operations" under Campbell's leadership. Nearly two hours later, they finalise the details of this most astonishing political manoeuvre.

Nicholls and Seeney are locked in. So too is the LNP hierarchy. After much deliberation, Campbell's long-serving deputy on council Graham Quirk agrees to take over as Lord Mayor. A media conference is scheduled for 10:30am the following morning; this will be the moment he publicly confirms the weeks of rumours and political intrigue.

The announcement

In front of a jostling media pack outside Lang Park on the morning of 22 March, Campbell reveals the scale of his plan to the people of Queensland:

> For some time now I've been deeply concerned about the way that Queensland is heading. I've been a very hard-working and committed servant of the people of Brisbane but as I look across at other things that are happening in the state I am very worried. I've thought long and hard over the last three months because on many occasions people in the community, in Brisbane but also across the state have said to me that they want me to consider putting my hand up for state politics.
>
> So after a lot of soul-searching today I come here with this announcement. I'm announcing today that I intend to nominate for preselection for the state seat of Ashgrove. Should I be successful in gaining preselection with the Liberal National Party, it's then my intention to resign the Lord Mayoralty and to then launch a leadership challenge for the leadership of the state LNP team. I do that having a lot of respect and a lot of time for Mr John-Paul Langbroek, but I believe that I am the one to lead the team forward. We need to deal with a very bad Labor state Government that has given us all sorts of problems across Queensland. I am saying today that I am prepared to do the hard yards, I'm prepared to do this in a difficult and probably complex way but I'm doing it because I want to help the people of Queensland and take this state forward.

The response to his announcement ranges from gobsmacked disbelief and profound skepticism to jubilation from party supporters and kudos from those who admire the crazy-brave nature of the move. Political pundits pontificate that it won't work. Renowned psephologist Malcolm Mackerras calls it "unprecedented" and predicts the move "favours Premier Bligh to win the election"[10]. Griffith University political scientist Paul Williams acknowledges Campbell's "enormous gravitas and kudos because of his performance during the floods", but says the switch the state politics is "fraught with all sorts of problems and may well backfire."[11] ABC election analyst Antony Green points to the Canadian Parliamentary system, where party leaders can be elected by leadership ballots of the political party, rather than the Parliamentary team:

> To avoid any hint of scandal, it may be an easier course for Campbell Newman to campaign for Premier while not an MP. As long as the LNP is prepared to support this unusual campaign for office, there is nothing stopping Newman or the LNP from acting in this way.[12]

As was so often the case in his political career, former premier Peter Beattie steals the daily media show with his quip to the media that "it's either the smartest thing the LNP has ever done, or the dumbest."

Labor is shell-shocked. They had feared this move and instinctively knew it would happen. But they had no idea it would happen now, in this way. Bligh and her Ministers, together with Labor's state director Anthony Chisholm, blitz the media in the hours and days after the announcement, attempting to capitalise on the complexity and confusing nature of Campbell's move. It has little impact.

Preselection

On 3 April, nine days after publicly confirming his intention to run for state politics, Campbell is literally on the edge of his plastic seat inside the Ashgrove Bowls Club. He and Lisa fought bitterly earlier that morning. They do not speak to each other on the short drive to the preselection meeting. At the entrance to the path leading up to the club's dining area, the assembled TV crews capture them momentarily pausing and exchanging a few brief words and a kiss.

Inside, the place is packed with supporters, branch members and the media. Taking her seat next to her husband, Lisa notices the speech notes he is holding are shaking. He is incredibly nervous. This is their point of no return. Temporarily casting aside her anger, Lisa places her hand on his knee. She wants him to know she is there for him. The TV cameras focus in on the affectionate moment. Up on stage, Lisa locks her gaze on her husband. In this most critical of moments, Lisa wants him to know she is there to provide him with any strength he may need. As the LNP dignitaries and assembled party members look on, Campbell tells them:

> I solidly commit that we will make this great state once again 'Can Do' Queensland. This is a historic moment, a significant moment in the history of Queensland. I pledge to be a great local member and, if given the opportunity, a great Premier of Queensland.

After some formalities lasting less than 10 minutes, Campbell is unanimously preselected as the LNP candidate for the seat of Ashgrove. He receives a rousing standing ovation, and Lisa embraces him. With the next Local Government elections due on 31 March, he is finally able to resign as Lord Mayor and avoid a by-election. He signs his resignation letter for the cameras right then and there and officially hands over the reins to Graham Quirk.

The myriad pieces of this momentous and elaborate political puzzle had fallen into place. With his preselection for Ashgrove confirmed, the die is cast. There is no turning back; he had crossed the Rubicon into the political unknown. From this moment on, the course of Queensland and national politics was set to change in ways no-one, least of all Campbell, could predict.

2

NEWCOMERS

1840-1975: History of the Newman and Mullett families in Australia

Campbell Newman was standing in line at a polling booth, watching determined voters file in and out of the school hall. As he strode into a voting cubicle, Campbell sensed this particular election was more significant than any other in living memory. For him, the ramifications and details were hazy, but the heightened sense of expectation among the voters in the hall was palpable. They had all been through one hell of an election campaign, a "sustained, year-long effort of persuasion and promotion" as one academic later described it.[13] Campbell looked around the hall one last time and then glanced up at his father, Kevin. With pencil in hand, Newman Snr marked the blank square next to his local MP. After much internal deliberation he voted for the incumbent, the Member for Werriwa Gough Whitlam. Judging by discussions around the dinner table, the nine-year-old Campbell was certain his mother Jocelyn was also going to vote for the Labor MP. It was time for change after more than two decades of conservative rule.

Later that December 1972 election day, Whitlam became Prime Minister of Australia with a narrow nine-seat victory. Kevin's unexpected decision to back Whitlam had been sealed a few months earlier when the then Opposition Leader visited him and his troops at Holsworthy Barracks, located within his electorate. At the invitation of Kevin – a Lieutenant-Colonel and the Commanding Officer of 5RAR – Whitlam was there to address a small assembly of officers and outline Labor's Defence policy. Having spent the past two decades of his life in army service, Kevin wanted Whitlam to clear up concerns about Labor's stance on Defence matters and the Vietnam War, where Kevin had been fighting some five years earlier. Kevin wanted his officers to be informed, and his own questions settled, before voting at the ballot box on 2 December.

Whitlam's talk at the officer's mess was well received. Kevin was impressed with the Labor leader's grasp of issues impacting Defence personnel. Whitlam further cemented the Lieutenant-Colonel's support with a follow-up letter mailed from his Canberra office in the days after his visit. Received on 11 August, less than four months before the election, the one-page handwritten note outlined an earnest pledge by Whitlam. He promised to address the "needless variations" between state education curriculums, which caused confusion for the school children of "servicemen and Commonwealth public servants and, say, bank executives". Whitlam thanked Kevin for his "generous remarks and valuable suggestions" during his visit to the barracks and ended the note with a steadfast flourish: "We are determined to set it right".[14]

Inviting the Opposition Leader to the barracks was one of the first forays into politics Kevin had ever made, and he was reprimanded for it. According to Kevin, the then Minister for the Army Bob Katter Snr "gave him a rocket for daring to invite a politician to an infantry battalion".[15]

The encounter at the barracks and his subsequent vote for Whitlam would change the Newman family's journey in ways they couldn't have imagined.

Origins of service

Less than three years after voting for him, Kevin himself would leap onto the national political stage and herald the beginning of the end for Gough Whitlam's Government. Transferred south and promoted to Deputy Commander of 6 Military District (encompassing all of Tasmania) at the end of 1973, Kevin had become troubled by his earlier decision to vote for Whitlam. The increasingly profligate Government was a runaway train fast heading for a crash. The mounting debt and deficits, the scandals, and the ill-disciplined approach to governance all disturbed Kevin. As a leader of lower paid officers, he sensed the hip pocket consequences for average families. He had served in the army for two decades. The state of the nation under the Whitlam Government convinced him to answer a new call of duty in the political arena.

He was already preselected by the Liberal Party in the seat of Bass when an extraordinary opportunity was thrust upon him in June 1975. The sitting Labor MP for Bass and Deputy Prime Minister Lance Barnard had suddenly retired, sparking a by-election. Kevin won that fight convincingly, providing the impetus for the Fraser Opposition's decision to block supply in the Senate. Kevin's victory had been the prelude to Whitlam's dismissal as Prime Minister less than six months later.

His rapid and unexpected ascent into Federal Parliament took another twist when Kevin was elevated to the outer Cabinet as a Minister in the new Fraser Government after the general election of 13 December 1975. Kevin's inner drive for service and sense of duty to correct the mistakes of a disastrous Labor Government had far-reaching consequences beyond his own political career. Starkly similar motivations drove his son Campbell to forge a parallel path into public office 30 years later. Kevin's service in public office also fostered the ambition of his wife Jocelyn, who became a federal Senator in the mid-1980s. But the roots of Campbell Newman's family tree provide little indication of both his and his parent's unwavering drive to serve the community in political high office, a vocation and a passion that would last for a cumulative 40 years.

The Mulletts

Jocelyn Margaret Mullett was born into a middle-class Melbourne family on 27 July 1937, the second eldest of four children to parents Lyndhurst "Lyn" Mullett and Margaret Eileen Maughan. Her eldest sibling had died at birth in 1932 and her parents waited five years before having Jocelyn. Lyndhurst Mullett, born in 1904, was a well-to-do solicitor based in his office in the heart of Melbourne. His firm, Mullett & Langford Solicitors, had two branches; the central office at 395 Collins St and a smaller practice at the town of Healesville, about 50km north-east of Melbourne's CBD.

Like her father, Jocelyn would study law at the University of Melbourne, and for a brief interval she later worked at his firm. When Lyndhurst had enrolled at Melbourne University in the early 1920s, tertiary study was either out of reach or of little interest for most Australians. At the time, less than 3000 students were enrolled at the institution in a state of more than 1.5 million people.[16] In the only familial clue hinting at the future political career of his daughter Jocelyn and grandson Campbell, Lyndhurst ran as an Independent candidate in two state seats at the Victorian state election in 1952. A legislative loophole allowed him to run in two seats at once; in Box Hill he received 9.5 percent of the primary vote, while over in nearby Evelyn he garnered 822 votes, or 4.7 percent. That was his sole tilt at public office.

There were connections between Lyndhurst and the machinations of government both in his legal career and in the work of his father, Albert Mullett. Albert, born in Adelaide in 1864, became the Government Printer in Victoria during the Federation's infancy, servicing the needs of the State Parliament and public service from 1911 onwards. Albert's success had afforded Lyndhurst the opportunity to study law at Melbourne University. Albert went on to become the Commonwealth Government Printer and he worked in that role until 1925. Among a range of publications credited in his name, Albert published the 598-page 1914 tome titled "The Commonwealth of Australia, Federal Handbook, prepared in connection with the eighty-fourth meeting of The British Association for the Advancement of Science".

Albert, like his son Lyn after him, was a respectable and steady man, dedicated to building a better life to bequeath to his children. Albert's father – the Seafaring Captain James Robert Mullett – had taken an altogether different approach to the fixed and sturdy life of his descendants.

In Captain Mullett, we surely find the exception that proves the rule of the stable, grounded family unit headed by Kevin and Jocelyn. Everything they came to stand for was absent in Captain Mullett's wild and restless life: their dedication to each other in a marriage of almost 40 years; their military, community and national service; their family life in suburban Australia; and devotion to their children Campbell and Kate.

Captain Mullett was born in London in 1840 and sailed with his family to Adelaide soon after. By the time he was 24, he had sidelined his marriage and children by signing up for a job as a seaman. He boarded a ship bound for the northern hemisphere, and rarely came back. During his travels he met and married an American woman, in what may have been a bigamous relationship; no-one knows whether he had ever divorced his Australian wife. On a trade trip sailing between England and South America transporting bat guano, Captain Mullett chanced upon the career that would bring him fame and fortune in the United States. Captain Mullett became America's chief supplier of sea lions for public exhibitions, supplying dozens of zoos and wildlife parks and garnering media attention in major newspapers such as the *New York Times*. Over the course of his 40-year career, Captain Mullett claimed to have captured more than 1,000 sea lions for display in zoos across the United States, Europe and Australia, and "received a little over $1 million" for his efforts.

The Newmans

Compared to the sea-faring adventures of Captain Mullett, Kevin Newman's side of the family featured a distinctly less colourful, more working class background. The family's Australian story began on the shores of Sydney in 1854.

Kevin's great-grandfather, Herman Numan, was a German cook working on board the Dutch Indiaman ship Doctrina et Amicitia that sailed from London on 25 November 1853, and arrived in Sydney in mid-March 1854. His future wife was a fellow passenger on the vessel. Dublin girl Hannah Maunsell was just 16 when she made the same journey to Australia, leaving behind her family's tragic past. Both of her parents perished within six months of each other in 1848 during the height of Ireland's Potato Famine, which would kill over a million people between 1845 and 1851. Hannah travelled to Australia with the Blake family, including her half-sister and half brother-in-law. Within eight weeks of landing in Sydney, Herman and the 17-year-old Hannah were married at St Andrews Church on George St and took up residence in the southern Sydney suburb of St Peters, close to where Sydney Airport is located today. Herman found work where he could as a labourer until more secure employment came with the construction of the brickworks close to their home in the early 1870s. He became a shell gatherer, a title given to men who collected oyster shells and burnt them to create lime for the brickworks.

Herman and Hannah's son Henry Newman, born in 1863, would later take up a job as a young engineer and labourer at those brickworks, keeping the steam engines running to power the kilns and machinery. Henry's son – Henry Eugene – was born in 1892. As a teenager he started his trade as a tiler, and it was while plying his trade in the early 20th century that he spied an exciting business opportunity in Sydney's booming population.

Back in the mid-1850s, when Henry Eugene's grandparents first landed in Sydney, the fledgling city was home to an estimated 50,000 people or less. But over the next two decades, the nation's gold rushes fuelled dramatic growth in the number of new residents. According to data collated by Professor Peter Spearritt, Sydney's population grew to 137,000 in 1871 and nearly tripled to more than 380,000 people in 1891. At the turn of the 20th century, the city's population had climbed to an estimated 480,000 people. By 1921, when Henry Eugene was capitalising on the city's insatiable need for new housing as a builder and developer, Sydney's population had ballooned to nearly 900,000 people.[17]

The enterprising Henry Eugene built a string of properties in the eastern suburbs and the north shore of Sydney in suburbs like Dover Heights, Kensington, Randwick, and Castlecrag. He had a consistent crew of about 20 workmen across three decades. His daughter Lorna later said that while her father was "not a great businessman", he did well enough to ensure his family was "always comfortable". As a symbol of the family's affluence, Henry Eugene bought his first car in 1927. The family never went without a vehicle from that point, including throughout the Great Depression when Australia's unemployment rate doubled to around 21 percent in 1930.

By the time Henry Eugene's son Kevin (born on 10 October 1933) was old enough to attend school, the family was prosperous enough to send him to the prestigious Scots College in Bellevue Hill. The school's motto is "Utinam Patribus Nostris Digni Simus", translated as "O that we may be worthy of our forefathers".

Campbell reflected on his grandfather Henry Eugene's aspirational spirit:

> I think Henry Eugene demonstrated the philosophy of the conservative side of politics. They were very much working class people who worked incredibly hard and displayed some entrepreneurial spirit to provide a better life for their children than what they were brought up with.[18]

When Kevin met Jocelyn

As a high school student, Kevin most enjoyed his time and duties as a member of the Cadet Unit – being outdoors, learning to shoot a rifle, and working with his hands. After high school, the experience with the cadets and the encouragement of senior master Norm Pinwell led him to apply for a position at the Royal Military College at Duntroon, the famed army school near the north-eastern shore of Lake Burley Griffith in Canberra. The federal government established the military college in the early 1900s on a working sheep station owned by the prosperous Campbell family. The Canberra suburb is named in their honour, and the family's impressive sandstone homestead became the officer's mess hall at the military college. The college accepted its first intake of students in mid-1911, with 32 cadets from Australia and 10 from New Zealand. But when the First World War broke out in late 1914, those inaugural students had not yet completed the four-year course. They were sent to Gallipoli regardless. During combat, an estimated 100 of the 158 Duntroon graduates sent to the war on active duty were killed or wounded.[19]

At the time of Kevin's enrollment in 1952, the college curriculum had reverted to four-year terms following the end of the Second World War. His first role after graduating from Duntroon at the end of 1955 was in Tasmania, training national servicemen. He didn't stay there long. Within a year he would get his first taste of active duty on foreign soil in the Malayan Emergency, a war sparked eight years earlier in 1948.

The Malayan Communist Party had murdered three European rubber plantation managers in the north of the country, an incident believed to have been motivated by a Soviet plan to expand communism around the world. The British colonial Government declared a state of emergency shortly after the murders and called for its Commonwealth allies to join what would become a prolonged guerilla war. Australia joined the fray in 1950 and was beginning the slow transition out

Newman family home in St Peters, Sydney circa 1928, where Campbell's great-great grandparents and great-grandparents both lived while working in the nearby brickworks

Kevin Newman circa 1938

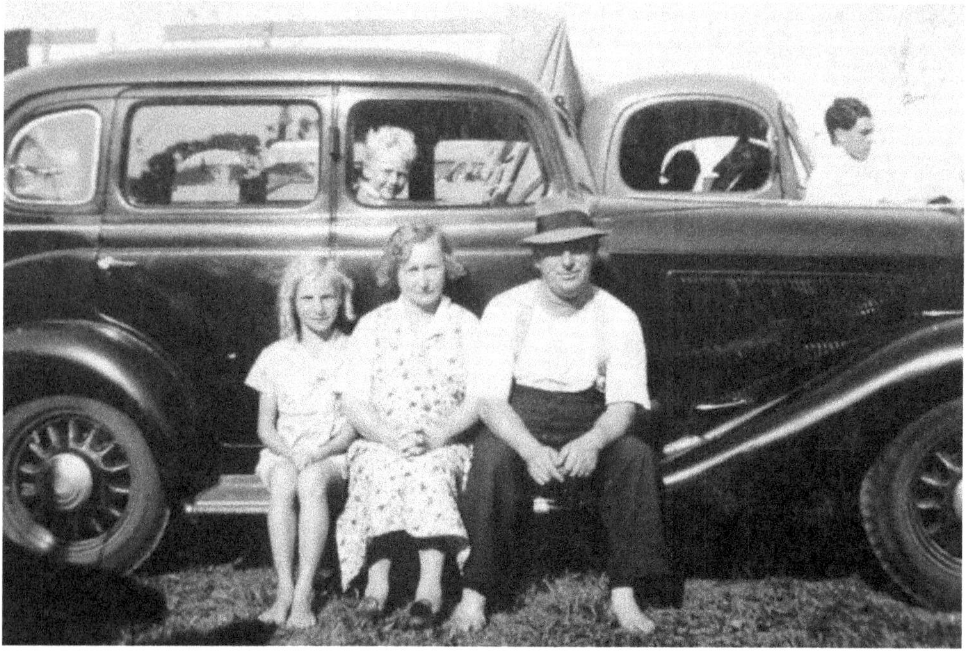

Newman family on the south coast of New South Wales circa 1938. Kevin is in the car, with his sister Lorna and parents Ruby Veronica and Henry Eugene pictured in front

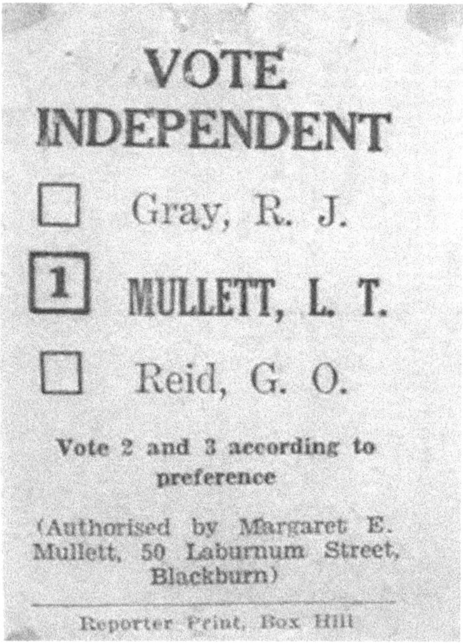

VOTE
INDEPENDENT

☐ Gray, R. J.
[1] MULLETT, L. T.
☐ Reid, G. O.

Vote 2 and 3 according to preference

(Authorised by Margaret E. Mullett, 50 Laburnum Street, Blackburn)

Reporter Print, Box Hill

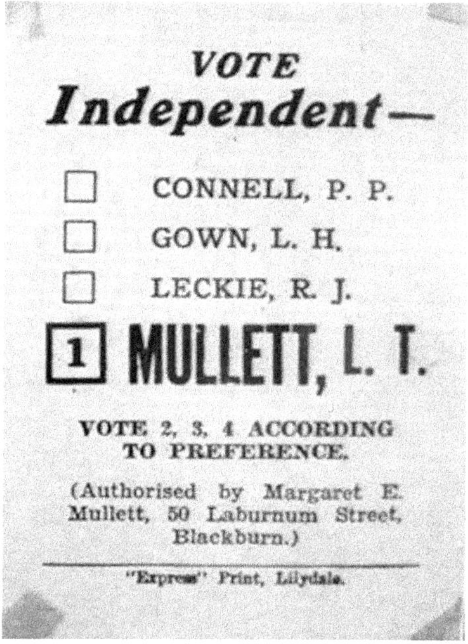

VOTE
Independent—

☐ CONNELL, P. P.
☐ GOWN, L. H.
☐ LECKIE, R. J.
[1] MULLETT, L. T.

VOTE 2, 3, 4 ACCORDING TO PREFERENCE.

(Authorised by Margaret E. Mullett, 50 Laburnum Street, Blackburn.)

"Express" Print, Lilydale.

Ballot papers for Lyndhurst Mullett, who ran in two seats simultaneously at the 1952 Victorian state election

The wedding of Kevin and Jocelyn Newman in 1961

Kevin and Jocelyn Newman with baby Campbell in Canberra, 1963

Jocelyn, Kate and Campbell outside the family's home in Deakin in 1965

Two-year-old Campbell outside the family home in Deakin in 1965 and, right, Campbell and Kate Newman in Draytons School uniform, England, 1971

of the conflict by the time Kevin was shipped there as a platoon commander in 3RAR Company in 1956. The 3RAR spent six weeks training in the art of jungle warfare before waging campaigns to drive the insurgents back into the jungle around Perak and Kedah. After 18 months of service, Kevin returned home as the communist forces were brought under control. Australian War Memorial records show that "by late 1959 operations against the communists were in their final phase."

Shortly after his arrival back in Australia, Kevin was promoted to captain and stationed as an instructor at the School of Infantry in Seymour, Victoria. The paths of Kevin Newman and Jocelyn Mullett first crossed at this time.

After graduating from Melbourne's Presbyterian Ladies College, Jocelyn was studying law at Melbourne University. She was a high-profile, active participant in campus life, leading fundraisers for charities and editing the student newspaper *Farrago*. Edwina Gatenby, a childhood friend of the family, told a Fairfax reporter in 2000:

> The image I have of Jocelyn when she was at university is of someone who really sparkled, she was slightly flirtatious, with a real twinkle and love of life.

In her final year of study in 1958 she won the Miss University competition. The following year, a close friend had persuaded her to meet an Army Captain at the Puckapunyal Army Ball. In the book *Partners*, edited by Anne Henderson and Ross Fitzgerald, Jocelyn remembered:

> I wasn't really keen. It didn't help when I learned that he had a moustache! But, against my better judgment, and dressed in the worst clothes my wardrobe could yield, we met.[20]

Despite her reticence, she was "swept off her feet". For his part, Kevin said the chance to meet a "graduated lawyer who had been glowingly described by our mutual friends" was a dream come true after his years at Duntroon and on the Malay Peninsula fighting the war. He later recollected:

> Despite my suspicions I played it safe and shaved off the moustache. But I considered myself a confirmed bachelor. Even the magic of the Pucka Ball didn't suggest I had found a mate for life.[21]

Jocelyn's parents didn't know what to make of the knockabout soldier their daughter began dating. They were relieved when she agreed to join the family on a grand tour of Europe. Jocelyn later wrote:

> Shortly after meeting Kevin I went to the UK with my family which was some relief to my mother who, to say the least, was suspicious of those 'service types'. Despite her well-meaning prejudice, absence did make the heart grow fonder and Kevin and I became engaged shortly after my return early in 1961.

Jocelyn was so confident of their fate together she had bought a wedding dress during her trip, months before they got engaged when she was back in Australia. During her absence, Kevin was shifted from his posting in Seymour in Victoria up to Sydney. Jocelyn promptly made the move up to be with him, and she rented a flat in Strathfield. Jocelyn, who worked as a law clerk in Sydney, fondly remembered the young couple's delicate balancing act of maintaining respectability before they were hitched. She remembered being "well-protected by my dear middle-aged landlords", who would discreetly knock on her door to "suggest that Kevin should perhaps be getting ready to leave for his barracks".

They didn't have to keep up appearances for long. Kevin and Jocelyn flew to Melbourne and were married on 1 July 1961. They started their new life together at Duntroon, where Kevin was an instructor. When Kevin was transferred as a staff officer to the Department of

Defence's nearby Army Office in 1962, they built their first home, choosing a vacant block in the suburb of Campbell.

Children and war

Shortly after he was born in August 1963, Kevin and Jocelyn's first child made his public debut in a pram wheeled out at the number one oval at the Royal Military College at Duntroon, where the college's popular rugby union team was playing. Campbell Kevin Thomas Newman was born in the Royal Canberra Hospital early on the Monday morning of 12 August. To commemorate his birth, cadets at Duntroon gave the newborn a military-inspired keepsake – a pewter beer mug engraved with the words "To Campbell Newman, from SOVCOY, 1963". SOVCOY, or Sovereign's Company, was the title bestowed on Duntroon's Champion Company of cadets each year, awarded for high performance in a series of sporting, shooting and drill events at the Lee Shield Competition. Two decades later, the heirloom would sit on a mantle in Campbell's room at the college when he was part of Sovereign's Company in 1983.

In 1965, Kevin, Jocelyn and two-year-old Campbell welcomed a daughter and sister Kate into the family. After the birth of Kate, they moved to Queenscliff in Victoria for a year while Kevin studied at the Army's Australian Staff College. His graduation meant they had to move again. Accustomed to postings between Sydney, Canberra, Melbourne and Tasmania, this time they headed much further north to Enoggera Barracks in Brisbane, where Kevin was appointed the Operations Officer of 2RAR. They loved their first few months there, settling into a high-set family home on Mountridge St in the north Brisbane suburb of Everton Park.

But their self-described "quiet" life was shattered in late 1966 when Kevin received word he was being sent to fight in Vietnam. He arrived there as the Operations Officer and Support Company

Commander of 2RAR in April 1967, working out of the Australian Task Force Base at Nui Dat in the country's south-eastern region. Kevin later wrote of his departure:

> Our pleasant and happy family life was shattered when I was posted off to become the operations officer in the 2nd Battalion of the Royal Australian Regiment preparing to enter the war in Vietnam. Mixed feelings for me because my whole training and experience since leaving school was aimed at this very task: as an infantryman to help lead a battalion in war. The parting was dreadful. Fifteen years of intense military training and fashioning could not diminish the wretchedness of that goodbye as I set off for a year at the Australian base at Nui Dat in Southern Vietnam.

With Kevin serving in Vietnam, Jocelyn and the two kids moved back to Melbourne where they could be close to her parents and extended family and friends. She took up work in her father's law office in the city. Jocelyn went back to practising law to "have a distraction from the anxiety of having Kevin in Vietnam". Despite support from her family, and her mum in particular, life was not easy for Jocelyn. Campbell and Kate were toddlers, and the community still frowned upon mothers who "deserted" their children to head to work. While he was away fighting the Viet Cong, Kevin was also aware his wife was bearing the brunt of anti-war sentiment back home. He recalled:

> We didn't realise that in some ways I had the easiest part of the separation. Old friends, professional colleagues and various community organisations were not backward in voicing their criticism or demonstrating their hostility towards a wife who happened to be married to a soldier fighting the Viet Cong. In the end, Joc was forced to conceal her husband's job and his whereabouts, not only to friends and acquaintances but to tradesman and shopkeepers, etc, so that the nastiness could be avoided.

Kevin gained high praise for his efforts in Vietnam. Fellow veteran Barry Seeley, who served alongside him in Vietnam in 1967, told *The Courier-Mail's* Des Houghton that Kevin was responsible for "planning all the military operations at Nui Dat". Seeley remembered Major Newman had "plotted a two-day onslaught to flush out the enemy hiding in several villages in Phuoc Tuy province" and described him as "highly effective and very popular with the troops."[22]

During the period Kevin was away, Jocelyn and the kids kept in touch via regular tape recordings. He would sometimes read children's books onto tape for Campbell and Kate to follow. Jocelyn later recalled:

> News of operations by Kevin's battalion and the reports of dead and wounded meant that I never could escape fear and worry about his safety. But we were great correspondents. We used tapes extensively. Kevin would record not only news and gossip but would read stories which the kids would follow in their books. The kids and I would respond by return tape. It helped keep all of us close. The intimacy of the tapes was only spoilt when the sounds of guns firing out of the task force base inadvertently provided a chilling background to the story-telling.

While the circumstances of their parting in April 1967 and the intervening period apart were distressing, the family's reunion in June 1968 was described by Jocelyn as a scene straight from "Gilbert and Sullivan". Jocelyn expected to embrace him at Melbourne Airport upon his arrival on a mid-morning flight. Instead, Kevin climbed through her bedroom window at about 4am earlier that same day. Kevin later joked about the circumstances of the "triumphant warrior home from the wars". He was "really cut to the quick" when Kate came into the bedroom and demanded to know "who the strange man was in her mother's bed".

The period following Kevin's return was extremely difficult for the couple. Jocelyn remembered the "joy of his safe reunion was soon tempered by problems":

> I had looked after the kids, practiced as a solicitor, run the home and put up with the sniping about my unmentionable relationship with a killer in Vietnam. Now we had to adjust to a dad who had literally left the battlefields only hours before he was to take up a normal suburban life again. No counseling in those days. Gradually the children began to cope with a strange man in the house, and I adapted from being a sole parent.

Upon Kevin's return to Australia in June 1968, the Newmans were shifted back to Army HQ in Canberra. They built their second home at Deakin, not far from Parliament House. A childhood friend Rowan Dean reflected on this period in a tongue-in-cheek article published in *The Courier-Mail* on 12 January 2015. Dean and his childhood friend Simon, who both lived on the same street as the Newmans, first encountered the young Campbell in the "cicada-screeching heat of a long, hot January summer" in 1969:

> That's when the new kid rode into town. A little feller with an egg-shaped noggin and piercing blue eyes. I was 10. Simon 9. A five-year-old spelt trouble; the kid would hold us back for sure. But Campbell's parents were big shots on the local scene. We had no choice – we took him under our wing.[23]

European adventure

The inexorable upheaval of military life imposed another move upon the Newman family in April 1969, a few weeks after the five-year-old Campbell had started in school at Forrest Primary in Canberra. Instead of the typical domestic army transfer, this time they embarked on an 18-month adventure few Australian families at the time would ever experience. The army had posted Kevin to the British School of Infantry as an exchange instructor. They were moving from the dry scrubland of suburban Canberra to the grasslands and chalky plateaus of Wiltshire, a county in the South West of England most famous as the home of Stonehenge. They would live in a small town called Warminster, near the largest military training area in the United Kingdom.

In April 1969, the Newman family departed on the five-week journey to the UK on board the Italian passenger liner Angelina Lauro, refitted for cruising after previously being used as a floating hospital during World War II. They stopped at ports in Perth, Singapore and Cape Town, where Campbell was kept in the ship's medical ward with a bout of measles while the rest of his family explored the South African city. Campbell recalled a fancy dress evening onboard the ship when Kate was done up as a Fisher-Price music box toy, and he was a lighthouse, complete with a handheld torch he used as a beacon lamp. Apollo 11 landed on the moon halfway through their trip, and their course was diverted away from the Suez Canal to avoid the pitfalls of the War of Attrition between Israel and Egypt, launched just a few months before the ship's scheduled arrival there. After a journey Jocelyn described as "indulgent and blissful", the Newman family arrived in England.

If the painful separation caused by Vietnam could be described as a family wound – a wretched period Jocelyn later described as "traumatic" and the "nearest thing to a crisis that our marriage had to face" – their time in Warminster was the balm they needed to heal it. During the two-year posting, they explored Europe and enjoyed a healthy social life, with Kevin reveling in his experience as an observer during an armed rebellion on the Arabian Peninsula. The family even bought a Kombi campervan and in between Campbell and Kate's studies at Draytons School they went on driving holidays throughout the United Kingdom and nearby European destinations.

Back home in Australia

Their home journey just after Christmas in 1971 happened in a virtual instant compared with their five-week sea voyage back in April 1969. Travel had been revolutionised in the months before their departure with the Boeing 747 jumbo jet now commanding the skies. The family hopped on and off flights on the way back home, stopping in Rome, Athens, Istanbul and Hong Kong before touching down in Sydney in late January 1972.

Upon the family's return to home soil, Kevin was promoted to the rank of Lieutenant-Colonel and named Commanding Officer of 5RAR at Holsworthy Barracks in western Sydney. The family lived in the "sticks" at Moorebank, surrounded by bushland where Campbell and his new mates loved to ride their bikes for hours on end. Campbell, now aged nine, attended Moorebank Public School on Anzac Avenue, his third school in four years.

In the December of the family's first year at Moorebank, Kevin – with Campbell in tow – walked into a polling booth and voted for Gough Whitlam at 1972's "It's Time" election. During their two years in western Sydney, the family hit its stride though Jocelyn expressed some personal regret at professional opportunities lost in the role of an "Army wife". Around this time, she applied to be Gough Whitlam's first Woman's Advisor. Whitlam's chief of staff Peter Wilenski signed her letter of rejection. Jocelyn later reflected on this period:

> Minor hiccups and the Vietnam trauma aside, Kevin and I had fashioned a fine family life. The children were happy, intelligent and healthy and we all loved each other dearly. But I quickly discovered that the Army and the life we lived in it was really all about being part of a special tribe, albeit a tribe that provided much professional satisfaction for the warriors, but demanded special application by the camp followers, that is, the wives. The Army and its families lived

in barracks and specially built married quarters. This put us outside suburban Australia. There was a rank structure, white gloves and general's wives and conduct and disciplinary codes which sharply divided the practitioners. All of this subtly extended into the families, creating a pecking order to which I, of course, had never been accustomed.

Except in the early years and during the Vietnam year there was never a chance of pursuing a career in the law. In those times it was generally understood that the wife accepted her role and got on with supporting her husband. The truth was that at times I did feel that I had wasted years of education and experience and that life as an Army wife, mum and housewife left me unfulfilled.

It was the family's next move that would in many ways shape their collective future for the next four decades. At the end of 1973, Kevin was named the Deputy Commander of the 6th Military District, overseeing the army's operations in Tasmania. Campbell, now 10 and entering his fourth school in five years, fondly recounted the lack of corporal punishment in his new classroom in Hobart. In contrast to the strict discipline administered at his small school in the western suburbs of Sydney, the Friends School in the northern suburbs of Hobart was run by the Quakers, whose religious beliefs forbade corporal punishment.

> We lived at the Anglesea Barracks in Davy Street in the centre of Hobart and every morning to get to school we'd have to walk to Sandy Bay Road outside the barracks, catch a bus into town and then change buses in the heart of the city to get to school at New Town. For kids like us from the sticks, it was a big change into what seemed like us to be a big city.

With a view to transitioning out of the Army into a new career, Kevin and Jocelyn bought a farm at Kindred in 1974, just outside Devonport in the north of the state. It was a dairy farm, but inspiration from the family's stay in the UK led Jocelyn to consider establishing the property as a Suffolk sheep stud.

Instead, the Newmans saw a future in cash cropping and introduced potatoes, beans, peas, broccoli along with a few head of sheep and Hereford cattle. Jocelyn was heavily involved in the management of the farm, driving to Kindred on day trips to inspect progress on the property's various activities and staying up late at night preparing the farm's accounts. At around this time she was also offered a job with a Launceston law firm, but declined. She couldn't fit in all of the work she was currently engaged in.

As a young boy, the farm was a playground for Campbell on weekends and school holidays. He learnt to drive tractors, build fences and earned his first money irrigating the crops. Later, as he progressed through high school, he wanted to work in agriculture, as an engineer or agri-scientist. The owners of their neighbouring farm, Max and Judy Baker, described the family as "very sincere, very nice". Mr Baker told the local newspaper:

> I guess you can scratch your head and grin and say politicians all want putting in a bag, but they were two people (Kevin and Jocelyn) who tried. They were very nice people, very sincere people, very good people.[24]

Since their return from England several years earlier, Jocelyn, now in her late 30s, had developed a passion and flair for house design. On the Kindred farm, she seized the opportunity to build her dream home. This was going to be the setting of their steady and secure life going forward, a place to settle after so many Army postings and so much upheaval. The couple became keen gardeners, and Jocelyn was passionate about old and rare varieties of roses. Campbell and Kate enjoyed their regular trips to the farm in between schooling endeavours in Hobart.

And then, out of the blue in 1975, the 42-year-old Kevin decided he wanted to run for Parliament.

The Newmans enter politics

After sounding out key party officials, Kevin had his mind set on winning preselection for the federal seat of Bass, based around the city of Launceston and surrounding rural areas. As a Hobart resident living some 200 kms away from the seat at the time, Kevin was an outsider and had to convince the Liberal State Council he was the right man for the job to take on the long-term Labor incumbent Lance Barnard, who also happened to be Gough Whitlam's Deputy Prime Minister. In a hotly-contested preselection ballot featuring a staggering 20 candidates on 10 May 1975, Kevin was chosen as the Liberal Party's representative in Bass. His political ambition ran up against army regulations, and Kevin dutifully issued a letter of resignation from his high-ranking position.

At the time of his preselection, Deputy Prime Minister Barnard had held the seat for the two decades. His father, Claude Barnard, had earlier held Bass between 1934 and 1949. Barnard's other role in Cabinet as the Minister for Defence heightened the drama of the contest with Kevin, the then Deputy Commander of Tasmania. Kevin later recalled:

> Gough Whitlam was in all sorts of trouble. His Government's performance stirred me up enough to get involved. Encouraged by the Liberal Party I stood for pre-selection to run against Labor's Lance Barnard. Many thought the Liberal Party was mad. They argued that it might be fine to have the Military Commander stand against the Defence Minister but that would be swamped by the heavy disadvantages of endorsing a stranger, a mainlander and, worse, a resident of Hobart.

Jocelyn went back to practising law to support the family while Kevin pursued his fledgling political career:

> The decision to leave the Army and stand against Lance Barnard was courageous to say the least. But, taking a great gulp, I supported Kevin's resolve to have a go. Looking back it was probably a stupid decision based on a very ignorant assessment of what politics was all about. We had great faith that together we would conquer the difficulties even if we had no idea what they might be. When Kevin was pre-selected by the Liberals it looked as if I was going to be the principal breadwinner until at least the election was called which at that time was still 18 months away.

The Newmans didn't have to wait 18 months. Kevin was driving back home from a Liberal Party meeting in Lilydale when he heard the shock news of Barnard's resignation on ABC Radio's 10am news bulletin. After weeks of rampant speculation, Barnard had announced his resignation in a speech to the House of Representatives the night before, on the Monday evening of 2 June 1975. He cited his wife's health and his own intractable problems with hearing in his right ear, caused by a war injury suffered during his service as a gunner in the Second World War.

The Canberra Times political correspondent Gay Davidson analysed the electoral landscape of Bass in a newspaper column shortly after Barnard's resignation:

> The electors (of Bass) are primary producers, food processors, textile workers and Launceston and country town dwellers. The Australian Government is not popular with them, as evidenced by Mr Barnard's all-time-low majority of only 3,500 in the 1974 elections. Unemployment has grown since then and the state Labor Government has lost popularity. There are very few in Canberra who believe Labor can hold Bass in a by-election.

Jocelyn remembered the upheaval and excitement of the family's first political campaign:

> With the by-election life changed dramatically. In the three or four weeks of the campaign we were both swept into a frantic razzle-dazzle which was both exciting and daunting. Of course, my Law career came to a sudden end once again. In contrast to the measured and unspectacular life as an Army mum and solicitor I was centre stage with Kevin in a national event. Whitlam had been in serious trouble and Fraser, newly elected as the Leader of the Opposition, was determined to make his mark. The press swarmed into the electorate. All the principal journalists from the Canberra press gallery regularly came and reported. Practically every member of the Coalition campaigned. People we had never heard of found their way to Launceston just so they could go out door-knocking for us. It was exhausting, exhilarating and, looking back totally unreal.

Campbell later recalled in an interview with *The Courier-Mail* the excitement of experiencing the campaign as an 11-year-old:

> I remember going to the television station in Melbourne and filming ads for the campaign. I remember driving around doing electioneering. All the cars had two-way radios. It was all very exciting.

Writing in *The Canberra Times* just days before voters went to the polls, Davidson described the candidates of both major parties as "unimpressive":

> John Macrostie, the Labor man, began his campaign with 'Keep a local in Bass', and journalists seeing and portraying him as a Norman Gunston found it all too easy to believe that was just what the electorate would do. He is still (understandably) too aggressive against blow-in journalists. Kevin Newman, the Liberals' man, starts under a handicap. He is a mainlander

> who has been in Hobart for the past couple of years … Even the local newspaper editorialising that the residential thing was immaterial and should not be held against Mr Newman did not read very convincingly. Mr Newman is certainly easier to talk to, more confident, but I suspect his acquisition of some of the language of politics is very recent — for instance he spoke of tariffs and devaluation being responsible for a drop in employment at a tin mine.

Bill Raine, a long-serving Liberal Party member who was in Tasmania during the by-election, recalled:

> Polling day on June 28 was a wet and miserable winter's day, yet all the booths were more than adequately staffed by enthusiastic Liberals. On the other hand, several of the Labor workers gave up and went home, leaving their how-to-vote cards under a stone on a post.

Labor supporters sensed the result long before the closing of the rolls. Kevin trounced Labor's Macrostie with a massive 14.3 percent swing. The Newman family moved to Launceston, the power base of Bass, though Campbell stayed behind as a boarder at Friend's School in Hobart until the end of the 1975 school year.

Kevin's victory was a watershed moment for Australian politics. With less than a fortnight to settle into his new Parliamentary career, he became a witness to a political train wreck. The troubles swirling around the Whitlam Government sharpened and exploded into a full-blown crisis soon after he was elected:

> After a record-breaking result, I was sitting in the maelstrom of the Parliamentary events which followed the 9th July special one day sitting of Parliament called to debate the loans affair. Thrilling stuff for one who had been a member of a political party for only a few months.

Six months after the Bass by-election, the Whitlam Government was dismissed from office by Governor-General Sir John Kerr on 11 November 1975. Kevin wrote more than two decades later that, as a politician, he was "wet behind the ears":

> Apart from Parliamentary procedures I really had no idea how politics and the party system worked. In the following months I learnt the hard way.

3

WHAT IT TAKES

1976-2002: Kevin and Jocelyn Newman in politics, Campbell's army and private sector career

When Campbell entered his final period of schooling in 1976 at Launceston Church Grammar, the 13-year-old had already been in four different schools in seven years. His enrollment in the fifth school of his educational life at Church Grammar meant he had studied in classrooms in Canberra, England, Western Sydney, Hobart and, finally, Launceston. With Kevin in Federal Parliament and the kids settled into a comfortable routine at their new school, the Newmans were finally free of the biennial moves imposed on military families.

Campbell began weighing up his future. He was considering some type of career in the agricultural sector, with a focus on engineering or a scientific discipline. His interest in those endeavours stemmed from his visits to the family farm, and over time he developed an interest in using engineering and science to find new ways of improving the food industry's productivity.

Another keen interest at the time was borne out of his new school's regular excursions into the spectacular highlands of Tasmania. They went white-water rafting, caving, and canoeing. The trips opened up a world of adventure and exploration Campbell wasn't exposed to in earlier schooling. Bushwalking and exploring national parks became a lifelong avocation.

Minister Kevin Newman

While Campbell was turning his attention to future endeavours, Kevin was commuting back and forth to Canberra and managing a string of ever-changing ministerial portfolios. Prime Minister Fraser was prone to regularly shuffling his Cabinet, to the detriment of momentum and continuity. At different intervals during his eight years in Parliament, Kevin would oversee seven departments. Appointed to his first Cabinet position on 22 December 1975, Kevin was named Minister for Repatriation, now more commonly known as Veterans' Affairs. It was an appropriate start in the Ministry for a returned serviceman.

Seven months later Fraser shifted him to the portfolios of Environment, Housing and Community Development, a role he would use to end sand mining on Fraser Island. As the architect of the federal "takeover" of the island, Kevin would confront an enraged Queensland Premier Joh Bjelke-Petersen, who labelled it "a political decision to appease Sydney and Melbourne conservationists".[25] The meeting was captured in a candid photograph published on the front page of *The Courier-Mail* on 11 July 1976. A defiant Bjelke-Petersen is on the phone at his desk while Kevin and two federal colleagues are forced to stand by and wait for him to finish.

In 1978, Kevin was appointed Minister for National Development, and a year later was shuffled again to Minister for Productivity. His final Cabinet role, announced in November 1980, was Minister for Administrative Services. In this portfolio, two key policy initiatives that would have long-lasting effects took place.

First, the portfolio meant Kevin had responsibility for the Australian Federal Police, and his early work led to the establishment of the Australian Bureau of Criminal Intelligence, the first serious attempt to co-ordinate the activities of state and federal police agencies. In its modern day guise, the ABCI played a role with its state counterparts in the fight against criminal bikie gangs.

Second, the role of Administrative Services Minister allowed Kevin to influence the economic policy debate raging within Coalition ranks at the time. The Government's direction on economic policy was increasingly split between a cautious Fraser wary of inflicting short-term pain on industries and the "dries", a group of MPs advocating free market reforms and swifter tariff reductions. The dries were particularly inspired by the "patron saint" of free market economics Milton Friedman, who addressed the Coalition's shadow front bench during Friedman's influential visit to Australia in April 1975. The split between the two schools of economic thinking within the Government was highlighted in Cabinet discussions over subsidies and tariffs in mid-1982. Kevin was party to a joint Cabinet submission with Phillip Lynch – the Minister for Industry and Commerce and the Government's chief proponent of protectionism – titled "Approaches to general reductions in protection". With the approval of Fraser, the Newman-Lynch submission recommended the Government maintain the status quo. A Cabinet minute dated 6 July 1982, noted the decision:

> The Cabinet agreed not to proceed with a program of further reductions in protection at this stage, noting that careful attention would need to be given to the public presentation of this Decision.

This decision, and an earlier Cabinet vote to continue high levels of protection for the car industry, deepened the philosophical split within the Government. John Howard, Treasurer at the time, described this period as a "major development in the internal debate on economic policy within the Coalition". Howard was increasingly sympathetic to free market policies, and the dries courted him to challenge Fraser for the leadership, an overture he rejected. Howard explained in *Lazarus Rising*:

> The dries had become increasingly disillusioned with the

Government's direction because they felt that decisions often failed to reflect the economic principles in which they believed. To their credit they maintained intellectual consistency, irrespective of political circumstances, in the arguments they put to me both in private and in the party room. They were quite an impressive bunch who wanted the Government to practice as well as preach the values of the free market.

Kevin's stance on economic policy was shaped by his electorate. In a region brimming with textile workers and small manufacturing businesses reliant on textile tariffs, he fought against the Whitlam Government's heavy tariff cuts during his 1975 by-election win. He knew the economic dries were advocating for change that was inevitable and ultimately necessary. But he wanted to ensure his constituents were given support and time to transition into the brave new free market world.

Jocelyn and the kids

Apart from the duties of motherhood and managing the house, Jocelyn was reveling in her new life as a community advocate and political partner. The family had bought a terrace house, a "fixer upper" as Jocelyn described it. Her renovation work evolved into a lifelong vocation restoring and protecting old cottages, as well as a leadership role in the local branch of the National Trust of Australia.

Jocelyn recalled being "swept into community affairs with a vengeance", meeting constituents, joining charity organisations and attending functions. She became increasingly involved in social causes, with a particular passion for child protection and domestic violence, fuelled by her confronting experiences in family law. In the face of fierce opposition from nearby residents, she led the fight to build Launceston's first women's shelter:

In doing so I struck some awful prejudice amongst some

of the citizens close to the old home where the Shelter was to be set up. A vigorous campaign was waged against the Shelter as not being 'desirable' and 'not proper for a genteel suburb'. We stuck to our guns and, with the help of the then Deputy Labor Premier, Michael Barnard, the Shelter was established.

Despite their father's absence on Parliamentary and Ministerial duties, the Newman children also thrived. They had a new-found sense of place and stability in schooling. The Tasmanian education system at the time required students to attain four "level 3" subjects, a benchmark Campbell reached at Launceston Church Grammar in year 11 in 1979. The achievement meant he could've commenced his university studies early, but instead he chose to finish year 12. At this point he actively began looking for a job.

At the start of his final year in school in 1980, the 16-year-old applied for an engineering cadetship with the Tasmanian Electro Metallurgical Company after seeing the position advertised in a local newspaper. TEMCO, a division of BHP, was a manganese alloy smelter at the mouth of the Tamar River. When Campbell applied for a cadetship the operation was at its peak, employing more than 450 workers. As one of the youngest applicants, he was told he had narrowly missed out to an older boy. Regardless, the job application process had solidified his thoughts about choosing engineering as his future career path. A few months later, at the beginning of the mid-year school holiday period, he stumbled on to another advertisement that determined his career course for the next 13 years.

Campbell at Duntroon

While reading *The Bulletin* magazine during the school break, Campbell was intrigued by a double-page spread spruiking cadetships at the Royal Military College at Duntroon, the same institution his father had graduated from 25 years earlier. Campbell said the advertisement made a cadetship sound "very attractive":

> You got paid, you could study engineering, and it wasn't a mystery to me because dad had done it. It appeared to be a very comfortable option for me. I'd never had any thoughts of being in the army. But much to the delight of my parents, who had never suggested it to me before, I announced to them I was interested. In fact they first found I was applying when I showed them the forms I'd gone and collected myself from the army office in Launceston.

A battery of tests in the army's selection process followed in an extremely competitive environment. Campbell travelled by bus to Hobart for tests, and later flew to Melbourne and a nearby Army Barracks for a final round of literacy, numeracy, psychological and medical tests. He passed the tests, and was selected for the 1981 intake at the Royal Military College at Duntroon. A stern looking young Campbell is pictured signing his enlistment form in the presence of an army recruiting officer in *The Mercury* on 20 January 1981, next to an article that read:

> In the largest intake of recruits from Tasmania, four youths yesterday enlisted for officer training at the Army Royal Military College at Duntroon, Canberra. Among them was Campbell Newman, son of the Minister for Administrative Services and the Minister assisting the Minister for Defence, Kevin Newman.

The Royal Military College at Duntroon's primary aim was to turn cadets into commanders, capable of leading Australian troops in the field. The institution's motto is *Doctrina vim promovet*, translated to Learning Promotes Strength. Through its tertiary education partnership with the University of New South Wales, the college aimed to give its cadets both the skills and resilience to lead soldiers in combat as well as the formal qualifications to succeed in the private sector. University researcher Dr John Connor held a slightly harsher, one-dimensional view in a 2013 conference paper, asserting that military training academies "strip the individuality of a trainee then re-build them in the image of the warrior."

Little wonder that the teenager out of Tasmania was more than a little overwhelmed and fearful when he stepped off a plane and onto the Duntroon college bus on the steamy Monday afternoon of 19 January 1981:

> It was stinking hot, and I felt sick in the pit of my stomach. We were picked up at the airport and taken to the barracks. You get off the bus and immediately you are set upon by people shouting and screaming at you. 'Stand to attention', 'get your hands by your sides', 'grab your bags and follow me, left, right, left, right'. Your arms are nearly dropping off because your bags are so heavy, you're drenched in sweat walking up this hill, no-one's helping you. When you get to the top of the hill, you walk into a three-storey brick building and people are just screaming at you. 'Stand fast', 'stand to attention', you walk past and they yell 'why didn't you excuse yourself', 'get it right', 'try it again' … then you went down to the mess hall for dinner and people are yelling and screaming at you there. That was the environment you walked into and the way people conducted themselves. Our first week was spent on the introductory stuff, haircuts, inoculations, getting our uniforms and our SLR rifle. From the second week on we went straight into training and out on field exercises at the Majura Training Area north of Canberra Airport. We were being trained by Vietnam veterans who less than 10 years earlier were over there fighting. It was very demanding. A few of the cadets I arrived with left after the first few weeks.

When he returned to his barracks after one particular field exercise in the nearby Majura bushland, Campbell was presented with an unexpected opportunity to back out of the four-year commitment Duntroon demanded. A telegram stuck under the door of his dorm room contained an offer to study civil engineering at Sydney University. Before he was accepted into Duntroon, he applied to other universities. He remembered:

> I was standing there reading this telegram from mum and dad asking me what I wanted to do about this offer from Sydney Uni. It was an escape hatch. I could've pulled the pin. It was a hard decision to make. I decided to stay at Duntroon. I guess I wanted to prove I could do it.

Campbell made it through to the annual Lanyard Parade, held five weeks after cadets first arrive at Duntroon to formally admit them to the Corps of Staff Cadets. With this induction milestone behind him, Campbell began his degree in electrical engineering through the UNSW. Lectures and course work dominated the cadet's schedule from Monday to Friday, with military training one afternoon a week, and sports on Tuesday and Thursday afternoons. Saturday was reserved for compulsory sport and military training activities while Sunday provided the only respite from the strict routine. Adjusting to the tightly structured schedule proved difficult for a young man who was more accustomed to exploring the farm and countryside during his family's recent years in Tasmania.

In his first year at Duntroon, Campbell caught up regularly with his father in the nation's capital. He broke his hand while playing hockey – his only team sporting endeavour then and since – and formed friendships that would last into adulthood. One of his first and closest mates at Duntroon was Stephen Chong, a Singaporean exchange student and cadet two years his senior who Campbell described as his "older brother". He also formed a bond with cadet Andrew Wilkie, two years his senior. The pair had met in unusual circumstances a few months after Campbell's arrival at Duntroon.

Earlier in the first term of 1981, Wilkie and four other cadets had snuck out of the college to steal a banner from anti-uranium protestors camped out in a tent embassy on the lawns of Parliament House. To their embarrassment, the cadets were caught in a citizen's arrest after the protestors gave chase. The police were called, and punishment was doled out by the college. The incident made it all the way to the floor of Federal Parliament when Opposition Leader Bill Hayden used a spot in Question Time to ask the acting Minister for Defence to outline what punishment the boys had received. Hayden appeared to be suggesting the cadet's behaviour was part of some broader fascist culture within the military and Coalition Government. The Acting Defence Minister bearing the brunt of Labor's venom was none other than Kevin Newman:

> My dad was the one up in Parliament defending the cadets, saying the boys had been dealt with, it was nothing more than hijinks and pranks, no-one was hurt, that type of thing. Well shortly after my dad did that, I got a visit late at night from these older cadets, three of them. They were senior people in the 3rd Class. I didn't know who they were. I was quite scared. They looked at me, extended their hands and said 'Staff Cadet Newman … put it there. We want to thank you, your dad saved us, we weren't kicked out'. One of those cadets shaking my hand was Andrew Wilkie.

While Hayden had called for Cadet Wilkie's head at the time, eight years later in 1989 they would form a close bond at Yarralumla where Wilkie served as Governor-General Hayden's Aide de Camp.

At the end of Campbell's first year, the cadets were sent out for an obligatory military training exercise. They camped out in the dense heathland and sandstone escarpments of the Tianjara plateau, south-west of Nowra, for nearly three weeks. Campbell said the cadets who took part in that expedition would never forget it:

> I think the weather on that trip was a bit like being at the Somme, it rained and rained, particularly the last 10 days. It was absolutely miserable, a very tough time. We were in trenches that would flood with water. We went through some pretty rough times with those end-of-year expeditions.

As Campbell entered his third year at Duntroon in 1983, the college was rocked by a bastardisation scandal that would reverberate through the ensuing decades. It started with the newest crop of 4th Class cadets, who were being put through their paces after arriving at the college on 24 January. Three weeks on, the new cadets were among those involved in a wild brawl at a college swimming carnival. Four cadets were hospitalised with injuries. In his research on that period at Duntroon, Dr John Connor found that 18 of the 153 Fourth Class cadets had dropped out by April.[26] Three of them approached *The Age* newspaper to tell their story, alleging they had suffered institutionalised "brutality" and "sadism". Other cadets came forward in the days after the first front page story was published on Saturday, 2 April 1983. A cadet called "David" who had quit the college the year before told the newspaper he had suffered acts of humiliation and witnessed bashings in the gymnasium that left "blood and holes" in the wall. The furore lasted for months. Two investigations resulted in 14 senior cadets being charged, with five of them expelled from the college. Andrew Wilkie was one of the senior cadets disciplined for inappropriate behaviour (unrelated to the above incidents), and some of his antics were dragged up in the media some 30 years later in 2011.

Campbell remembered episodes of so-called bastardisation and hazing during his time at Duntroon. He was part of the system and culture of the place. One example included first year cadets being put in a closed cupboard to see how long they could last while a piece of burning toast smoked them out. Campbell was once told to do the "cuckoo clock", which involved huddling up in the dark space at the top of an inbuilt wardrobe and, at the stroke of 10pm, sticking your head out and saying "cuckoo, cuckoo, cuckoo". Campbell was never "a stand-out or got in trouble" for any incidents the way some other cadets during his time were.

Kevin retires from politics

While the Duntroon scandal played out in the nation's media, Kevin Newman's career was winding down in parallel with the fortunes of the Fraser Government. When Bob Hawke trail-blazed his way to victory over Fraser at the March 1983 election, Kevin read the writing on the wall. Nearly 60 years of age, Kevin's health was deteriorating. He had contracted the autoimmune disease lupus, and it was affecting his lungs and, at times, making it difficult to breathe. He wanted to spend more time at home with Jocelyn but battled on in the Parliament for another 18 months before settling on a decision. When Hawke called an early election for 1 December 2004, Kevin was handed the ideal opportunity to exit politics. Six weeks before polling day, he resigned from the Parliament. The Hawke Government went on to be comfortably re-elected against the Andrew Peacock-led Coalition.

Kevin later reflected on the ups and downs of his Ministerial career:

> One of the ministerial jobs, National Development, was somewhat of a nightmare. During this period the world went through an oil crisis and Australia went through tough shortages particularly of distillates and aviation fuel. The most enjoyable and satisfying responsibility was for the Australian Federal Police (as Minister for Administrative Services). The community had woken up to the increasing dangers of Organised Crime and the drug trade. Following a number of scandals in state government forces I was convinced that the only force largely untouched by corruption was the AFP and that they were best suited to spearhead action against

the crime bosses. To meet the challenge I wanted a more effective force: stronger leadership, better training, improved intelligence and increased cooperation with the state forces which did not have a very high regard for the Federal Police. By the time we went out of office we were well under way in achieving these objectives. We also wanted to have a strong Crime Commission with wide powers. After we left office this was established but with much weaker authority and organisational strength. I feel that our model would have at least kept the situation in check. I raised the ire of the PM and some Cabinet colleagues when I asserted on national TV that there were politicians, policeman, business men and public officials who had been corrupted by organised crime in Australia. The remarks also brought on an attack by the Opposition in the Parliament. Time, along with the jailing and sacking of magistrates, policemen and politicians have now proved the point I was making. In 1984, due to ill health, I retired from politics.

At the start of 1984 Campbell too was entering the final phase of his current station in life. Now a 1st Class Cadet, the last year at Duntroon, he would turn 21 in August. For the first half of that final year, Campbell struggled under the immense pressure of juggling his tertiary studies and full-time military training. While many other 1st Class Cadets had attained their university degrees after three years, the engineering and Honours students still had one year to go before graduating. He recalled:

> It was a very demanding year. Your fourth year at Duntroon is full time military training. We did a lot of time out in the field on exercises and we had a lot of tough instructors who really put us through our paces. They really did. To be honest there was a point where I almost didn't make it. I was a very shy kid. Very shy. And at Duntroon there was a fear of failure or a worry for me about whether I could do those things.

> In that final year when they're really looking at whether or not you've got what it takes to be a leader in the military, a leader in combat, they put a big question mark over me for the first three months or so in that final year. One or two instructors thought I didn't have the goods. They didn't believe I was confident or assertive enough. I was put under a lot of scrutiny. They weren't training you as an engineering officer, we were trained as infantry officers. The training was meant to prepare you to lead an infantry platoon of soldiers in combat operations anywhere in the world, at the pointy end. You had to be able to go out there and do that, it was mandatory to know how to run platoon attacks, participate in company attacks, know how to sight machine guns, look after the whole gamut of the administration of a group of people. It was intense training. Luckily I asked for extra help and training and assistance and realised what I had to do. By the middle of that final year I got my act together, I was doing OK, and they decided I could graduate.

Throughout his four years at Duntroon, Campbell formed habits that would last a lifetime; a commitment to running and exercise, the courtesies of punctuality and appearance, the discipline of routine:

> A lot of those things like punctuality, polishing shoes, ironing your shirt, all those basic things were drilled into you at Duntroon. Mum didn't teach me how to iron a shirt, the army did. It's fashionable to sneer at this stuff today. But if everybody decided they weren't going to turn up on time, nothing would ever get done.

Despite having a year of study remaining on his engineering degree, his time as a cadet at Duntroon was complete. In the first months of 1985, Campbell was ready for adventure. In echoes of his family's sojourn to the United Kingdom 15 years earlier, Campbell arranged to be seconded to the British Army with two fellow

Duntroon graduates. They spent nearly two months embedded in the 35 Engineer Regiment at Hameln, Germany, taking part in patrols along the frontier separating the Federal Republic of Germany in the West and the German Democratic Republic in the East. Campbell recalled patrolling the barrier that stretched nearly 1400 kilometres from the Baltic Sea in the north to Czechoslovakia in the south-east:

> The Brits were basically preparing for the Russians and East Germans to come rolling across the border to take over Western Europe so we were there in the middle of what was a real Cold War setting. I remember looking over at the Soviets and East Germans in their watch towers as we patrolled the fence. The countryside was covered with snow, and from memory it was the worst winter since 1944.

Upon his return to Australia, Campbell spent the rest of 1985 finishing his engineering degree, graduating with honors in December. In 1986, Campbell's path would intersect with his father's past again, this time at Enoggera Barracks. Kevin had been stationed there twenty years earlier in 1966. Campbell, now 22, was made plant troop commander of about 45 men in the 20th Divisional Engineer Support Squadron. A number of soldiers under his command were Vietnam Veterans. Campbell recalled:

> We built roads, bridges, got involved in airfield construction. We were a little construction unit. We had scrapers, bulldozers, graders, fuel tankers, trucks. We built an airfield and a causeway at Tin Can Bay, took part in a big exercise at Mt Isa, we went to Darwin to help the Air Force clean up an old bombing range. We worked with the Lions Club and local council to build a road on the border of Queensland and New South Wales, went to Cooktown to provide support to the biggest military exercise in Australia since World War 2 where we did things like road maintenance, managed the water supply and other logistics. It was a very happy two years.

Senator Jocelyn Newman

In the same year Campbell was following in his father's footsteps at Enoggera Barracks, Jocelyn's professional life spectacularly overlapped with her husband's former political career. Federal Liberal Senator Peter Rae had represented Tasmania since 1967. In a shock announcement in his 19th year as a Senator, he resigned the post in January 1986 to contest the state election in February. The opening presented a stunning opportunity for Jocelyn, who nominated for the vacant spot in a field of Liberal Party candidates. To her surprise, she won it. State Parliament endorsed her nomination in March. Her elevation to the Senate meant the Newmans were only the second married couple to have served in Federal Parliament. Another pair of conservative Tasmanian politicians – former Prime Minister Joseph Lyons and his wife Enid (the first woman elected to the Federal Parliament in 1943) – were the first.

Kevin gave his "wholehearted support" to Jocelyn's new career move. Jocelyn had been by his side during two successful careers. Now it was her turn. But her entry into the political arena was not as high-profile or initially rewarding as Kevin's dramatic appearance on the federal scene a decade earlier. She would serve in Opposition for the first 10 years of her political career, first under John Howard, and then Andrew Peacock. Shortly after Jocelyn was sworn in, Howard gave an interview to Fairfax journalist Anne Summers in Washington, uttering the now legendary phrase "the times will suit me":

> Governments on our side of Parliament in the past have been too timid about change. They've thought people on our side of politics must always be cautious about change. I think that is wrong. I think you've got to be selective about change, be willing to hang on very hard to certain things but be willing to radically change other institutions.

Tackling the obstacle course at the Royal Military College at Duntroon in 1983

At the controls of an M2 Bridge and Ferry Unit on the Weser River, West Germany in 1985

Training in nuclear, biological and chemical warfare on the Barkly Tableland west of Mt Isa in 1986

Campbell and Lisa's wedding day in July 1991, with Frank and Elizabeth Monsour (left) and Kevin and Jocelyn Newman (right)

Investiture Ceremony for Kevin Newman upon receiving his AO with Jocelyn and granddaughter Rebecca in Hobart September 1994

Campbell with Sarah (left) and Rebecca (right) in their Warmington Rd home in Ashgrove, September 1997

Rebecca Newman wearing a Kevin Newman campaign t-shirt with her sister Sarah at the family home in Ashgrove in 1998

Grainco Australia's executive team at the Melbourne Bulk Commodity Terminal in 2000

Campbell meets Lisa

As Jocelyn learned the ropes of her new political career, Campbell was leading Operation Hard Slog III. In charge of 18 men on a gruelling walking expedition across the Tanami Desert in Central Australia, it was Campbell's job to make sure everyone made it through to the end of their entirely self-sufficient, self-contained trip. The troop was pushed to the limit in the 15-day 550km east-west crossing of the Red Centre. Participants kept a tally of tyre punctures on the support vehicles, recording a grand total of 199. The expedition became one of Campbell's fondest memories of his army career. Not long after the trek across Central Australia, a chance encounter in August 1987 would prove to be a life-changing event for the young officer.

In the midst of an introductory gathering in the carpark of the Enoggera Barracks between army officers and nurses trained at the nearby Mater Hospital, Campbell Newman met Lisa Monsour. Lisa was born on 15 August 1963 at the same hospital she was now nursing at. The eldest of six children born to Frank and Elizabeth Monsour, Lisa followed her parents into the medical profession. Her father had become a renowned Oral and Maxillofacial Surgeon and educator, while her mother had trained as a nurse at the Mater. As their eldest child, Lisa was incredibly close to her parents. They utterly adored her. Any man who wanted to court her faced an almighty hurdle in Frank and Elizabeth. Campbell and Lisa were destined to meet at the time they did. Their overlapping circle of friends in the small world of late-1980s Brisbane included one of Campbell's fellow army engineers who would soon start a relationship, and later marry, one of Lisa's nursing colleagues. Campbell and Lisa soon discovered they were born just three days apart in 1963. There was a certain spark between them on that first encounter, but not enough to indicate love at first sight. Campbell explained:

> Throughout 1986 I had a big love affair with a girl in Sydney,

and I thought I was going to marry her. But it fell apart, and I was feeling very sad and sorry for myself for the first few months of 1987. A fellow officer Peter Ruff and his partner Cathy had organised for a group of guys from the barracks to meet up with a group of nurses from the Mater Hospital so we could all go to the Ekka (Queensland Show) together. We all met in the carpark outside the engineer officer's mess at Enoggera, and that's when I met a girl by the name of Lisa. We went to the Ekka, and then afterwards to a club called The Underground on Caxton St, across from Lang Park. We danced a fair bit of the night away and I remember that as we were leaving, after midnight, Lisa said to Cathy 'thanks for forgetting my birthday'.

It would take two years for them to progress beyond a platonic friendship. By then Campbell was stationed with the 19th Chief Engineer Works in Sydney, a dream job for a young army engineer. During his first year there in 1988, he lived at the Randwick Barracks, moving to an apartment in Vaucluse with two mates in 1989. He worked on civil engineering projects like roads, bridges and airfields. He went to a remote part of the Solomon Islands to design an airfield and to Papua New Guinea to help develop a wharf at what became the Manus Island detention centre. In the middle of 1989, Campbell took part in a selection process to take over as Aide de Camp from Andrew Wilkie at Government House. The prestigious role was always awarded to an officer from one of the three Defence disciplines. Campbell and two other officers went through an intensive recruitment process, spending time at Yarralumla, being interviewed by Bill and Dallas Hayden. They were also scrutinised by the long-serving Official Secretary to the Governor-General David Smith, the man who had read aloud the proclamation to dismiss Whitlam 25 years earlier. Campbell was beaten to the role by fellow officer Warwick Jones.

Being invited to participate in the selection process for Aide de Camp at Yarralumla was recognition of a young officer's standing in the army. Campbell had reached a point in his military career where he was given a choice over his next posting. He decided on Brisbane, where Lisa was living. They had become an item a few months earlier at a 4th of July function. Peter and Cathy Ruff had invited Lisa to attend the function at the Engineer Officer's Mess in Sydney:

> I was still seeing other people, but Lisa and I started writing and calling each other more frequently and we were getting more serious. I vividly remember I made a conscious decision that Lisa was the one for me on New Year's Eve in 1989, six months after we first became an item. I was at a party in Launceston, she was in Brisbane. And the penny dropped. It was sort of like 'this girl's just great, she's the one'. So when I got the chance to move, I chose Enoggera Barracks in Brisbane and we became a proper item. Lisa lived in New Farm at the time. I moved all my stuff into the Army Barracks but I didn't spend a lot of time there.

Lisa's father Frank remembered that young Campbell was not "readily distracted" in the pursuit of his daughter's affections:

> Campbell had quite a presence, he was a military gentleman and had all of the good principles that career advocates. He was well-groomed, highly disciplined, and highly respectful. He was a young gentleman who had been courting Lisa for some time and he was, shall we say, absolutely committed to the pursuit of that goal. Lisa was very close to us, very close to her mother. She was precious to us and we weren't about to part with her lightly.[27]

Back at Enoggera Barracks, Campbell was working for Brigadier Rod Earle as the personnel staff officer on the 6th Brigade headquarters. It was a role he described as the "junior woodchuck HR manager". He travelled to Hawaii for a joint exercise with the US

Army and participated in the annual Shoalwater Bay training exercise on the Central Queensland coast. But his planned two-year stint in the role was cut short when he was hand-picked to be the Aide de Camp for newly appointed Major-General Denis Luttrell, who was chosen to head up the Army Reserves in May 1991. Campbell set up an office for the General at Victoria Barracks in Brisbane, and they travelled extensively visiting Army Reserve units around Australia. The time spent on planes and the 9-to-5 nature of the job allowed Campbell to start an MBA at the University of Queensland.

All the while, Campbell and Lisa's relationship grew stronger. They were in love and had become best friends.

Lisa would later tell *The Courier-Mail* she was attracted to Campbell's integrity, drive and "force of energy":

> He is a very passionate man. Every aspect of his life he takes on as a passion, and that appealed to me. And he is a kind-hearted man. I would never have fallen in love with someone who was not kind-hearted.

In August 1990, almost three years to the day since they first met, Campbell and Lisa were attending a fete at her old school St Rita's College in the Brisbane suburb of Clayfield. Campbell took Lisa off to the side, away from the crowds. He got down on one knee and proposed. They were married the following year in July 1991, at the chapel at the Enoggera Barracks. At the reception afterwards, held at the Queensland Club, Andrew Wilkie was the master of ceremonies and his Duntroon classmate Stephen Chong, by now an officer in the Singaporean Armed Forces, was his best man. They honeymooned in Port Douglas and lived in the home they had just bought on Warmington Rd in the suburb of Ashgrove. Some six months into their marriage, Campbell was offered a role he had desperately wanted a few years earlier:

> Sometime back in 1988 or '89, I had volunteered to go over

and be an observer during the ceasefire in the Iraq-Iran civil war. I was single, footloose and fancy-free and I would've gone in a heartbeat, but they knocked me back. Then, in 1992, when I had a child on the way and a wife who is half Lebanese, they rang me and said 'we want to send you as an observer to the Golan Heights (the disputed territory between Israel and Syria, where the United Nations operated a buffer zone monitored by its Disengagement Observer Force until 2000)'. At that stage of my life I just didn't want to do that, so I told them I wasn't interested.

One of the key reasons for staying put in Brisbane arrived shortly after he rejected the Army's offer. On 10 August 1992, Campbell and Lisa welcomed their first daughter Rebecca into the world.

In what would be Campbell's final year in the army, the 29-year-old was promoted to the rank of Major in 1993, working as the Operations Officer in 2nd Combat Engineer Regiment at Enoggera Barracks under the command of Peter Cosgrove. But after 12 years of military service Campbell wanted out, to the disappointment of his commanding officers including Cosgrove:

> I was promoted to Major at a fairly young age, but I'd had enough. I had my MBA, we were starting our family and I was looking for jobs in the private sector. I wanted to do my own things, I wanted a business career. I wanted to excel on my own merits, not just have to wait in line for a period of time before being promoted the way it happens in the army. At this stage of my life I wanted to translate my military skills into the private sector. I was interested in business, it sounded exciting to me, and I wanted to create wealth for the company I worked for and for my family.

Campbell's final report of his army career reads:

> Major Newman is a very impressive operations officer. He is eager, talented and shows an extraordinary level of

commitment. He works until things are done, respects deadlines and always strives for excellence. He is highly principled with a clearly defined sense of right and wrong. He holds views strongly and is not afraid to put them forcefully. You may not always agree with what he says, but you respect the conviction with which he says it. As President of the RTF (Army Relief Trust Fund) he has completely rationalised the account. He produced a constitution, a workable annual budget and he manages the operation rigorously through the committee. We are losing a fine young officer with considerable potential.

Campbell's exit from the army took longer than he had planned. The nation was still reeling from the recession it had to have. Prime Minister Paul Keating was trying to contain a run of budget blow-outs after narrowly defeating John Hewson and his proposed GST at the federal election in March 1993. The trend unemployment rate peaked at 10.7 percent in August that year. Job opportunities in the engineering and consulting game were scarce. Campbell remembered:

> I couldn't find a job anywhere, even though I had an Honours degree in Engineering, an MBA and a good CV. Finally, I saw an ad for PA Consulting Group, and after an extensive recruitment process I started work there in early 1994.

Tough as nuts

A few months before he started work with PA Consulting Group, Campbell was reunited with his parents and sister Kate in Hobart. It was not a happy occasion. The family had come together at a time of great personal stress. At the age of 55, Jocelyn had just been diagnosed with uterine cancer and required urgent surgery. Her strength of character masked the seriousness of her diagnosis. Friends at the time remembered her outright refusal to "wallow in self-pity". Staff recalled her editing and rewriting the consent form she was supposed to sign before her surgery – Jocelyn believed it was "a bit too general", so she wrote out a different form. Edwina Gatenby, a close friend of Kate, told Fairfax newspapers in 2000:

> I remember when she was in hospital…everyone was obviously shaken by it, but she was determined that there was no point lying around feeling sorry for herself, she was going to get better and life would go on.[28]

The family supported their matriarch through surgery and her subsequent recovery away from the pressures of Parliament. A few months after her return to the corridors of power in Canberra, the family would face an even more frightening shock in May 1994. In what doctors believed was unrelated to the uterine cancer scare, Jocelyn was told she had breast cancer, like her grandmother, mother and sister before her. Jocelyn later said she was "shattered that day" and thought she was "on the way out". Remarkably, she remained in Parliament. After spending less than six months on the backbench to recover from a mastectomy, she returned to the Shadow Ministry to do a job she had always coveted. In an offer she couldn't refuse from Opposition Leader Alexander Downer, she was appointed Shadow Minister for Defence in September 1994. Finally, she could utilise personal insights and experiences gained as an army wife in the 1960s and '70s. Her "stay at home" husband Kevin provided the perfect sounding board for the complex issues the Defence portfolio was renowned for. In her 2009 book *So Many Firsts: Liberal Women from Enid Lyons to the Turnbull Era*, Margaret Fitzherbert described Jocelyn as "unrelenting" in her approach to policy issues:

> Newman systematically attacked the ALP on Defence issues. Her file in the Parliamentary Library is distinctive for its sheer size and shows her unrelenting approach. It also shows clarity of thought and strong reliance on evidence in her attacks. Few Newman media releases arrived on a journalist's

desk without a raft of relevant statistics and quotes, all neatly attributed. Her capacity for attack and her genuine interest in policy – how it influences people, how it is developed in consultation with stakeholders, how it is presented to Parliament – made Newman a natural in Opposition. Her performance meant that, aside from when she stood down between May and September 1994 due to ill health, Newman was a given in any iteration of the Liberal frontbench, under any leader.

During the period of his mother's diagnoses and recovery, Campbell was getting used to his new career in the private sector. For the first seven months of his job at PA Consulting Group, he worked as a fly-in, fly-out consultant on a maintenance improvement project at the Moura Coal Mine in Central Queensland, jetting in on Mondays and returning home on Fridays. While Campbell was taking a break in Port Douglas with Lisa, their daughter Rebecca and his mum Jocelyn during a weekend in August 1994, explosions killed 11 miners at the site and forced the closure of underground mining operations there. Later that same year, Campbell was sent to Tasmania to work for the Hydro-Electric Commission.

At the height of Jocelyn's health crisis, the Newman family was given at least one reason to celebrate when Kevin was named an Officer of the Order of Australia in the 1994 Queen's Birthday Honours. In the decade since his retirement, Kevin had become a director of the Stockman's Hall of Fame, president of the National Trust of Tasmania, a member of the Board of the Menzies Foundation and chairman of the council of Old Parliament House in Canberra. He had a particular passion for community health, serving as Chairman of the Tasmanian Committee of Nurse Education from 1986 until 1989 and helping to establish the Menzies Centre for Population Health Research at the University of Tasmania. He was also Chairman of the Launceston Public Hospital Board from 1985 until 1989. Lisa Newman's father

Frank Monsour had become close mates with Kevin during this period. On his frequent visits to Canberra in various capacities as a healthcare leader, Frank would often joke that he outranked Kevin in the Army, despite not being a military man at all. Frank was a lifelong Army Reservist, but in his role as a senior Colonel Consultant for the Australian Defence Force's Office of the Surgeon General, he was of higher rank than Kevin, the retired Lieutenant-Colonel.

Frank recounted his friendship with Kevin:

> Kevin was a great gentleman, I held him in very high regard. He was extremely well liked, whether it was the Governor General or the man on the street, he could talk and get along with anyone. I liked spending time with him. I know how special and close his relationship with Campbell was.

Apart from his varied community service and board roles, Kevin enjoyed life as a self-described "supportive husband":

> I do it gladly although some of my friends still scratch their heads when they front our dining room for a meal cooked by me. There aren't too many New Age Guys in my generation.

Throughout 1995, Campbell worked on several small projects for PA Consulting Group, including a coal mine in the Hunter Valley. Later that year, the fortunes of PA Consulting Group rose in tandem with a resurgent national economy when it landed a big contract with Telstra in south-east Queensland, keeping Campbell closer to home. The most significant event of this year came with the birth of their second daughter Sarah, on 8 June.

At the end of 1995, Campbell was head-hunted by Grainco, a Queensland storage and handling company servicing the wheat and barley industries. Campbell worked on a range of major projects for the company, identifying expansion opportunities and building silos and facilities at sites in Melbourne, country Victoria, southern New South Wales and Brisbane. Just two years after leaving the army, Campbell was working his way up to the executive level in one of Australia's largest agribusinesses. Campbell later reflected:

> There was a lot of travel, a lot of scouting out new opportunities and ways to grow the company. I helped develop low cost pathways to get farmers' grain to port and out to overseas markets. Melbourne was a good example. Within a three-year period, I'd scouted the location by identifying the potential to use the existing dual gauge railway, got the approvals and had the silos and port facilities built. It was an exciting time to be in the industry.

Lesley Jenkin, who worked as Campbell's personal assistant at Grainco, said he "always demanded 110 percent but he gave 120 percent in return".

The most powerful woman in Australian politics

The political climate during this time favoured the Liberal-National Coalition. The Keating Labor Government was facing a revitalised John Howard, widely tipped to become the next Prime Minister following his famous "Lazarus with a triple bypass" comeback as Opposition Leader a year earlier in January 1995. The predictions came to pass at the election on 2 March 1996 with "Howard's battlers" swinging heavily to give the Coalition the second-biggest majority in Australian Parliamentary history, second only to Fraser's resounding win in 1975. Now that she finally had the opportunity to be the Defence Minister in government, Jocelyn was bitterly disappointed with the portfolio the new Prime Minister gave her:

> I had expected to get Defence. I had developed what I believed was a good reforming Defence policy and when that was not offered, I was very disappointed. Disappointment

was soon followed by shock and apprehension when I considered the ramifications of accepting Social Security. It was an area that I had never taken a deep interest in, but I was well aware that it was complex, political dynamite, and in need of reform. I discovered that it was a physically enormous portfolio, over twenty thousand officers and spent about a third of the national budget, forty billion dollars. Its operations and programs were based on a complex act and hundreds of regulations. As I met with the Department's head and his senior officers I began to appreciate the task that now lay before me. I had to work very hard on a very steep learning curve. Of course like dozens of new ministers before me the special incentive of getting on top of it all was the approaching first day of the new Parliament and Senate Question Time (on 30 April 1996).

Howard acknowledged Jocelyn's disappointment in his autobiography *Lazarus Rising* though he didn't know the hard-nosed Jocelyn had burst into tears after his phone call about her new Cabinet position.

In her capacity as the Minister For Social Security, rebadged as the Family and Community Services portfolio in 1998, Jocelyn was described as the most powerful woman in Australian politics. Ranked eighth in the Howard Ministry with control of 40 percent of the Commonwealth Budget, she had become the most senior woman in the history of Federal Parliament.

Go and see your father

Campbell was growing in stature at Grainco since starting work there three years earlier, and as the proud father of two girls, he was content with his place in the world. But his comfortable, busy life was thrown off its axis in July 1999.

Since the start of the year Kevin, now 65, had spent considerable time in a wheelchair recovering from an injury to his Achilles. He was unable to stay active and work his lungs, already weakened over the years from the degenerative autoimmune disease lupus. The flu he had picked up in early July developed into pneumonia, and he was hospitalised. Jocelyn was in Scotland at the time, investigating UK approaches to welfare reform. During an inspection of a slum clearance project in Glasgow, word came through from Kevin. He was getting worse, and he wanted her home.

At around the same time, Campbell was having a beer at the house of Shayne Rutherford, a Grainco colleague. They had just returned from a work trip to Toowoomba. Campbell remembers the moment Rutherford stopped their conversation mid-sentence to insist he drop everything to visit Kevin in hospital:

> We were having a beer and a talk, and our conversation turned to how my dad was sick. Shayne just stopped in his tracks and said: go see your father. I told him dad was fine, he was being looked after in hospital, and Shayne just said 'Go and see your father'. He told me he had always regretted not dropping everything to visit his sick father who had died before he got the chance to see him. He just kept saying 'you need to go and see your father'. I came home and talked to Lisa. She said 'your Dad's probably a bit lonely, go and keep him company. It's all been on your sister's shoulders, go and keep him company until your mum gets there on Saturday'.

Campbell caught a Friday afternoon flight to Canberra and went straight to the hospital to spend a few hours with his dad:

> I was with him at his bedside, having a good chat, talking about the building of our house, telling him about the work I was doing on a big grain silo down at the Port of Melbourne. He had an oxygen mask on, but he seemed fine.

Campbell stayed with his sister Kate, and they had dinner together. Their mum called during a stopover in Bangkok to check on Kevin's condition. She would be home early the next morning, a Saturday. Campbell also called Lisa, reassuring her about his dad's condition:

> I called and said Dad was in good spirits, and there was no need for Lisa and the kids to come down to Canberra. I think I said something like 'he's not going to pass away tonight or anything, he's fine. I'll be coming home tomorrow after I say hi to mum'. The next morning, it's about 8am and I'm in the shower getting ready to go out to the airport to collect mum. Then Kate comes in, she's very distressed, saying the hospital called to tell us Dad had just died.

Jocelyn's plane was still in the air circling above Canberra, waiting for the heavy fog to lift.

> I had to go to the airport to meet mum, but the plane was delayed and circling because of all the fog. Finally, they land, and she gets off the plane and walks up the airbridge with a big smile on her face. Then she sees me and as she got to me she realised what had happened. I took her into the Qantas Club, and she just collapsed. She was just sitting there crying. It was just terrible. She missed him by a couple of hours. These two people had been incredibly close and totally in love. It was an awful end. It was just so tragic.

At the time of his death, Kevin and Jocelyn had been married for just over 38 years.

To this day, Campbell has been unable to bring himself to watch video footage of his father's memorial service. Jocelyn described how Campbell felt about his father in interviews she did with News Corporation papers in 2011:

> As an individual, I think Campbell is a very loving man. He loved his father very dearly and was not afraid to show that, which is a nice quality in a young fella. He did not think it

unmanly to give his father a hug and be proud of his father and tell him so. He admired his father enormously. His dad could have said, 'Jump off the roof' and he'd have done it; they were real mates.

Tributes for Kevin flowed in from all quarters. John Howard and Opposition Leader Kim Beazley praised his diligent parliamentary service and dedication to his family. The then Tasmanian Opposition Leader and Bass Liberal MHA Sue Napier described Kevin as an "extraordinarily hard worker for the people of Bass."

Towards the end, Kevin himself appeared deeply satisfied with his lot in life. In the book *Partners*, published a few months before Kevin's death, he described the empowering feeling he and Jocelyn experienced when their serious illnesses forced them to confront their mortality:

> Over recent years we have each had to look a doctor in the eye while we were told that we were not immortal. That can be pretty hard to come to terms with. But it can also be enormously positive. The heightened appreciation of life, love, family and friends is something to be experienced. Every day is special and to be lived to the full. It also helps to put the problems in perspective. Political attacks, be they ever so cruel, are not really of enormous importance. Just to be alive and loved counts for more than fame and fortune. We think fortune has smiled on us. When we married, it was for love. But we all know that choosing a mate for life can be a pig-in-a-poke. For us a long marriage has worked: We have been blessed with great children and grandchildren; we have both had important and influential careers; but best of all, we are still 'best mates'.

Kevin was farewelled at a state funeral service in the white-walled chapel on the grounds of the Royal Military College at Duntroon on 22 July 1999. Cadets from the military college bore his casket. Prime

Minister John Howard delivered one of the eulogies, describing his former Ministerial colleague as a "man of duty":

> Kevin had a simple faith in his country, a love of his family, a proper sense of priorities and a belief that in the words of his Governor-General and Commander in Chief that if you live according to the principles of courage and faith and integrity you can endure the challenges, you can endure difficulties, you can make a difference.

From the time he graduated from Duntroon as an officer in 1955 right up to a few months before his passing, Kevin had served the nation in the army, the Parliament and in non-profit organisations for 44 years. Attending the funeral service with Lisa by his side, the solemn occasion sparked an ember in Campbell that would fire his future career in politics. When Campbell's time came, he wanted the eulogy at his own funeral to be about more than just his successful business career. He wanted his eulogy to live up to his father's before him.

Tasmanian Tiger

For the time being, Campbell remained focused on his career with Grainco. Over the next two years, he would climb its ranks to become general manager of operations with responsibility for projects in Queensland and Victoria and hundreds of staff. Just prior to his father's death, Campbell and Lisa had bought a block of land on the same street as her parents in the hills of Windsor in Brisbane's inner north. The design and construction of the house on a complex, sloping site, as well as Campbell's increasing workload at Grainco, provided welcome distractions in the wake of his father's death.

To fill the void left by her husband's passing, Jocelyn immersed herself in her work as Minister for Family and Community Services. In an address at the National Press Club on 29 September 1999, just two months after Kevin's death, Jocelyn announced a significant review of Australia's welfare system. In his 2008 research paper *The Centrelink Experiment*, Professor John Halligan wrote:

> ... while the unemployment rate in Australia was falling, the proportion of working-aged people receiving some sort of benefits was increasing. Thirty years ago, one in 20 working-aged people were receiving payments. It was now one in five – more than 2.5 million people. About 60 percent of these, under the current system, were not required to look for work or contribute to their communities in any way.

When the review's report was released in August 2000, it called for "fundamental change" with a greater focus on individualised service delivery, mutual obligations and a simplified income support structure. The rollout of welfare system reform after the report was released would be Jocelyn's final task as a Minister in the Howard Government. As a relatively new grandmother to Campbell and Lisa's girls, Jocelyn began to question her future after Kevin's death. Her passion for the cut and thrust of politics had diminished considerably since. Just as Jocelyn was beginning to sound out her intentions to retire to Howard, she was featured in a lengthy profile piece in the *Good Weekend Magazine* in *The Age* and *Sydney Morning Herald* newspapers on 18 May 2000. Under the headline *"Tasmanian Tiger"*, the article described her "iron grip on the welfare purse strings" and outlined her plans to "whip the welfare system into shape", alongside personal reflections of her health battles and the loss of Kevin. She was described by people who worked with her as a "fairly formidable person" and "tough as nuts". The one thing the article didn't pick up on was Jocelyn's growing desire to leave politics. Rumours of her intention to quit surfaced shortly after the profile piece was published. In a telling exchange with an ABC Radio reporter on Thursday, 15 June 2000, Jocelyn batted off questions about her future:

> (Reporter) ALEXANDRA KIRK: On a more personal level,

you've been a Senator now for 14 years and there've been plenty of rumours that you've had enough of politics. Do you think it's time to retire?

JOCELYN NEWMAN: Oh, I'll make up my mind when I have a moment to breathe. When I decide that politics is no longer for me, I guess I'll be telling the Prime Minister first and maybe you'll get to hear afterwards.

ALEXANDRA KIRK: But you haven't said that you want to continue.

JOCELYN NEWMAN: Oh, well, I'm 63 and I won't intend to go on forever. Everybody has a retirement age whether it's mandatory or voluntary. I haven't made up my mind about my future at this stage.

ALEXANDRA KIRK: You were very close to your husband and he played a very supportive role when he retired from politics and your career took precedence. Did you lose a lot of impetus for politics when you lost him?

JOCELYN NEWMAN: No, but it's not nearly so much fun without him.

She continued in the role for another 18 months. Just before Christmas 2001, Howard used a Cabinet reshuffle to help Jocelyn ease her way out of public office. She later resigned from the Senate on 1 February 2002. Howard wrote in his autobiography:

> Jocelyn Newman had indicated for some time her desire to retire. She had had terrible health challenges, especially from breast cancer. She had been a great minister, putting aside her real disappointment at not being given the Defence portfolio when we won in March 1996. Jocelyn had a dogged, battling style which appealed across the political divide to many people. She had, however, reached the point where she wished, quite literally, to retire and spend more time with her family in Canberra.

Jocelyn's policy achievements and personal tenacity were widely praised by all sides of politics. In a Valedictory motion in the Senate on 13 February 2002, the then Health and Ageing Minister Kay Patterson said:

> Time does not permit me to speak about her various achievements in the portfolios she was Minister for (Social Security, Family and Community Services, Minister Assisting the Prime Minister for the Status of Women). Her legacy as a Senator and Minister has been enormous. We all remember the very tough test she faced when confronted with breast cancer. I will never forget the press conference she called to say she was stepping down from the Shadow Ministry in order to have treatment. It was a sign of the respect in which she was held in the press gallery that there was hardly a dry eye among the normally tough operators behind those microphones and cameras. As if one challenge was not enough, it was not long before she had to face the second challenge of cancer and very drastic treatment which left her with side effects that could have been enough to lead most to think that the demands of public life were too much and it would be better to bow out. It was of course a terrible blow to her when Kevin died. He had been ill for some time, but he never complained. I know that his death dealt Jocelyn a dreadful blow. The toll of public life can sometimes be almost too great to bear, and surely this must have been one of the times that toll was too great. A less mortal would have packed it in – but not Jocelyn. Jocelyn said in her maiden speech: '… the example which my husband set of service to his electorate, his state and his country will be always before me. I hope I can one day claim the love and respect which his constituents came to hold for him.' All I can say is: Jocelyn, you can.

Into business and a new horizon of service and duty

In August 2001, six months before his mother's resignation, Campbell himself had resigned from his job, leaving Grainco with a plan to start up his own management consultancy business. His chief client was AWB Limited, working for them in logistics and business development in much the same way he had built up Grainco's operations. Other consulting work at the time included a stint back at Moura Coal Mine and an American company he had dealings with during his time with Grainco. But after a combined two decades of military service and work in the private sector, Campbell began lifting his gaze to a new horizon.

Consciously or not, the revelation he had experienced at his father's funeral service resurfaced. He wanted to do more than make money. Increasingly he thought about the linked concepts of service and leadership, and the fabric of life lessons he had constructed over the past two decades were coalescing into the imminent third phase of his career. His time at Duntroon, his military service, the Parliamentary careers of his parents, managing multi-million dollar operations at Grainco and running his consultancy business would all combine into a launch pad for his next major step.

While he didn't yet know when, where or how, Campbell's future direction was taking shape in his mind. He was going to make a run for politics.

4

TOP JOB FOR AN OUTSIDER

2002-2004: Campbell Newman runs for Lord Mayor of Brisbane

Some of the brightest future stars of conservative politics in Queensland were about to meet in a dreary office located deep within Brisbane's historic City Hall. They were gathered in the party room allocated to the Brisbane City Council Opposition. Paint was peeling from the walls. A rectangular boardroom table loomed large in the middle of the room. The cavernous atmosphere was at odds with the small gathering, a diminished Council Opposition of just eight members. Labor's Mayor Jim Soorley, a former Roman Catholic priest, had ruled the roost at council for the past decade. A cynic might say Soorley had allocated this unedifying space to the Opposition as just another psychological blow against his political opponents; a run-down office to match their decimated electoral stature.

Sitting around the party room table, the team of Liberal Councillors featured a future Federal MP, State Treasurer and Lord Mayor, plus a soon-to-be-anointed Queensland Liberal Party President and, finally, a Queensland Local Government Association President. For now, Jane Prentice, Tim Nicholls, Graham Quirk, Michael Caltabiano, and Margaret De Wit, plus three other Liberal councillors, were waiting for Campbell Newman to walk in to address them as a group for the first time. They had no way of knowing they were about to make decisions that would shape Queensland's future for the next decade and more. In a political ripple effect, they would also inadvertently alter the very nature of electioneering and style of conservative politics across Australia.

Campbell's address to the party room on that day was notable only for the response it garnered from Nicholls, who thought Campbell was too politically naïve and his planned approach to campaigning too soft:

> 'You need to be more of a dictator', Nicholls reportedly said across the table.

It was March 2002. The war on terror and debate over asylum seekers was dominating the national agenda in the aftermath of the 11 September attacks and the "children overboard" Tampa incident some six months earlier. Prime Minister John Howard was riding high after a decisive election win on 10 November 2001, recording one of the biggest swings to an incumbent government in the nation's history. Earlier that year, at the February 2001 state election, Premier Peter Beattie had won his own massive majority after weathering a political storm that had threatened to sink his Government. Claims of electoral fraud by Labor Party members in North Queensland had sparked the Shepherdson Inquiry in late 2000. That investigation uncovered a culture of electoral rorts and forced the resignation of Beattie's Deputy Premier Jim Elder and two of the party's backbenchers Mike Kaiser and Grant Musgrove.

By the time Campbell was due to address the Council Opposition party room in March 2002, the Beattie Government was dominating the Opposition in the Queensland Parliament on a scale similar to the Soorley Labor Council's command over the Liberals in City Hall. Beattie was the most popular state Premier in the nation. The Shepherdson Inquiry report handed down on 17 April 2001 was long forgotten. If a week is a long time in politics, 12 months is several lifetimes.

Against this backdrop of strong Liberal power on a federal level and Labor dominance on a state and local government level, the eight Liberal councillors awaited the arrival of their new Lord Mayoral candidate. Campbell was meeting with the Liberal councillors at City Hall to do what many believed was impossible. As an outsider, he needed to unite the fractured Council Opposition and convince them he was the best man to lead them at the 2004 Brisbane City Council election. The room was virtually cleaved in half between two warring factions; on one side sat Caltabiano, Nicholls and Quirk, and on the other the five female councillors De Wit, Prentice, Geraldine Knapp, Carol Cashman and Judy Magub. Tension filled the air. Over the past two years, these members of a depleted Council Opposition lurched from one internal fight to the next. The Queensland Liberal Party itself was struggling to stay afloat. On a state level, the Libs were reduced to an abysmal three seats in Parliament after securing just 14.32 percent of the primary vote at the state election in February 2001. This followed on from the March 2000 council election, where they had recorded the worst ever result for the conservatives at a Brisbane City Council election. Their candidate for Lord Mayor in 2000 Gail Austen was deemed an unmitigated disaster after an initial period of great promise. The proverbial wheels of Austen's campaign bus were never screwed on tightly enough. There was little in the way of structure and strategy to her campaign and the Liberal organisation was at its lowest ebb. Money was short, discipline was lacking and a cohesive message for the electorate was virtually non-existent. Despite internal Liberal Party polling showing Soorley was deeply unpopular, he smashed Austen and the Libs into electoral oblivion with 56 percent of the primary vote, increasing the Labor majority by picking up two extra councillors.

By the time Campbell came along, Soorley was presiding over a council dominated by his 18 councillors to the Liberal Opposition's eight. Commentator and former Liberal Party official Graham Young summed up the dire state of the Council Opposition by saying failure for the party had become a "comfortable habit":

> (The Liberal Party had) no money, too many messages, and none of them right, too little manpower, incompetent management, and constant internal faction fighting. The party is no longer capable of making a connection with its constituency.

That was the political environment Campbell was set to operate in as he walked into the Opposition party room meeting in March 2002.

You could go for that

Campbell's motivation to run for politics was sparked three years earlier at his father's funeral in 1999. But it was a chance conversation at a 2002 Valentine's Day dinner that led him to the Opposition party room for his first address to the group of Liberal councillors.

It was 15 February, a Friday night. Campbell was with Lisa, her brother Seb Monsour and his wife Megan at the prestigious Queensland Club to celebrate Valentine's Day, which had fallen the day before. Their dinner followed celebrations a fortnight earlier to mark the end of Jocelyn Newman's political career. She had retired from the Senate on 1 February. At their Valentine's dinner on that Friday evening, Seb was sitting directly opposite Campbell. Halfway through their meal, Seb casually asked: "Did you know the Liberal Party's looking for a candidate for the Lord Mayoralty?"

Campbell said nothing and instead turned to Lisa, seated on his right. She looked back at him and said what he was already thinking: "You could go for that". Lisa was aware of Campbell's desire to serve in elected office. They had discussed it on the flight back from his dad's funeral, though the idea had remained largely unspoken until now. Campbell was hoping for Lisa's endorsement and surprised by her decisive response. His new management consulting business was taking off, but he found himself wanting more than just a lucrative career in the private sector. And he was increasingly concerned at the Soorley Council's lack of action on pressing infrastructure and transport needs across Brisbane.

"Well, I might be interested", he said to Seb. "How do I find out more?" Seb told him the first port of call was Michael Caltabiano, the councillor for the district of Chandler and Liberal Party power broker. Seb pledged to set up a meeting between the pair and sound out party officials about Campbell's potential as a candidate. The timing felt right. The party needed someone new, a political cleanskin, to correct the disastrous mistakes of the 2000 campaign. Campbell matched the profile they were looking for: married with kids, successful army and private sector career, managerial experience, no scandals in his personal life. But as a potential Lord Mayoral candidate coming in from the outside, he would be starting from scratch on so many fronts. Campbell recalled:

> There was no money, no support, no policy, no unity, no nothing, absolutely nothing. It was a complete scorched earth.

He needed to curate a public persona and build his profile, select a team of candidates, raise money, door-knock the suburbs, devise policies, and train for media interviews, all while learning and discovering more about the city he wanted to lead. Having spent most of his time on the north side of Brisbane, the southern suburbs were mostly unknown territory. Importantly, he needed to visit leading business people across Brisbane in a bid to raise funds and rebuild the faith they had lost in the Liberal Party. The uphill battle of fundraising was critical to Campbell's chances; Labor had significantly outspent their Liberal opponents in recent council elections. But most business people were reluctant to throw their support behind anyone going up against the incumbent. Few people gave the Liberal Party any chance of winning the top job from Lord Mayor Soorley, and they feared retribution or being informally blacklisted if they backed his opponent.

The cumulative task confronting Campbell was monumental. But, like an army expedition across the desert or the logistical challenge of building a giant grain silo at a capital city sea port, Campbell mapped it out. He planned and strategised, breaking the task down into bite-sized chunks. One of the first steps – that introductory meeting with Caltabiano in his ward office in the Brisbane suburb of Carindale – went well. Putting aside his own mayoral ambitions, Caltabiano liked what he saw. He phoned Liberal faction heavyweight Santo Santoro, who was in Texas at the time, and convinced him Campbell was the right man for the job. Subsequent meetings were lined up with party officials such as Brendan Cooper, the then state director. There was just one formality left – Campbell needed to fill out the necessary forms to join the Liberal Party. An unnamed source quoted in *The Australian* said of Campbell: "He was not a creature of the Liberal Party".[29]

> My first impression was he was a completely self-driven man, completely independent and really the party was just there as an easel for him. He is an extraordinarily energetic and driven person ... who had great reasons for wanting to be Lord Mayor, very honourable, wanting to fix things.

The path was cleared for Campbell's preselection with other potential candidates quietly discouraged from standing. At this early juncture of his political career, Campbell described himself as a "complete babe in the woods":

> I had no clue about the factions, about them clearing the path for me in the preselection, the machinations of the party going on in the background. I knew nothing about all that.

Under the section titled "Why I would make a suitable candidate" in his official application for endorsement as the Liberal Party's Lord Mayoral candidate, submitted on 3 March 2002, Campbell wrote:

> Tertiary qualifications in business and engineering, a successful career in senior management in the private sector, experience of a range of large organisations as a management consultant and involvement in large complex change projects, (and) leadership skills gained from a 13 year career in the Australian Army, responsible for leading soldiers in demanding and stressful situations. I am energetic, pro-active and decisive and have the capacity to work under pressure for extended periods. I have a strong feel for the demands of a political career from my own family experience with both parents being involved in federal politics.

Campbell, Lisa and their two girls – nine-year-old Rebecca and six-year-old Sarah – arrived at the Greek Club in Brisbane's trendy West End early on Sunday morning, 17 March, for the preselection meeting. He was there to deliver his pitch to the party faithful; the Lord Mayoral candidate was chosen by a plebiscite of hundreds of preselectors from across metropolitan Brisbane. Despite being the only candidate, rules dictated that Campbell must go through due process. He told the audience:

> The current bunch of ALP commissars are running us into the Siberian tundra unless we in the Liberal Party do something about it. We have the opportunity, in around two years, to greatly influence the outcome for the city and this is what I want to speak to this afternoon. Lisa and I both carefully considered what standing for Mayor would mean to our family. Having carefully considered the implications it's important that you know that Lisa is right beside me in this endeavour. My career has been about leadership from the time, at the age of 23, that I had the honour to command 40

soldiers to when I had over 220 permanent employees and 400 casuals bringing in the Queensland grain harvest and shipping it to overseas export markets. My career has been about 'getting things done' in demanding environments, under pressure, delivering the results for people who have depended on me. My career track record speaks for itself. I will get things moving in record time and won't be distracted by the melodramatic antics of our opponents. Brisbane can have a fantastic future, but we have to break out of the ideological dead end of our opponents. They have no new ideas, they are trapped in a road block…their vindictive approach to those who would propose a different way, their high taxing and big spending budgets directed toward inner-city elites. What the heck are they doing about the big issues? We need to address the infrastructure needs of the city, we need to put in place a framework for economic growth, we need to put in place budgets to produce real outcomes and we need to do all this and preserve the essential quality of life that we all love in this town. In closing, you have a choice now. You can go for new ideas, new enthusiasm and new energy or you can stay with the old. I urge you to go for the new, I urge you to choose new leadership, I dare you to go for new ideas and I humbly ask for your support. I won't let you, the rest of the Liberal Party or the people of the great city of Brisbane down!

His speech was met with warm applause. Graham Quirk remembered sitting in the hall listening to Campbell's speech, thinking:

> Well this is a guy who really does have a chance. I had toyed with moving on. I had felt that, before Campbell arrived on the scene, there wasn't in my mind a great prospect of us returning to the administration benches. When Campbell came along he certainly gave me a new lease of life. He came

to the job well credentialed with his engineering background and had a real sense of energy and focus that I thought gave us a genuine chance.

Councillor Geraldine Knapp was also at the preselection meeting: "He got up and gave this speech and all I could think of was 'we're going to have to do something about that voice'."

In accordance with party rules, the Newman family was taken from the hall to a small adjacent room to allow members to openly discuss the merits of the candidate. It did not go quite as smoothly as Caltabiano and others had predicted. The Newmans could hear the proceedings and debate through the walls. Someone questioned the validity of running an unknown "blow in" – someone who had only just joined the Liberal Party – in such an important position. Liberal Party elder and former state president Con Galtos jumped up to speak in defence of Campbell, who he had grown to like and respect from their dealings together at Grainco over recent years. Campbell took the opportunity to talk to his two girls, telling them people would call their dad "all sorts of names and say all sorts of things" in his new adventure. The vote inside the hall was called and cast, confirming Campbell as the Liberal Party's new Lord Mayoral candidate. The Newman family re-entered the hall. The room was buoyant, enthusiastic. But there was little time to bask in the moment. His first media conference awaited outside. Campbell was incredibly nervous in front of the cameras, but he passed with flying colours. The next morning an FM Radio station lampooned the "funny" way Campbell walked, referring to his appearance on the TV news the night before. The challenge of leading a divided team in a media landscape constantly littered with trivialities was on display from day one.

The long campaign begins

The campaign took off at a furious pace in the days after his preselection. To brush up on his public appearance and speaking techniques, Campbell and other council candidates paid a visit to Jann Stuckey, an image and public speaking consultant and the Liberal candidate for the state seat of Currumbin. He also took the time to win over the group of female councillors, who were suspicious of Campbell. They wondered if he was a Santoro stooge. A few weeks into the long campaign ahead, Campbell received his first major profile piece in *The Courier-Mail* on 4 April 2002. In the article, his mother Jocelyn brushed away concerns about Campbell's political inexperience: "He has seen politics close-up and, therefore, goes into it knowingly. When you live with it as kids, it tends to put you off because you see what a hard life it can be."

Campbell told the same reporter:

> I don't have any self-doubts about my ability – and I don't mean to be arrogant and I won't be arrogant – but what I have got to do is convince people of that. The Newman approach to politics has always been about doing the job for the people we are representing.

In June 2002, just a few months after Campbell started in the role of Lord Mayoral candidate, the Soorley council released its Budget. Campbell was so nervous about providing his budget response to the Brisbane media pack that the sheets of notes he held were shaking:

> I had to sit there in the council gallery and listen to Soorley deliver his budget (in June 2002) with my heart racing. Then I had about an hour to go out the back to the Opposition party room and analyse the budget as quick as I could because the media was waiting outside for my response. In those days, there were four TV cameras, print journos, radio stations, lots of journos all there set up and waiting in King George Square. It was a very big deal for me at the time. I was so scared. I was catatonic with fear. I was wooden,

my knees were knocking together. It was my first big media conference. I was terrified.

Apart from media commitments, the pace of juggling family, work and campaigning became so frenetic Campbell hired an assistant. Helen Mathers, a 21-year-old university graduate, was brought in to work as a jill-of-all-trades across Campbell's consulting business and campaign team, her wage funded directly by the Newmans. Mathers became a crucial element of a campaign team that had begun to assemble around Campbell. His sister-in-law Heidi Monsour played a lead role handling the management of events and the administration of early fundraising activities. Greg Bowden was an early volunteer on the team. He and Campbell had formed a friendship at Grainco, where Campbell was in logistics and Bowden worked in procurement.

Together with the existing councillors, one of the team's first collective tasks was policy development. At this point in the four-year electoral cycle, the Opposition's policy cupboard was bare. Working closely with the councillors, in particular Graham Quirk, as well as independent experts where required, Campbell set about devising a suite of in-depth policies. The aim was to progressively release them over the next 18 months right up to the scheduled March 2004 election. They chose five key policy areas: Parks, sport and recreation; governance and administration; advancing the Brisbane economy; planning; and the biggest and electorally hottest of them all – transport and traffic. The policies were released every six months or so, peaking with their signature Moving Brisbane plan to tackle the city's traffic congestion woes with new infrastructure, bus services and various road upgrades.

Graham Quirk, the Opposition's spokesman for Transport and Traffic, was working on the Moving Brisbane policy before Campbell arrived on the scene. The centrepiece of the policy was an ambitious tunnel and bridge program called TransApex. Launched at Liberal

Party headquarters in Bowen Hills on a mild Sunday in July 2002, the Moving Brisbane announcement came complete with a new novelty for the time: CD ROMs that featured a slick sales video. TV news crews lapped up the announcement, running with the theme of 'Liberal Revival'. Campbell attended a business breakfast to sell the policy the following morning, with the scope and detail of the policy garnering wide praise. The team was on an early roll. At the same time, Campbell continued his management consultancy work for his major client AWB Limited, scouting for the potential to build new grain terminals at sites in South Australia and Western Australia.

The rollout of policies and some positive early media coverage helped with the next important and most challenging task. Given the immense scale of Brisbane City Council's footprint, they needed to fundraise hundreds of thousands of dollars to be viable in the long campaign ahead. But raising money for their campaign was difficult before they even began. The Liberal Party was so run down it was more hindrance than help at the time. Its assets amounted to one building and three staff. Business people viewed the party as a rabble, with rumours swirling it was on the brink of going bust. No-one wanted to throw money into that pit. As Campbell bounced back and forth between boardroom lunches and one-on-one meetings with business leaders in industries such as construction, transport, law and planning, he asked Bowden to help establish a stand-alone trust to take receipt of any donations. So far Campbell had been funding most of the campaigning activities himself. The key ingredient in the new fundraising trust was its isolation from the Liberal Party, giving donors the confidence that their cheques wouldn't be swallowed up and lost if the Party crashed. They named it the Forward Brisbane Leadership Trust, a separate legal entity with parameters in place to comply with political donation disclosure laws.

Through the second half of 2002, while Campbell and his team were out in the field, developing policies and pressing the flesh with donors, Labor was focused on finding a replacement for Mayor Soorley, who had signaled his intention to retire before Campbell was preselected. Soorley was increasingly on the nose, getting into public spats with firefighters and facing a backlash over his spending on international travel. But still he wouldn't nominate a date for his exit. While councillors such as Tim Quinn and David Hinchliffe were mentioned as contenders, the party also tried to recruit rising university star Sandra Harding, the then head of Queensland University of Technology's business school. She declined the party's approach, as did local lobbyist Mark Nolan and Premier Beattie's wife Heather.[30]

In stark contrast to Labor's leadership dilemma in the second half of 2002, Campbell and the campaign received a glowing endorsement in an editorial in *The Courier-Mail*. Under the headline "Liberals get serious about council poll" published on 20 November 2002, the editorial read:

> Nine months into his job as the Liberal Party's Lord Mayoral candidate, Campbell Newman has done enough to show he and his party are serious in their bid to take over the running of Brisbane City Council. It is still more than a year to the next council elections, and the Liberal Party has shown before how it can turn even the most promising start for a Lord Mayoral candidate into an excuse to shoot itself in its bullet-ridden feet. However, Mr Newman carries more substance than many previous conservative hopefuls for the lord mayoralty and, even though it is the four-time election winner Cr (Jim) Soorley he is battling at the moment, that probably will not be the case by the time ballot papers are drawn up for the 2004 poll.

Fundraising and campaigning ramps up in 2003

Campbell's campaign started swimmingly in 2003. Policies continued to be developed and released, while media coverage of his campaign efforts was mostly positive. The Forward Brisbane Leadership Trust continued to build its war chest, though progress on this front was slow. A profile piece in the *Gold Coast Bulletin* by journalist Michael Corkill – who would later work for Campbell as a media adviser – focused on the different styles of campaigning between the two sides, particularly when it came to personal attacks:

> Some of the Labor tactics are already out there. There's the 'parents have been politicians' and 'silver-spooner' jibes, that sort of stuff. As I said, I was in the army for 13 years and dug my fair share of holes. I crawled through the mud and did the route marches. I am tough, I am resilient and I have worked with the salt of the earth, the Australian soldiers. I certainly won't be involved in any muck-raking or tawdry, nasty little things. I have got no skeletons in my closet so they are going to have to look beyond and draw some really long bows. Maybe I shook hands with somebody once.

A distraction rattled the Liberal campaign in early 2003 when Council Opposition Leader Margaret De Wit announced to the Opposition party room she was standing down from the role. She had already issued a media alert to inform the wider world of her decision, and about 90 minutes after telling her colleagues she told the local press gallery. Some of the councillors had increasingly felt De Wit was taking too much of the limelight in the campaign, particularly in the media. With a still relatively low public profile, Campbell needed all the media attention he could get. But De Wit was crowding him out. De Wit's unilateral move to stand down as leader infuriated the team, who found out after she informed local reporters. The mantle of Opposition Leader in Council was passed to Graham Quirk, who flawlessly filled the role. Campbell was allowed to take the lead, particularly in the media. But the De Wit resignation had revived memories of party disunity and instability at a time when Campbell's team was approaching the business community for support. Despite the advances made since Campbell was preselected, fundraising remained a tough task. On one of his many visits to meet with business people since the campaign began in March 2002, Campbell remembered being seated in a boardroom with one of Brisbane's richest men. After some perfunctory greetings, the businessman proceeded to rip Campbell to shreds in a blistering verbal assault:

> He just launches into me, abusing me, told me what a lot of idiots the Liberal Party were, how hopelessly divided they were, what an idiot and a loser I was, why would he ever give us any money, told me I was a disgrace. It was just awful stuff, bully boy tactics. I felt totally demoralised.

Over time, however, the momentum within the team shifted up a gear. In March 2003, Campbell shelved his management consultancy business to concentrate full time on the final 12 months of the campaign. Donations started to steadily flow in to the campaign from mid-2003 as Campbell's star continued to rise and the team's detailed policy releases gained accolades and support. When they received the first big cheque of the campaign so far – a $5000 donation from Sir Robert 'Bob' Mathers – they were ecstatic, and redoubled their efforts. With less than 12 months to go until the election, everyone was lending a hand.

Campbell's mother-in-law Elizabeth, a frequent taxi traveller, handed over dozens of the campaign's policy CD-ROMs to unwitting cab drivers, while his mother Jocelyn rallied Liberal branch members to support her son via phone calls from her unit in Canberra. The former Senator had recently been appointed to the board of the Australian War Memorial and maintained an impeccable book of contacts. Despite all of the momentum and relentless campaigning, it was difficult to gauge how much closer they were to seizing the reins of City Hall. Their challenge was about to take on a different dimension when a new opponent arrived on the scene.

Dim Sim Quinn

On 16 May 2003, Soorley ended many months of speculation and division within Labor ranks by announcing he was leaving City Hall in the next 48 hours. The timing of his exit was a deliberate move to avoid a by-election. Under the current law, the Lord Mayor can immediately install a replacement from his own party if it happened within 12 months of the next scheduled election. Discussions about his replacement were held at a Chinese New Year function back in February. On the lush green lawn of Parliament House, Soorley, Beattie, deputy premier Terry Mackenroth and union heavyweight Bill Ludwig reportedly did a deal to anoint current deputy mayor Tim Quinn as Brisbane's next Lord Mayor. Graham Quirk knew about the deal before anyone else outside Labor's inner circle. Late one night shortly after the meeting of Labor heavyweights at Parliament House, Quirk received an anonymous phone call at his house. A male voice spilled the beans but refused to give his name. Quirk remembered the phone call as being too detailed to be ignored:

> At the time I wasn't absolutely certain that it was a legitimate call. But the person knew enough for me to be of the view that there was a fairly high chance of legitimacy to the call. So the next day in the council chamber, as the then Leader of the Opposition, I announced that this deal had been done on the lawn of Parliament House and that the powers that be, the state Parliamentary leaders and the backroom players in the Labor Party were going to install Tim Quinn as the next Lord Mayor. The look on some faces of shock and horror, particularly people like David Hinchliffe and Maureen Hayes who saw themselves as potential starters for the Lord Mayoralty at the time. As it turned out, the information I received in that anonymous call proved to be absolutely 100 percent correct.

In honour of the finger food apparently served at the deal-making function, the new Lord Mayor was nicknamed "Dim Sim Quinn". Though Campbell's team knew it was coming, the shift to Quinn as Lord Mayor changed the game less than 10 months before the election. Labor hoped the exit of the increasingly unpopular Soorley would boost their chances of retaining the mayoralty of a council they had dominated for over a decade. But just a month later Campbell and his team were handed a gift from the gods of political chance.

On the morning of 24 July 2003, the freshly minted Lord Mayor Quinn was rocked by a front page story in *The Courier-Mail* about a secret council flood report. The headline screamed: "Flood Cover-Up". The explosive article by star journalist Hedley Thomas exposed a secret report into flood levels the council had been hiding for the past four years:

> Expert studies showing Brisbane properties are at greater risk from a serious flood than previously believed have been covered up for four years by Lord Mayor Tim Quinn and the Brisbane City Council. The council also has failed to implement flood mitigation strategies recommended to protect ratepayers from life-threatening floods.

Lord Mayor Quinn was sideswiped. He had been the head of the committee responsible for Town Planning during the period the report was kept hidden. He stumbled for weeks dealing with the fallout. While Quinn struggled to find his feet in his new job, Campbell and his team were locking in candidates across numerous council wards, where they door-knocked and attended grassroots events together.

Ben Myers joins the team

By this stage, the coffers of Forward Brisbane Leadership Trust were filling up. The extra resources allowed for Campbell's former PA at Grainco Lesley Jenkin to be hired. She worked alongside Helen Mathers, who was now based at the Liberal Party HQ.

Ben Myers and Campbell take part in the first "Can Do" stunt in 2004 Brisbane Lord Mayoral election

Campbell celebrated his 40th birthday on 11 August 2003, just as trouble was brewing in the higher echelons of the Queensland branch of the Liberal Party. The state director Brendan Cooper had increasingly become embroiled in another internal party dispute. Towards the end of 2003, the factions flared up and the disunity spilled over, yet again, into the public domain. Things got so bad Cooper resigned. John Wanna from Griffith University later wrote that "factional warfare again dominated Liberal Party politics in 2003", with Cooper bluntly telling reporters he was "fed up with the factionalism and idiocy of the party".[31] The resignation of Cooper and public disunity sent a wave of panic through Campbell's camp just six months out from the council election. Seeking an urgent replacement, Campbell spoke to the ousted Cooper for advice on who might replace him on the campaign team. Cooper gave him three names. When Campbell pressed him for the top pick of the trio, Cooper nominated Ben Myers, a 30-year-old communications manager with the National Retail Association (NRA). Myers was keenly involved with the Young Liberals during his university years and worked for a time in Peter Slipper's electorate office, but he was no longer a member of the Liberal Party. In a later interview with *The Courier-Mail*, Myers said: "I'd never been involved in or ran any campaign of this scale and magnitude. I felt I lacked the experience and I was questioning myself whether I had the interest in doing it."

Campbell and Ben Myers had met on a couple of occasions during the Lord Mayoral candidate's rounds of local businesses and organisations over the past 18 months. But neither of them was sure Myers had the necessary expertise to run a major political campaign. Phone calls ensued between Campbell and NRA bosses Mark Brodie and Patrick McKendry. Graham Quirk spoke to Myers in a bid to convince him. Despite the urgent need for a campaign director, Myers delayed making a decision in the face of repeated calls from Campbell:

> I was in Melbourne when he rang my mobile and said 'what's

your answer?' I was still undecided, but it was one of those times when whatever comes out of your mouth, that's your answer. I said 'Yes' while walking along a footpath. Just as I said it, Patrick McKendry stopped me from stepping on a dead rat. I think there was an omen in it.

A friendship and political partnership that would last for the next 15 years began. Campbell later reminisced:

> There are so many things in politics that are about luck. You can work your arse off, but there are so many lucky things that need to happen. Looking back on it, if Brendan Cooper had continued on as state director I'm firmly of the view I would have had no chance of winning the Lord Mayoralty.

Despite the appointment of Myers and some momentum in the first half of the year, the campaign appeared to stall in late 2003. A devastating poll was published in *The Sunday-Mail* in mid-September, showing 87 percent of respondents didn't know who the Liberal candidate for Lord Mayor was. Of those who did, just 25 percent intended to vote for him. When the Christmas and New Year period was wiped off the campaigning calendar, there were just a handful of months left until polling day.

Myers called a campaign meeting to get things back on track. They discussed repositioning Campbell's brand. His sister-in-law Heidi reflected on his personality. Campbell was a dynamo, she said, always on the move, fixing things and finding solutions to problems both big and small. In the midst of the brainstorming session, they came up with the slogan "Can Do". And a new direction for the campaign was born. To mark the 100-day countdown to the election, due in March 2004, *The Courier-Mail* wrote:

> Newman has worked hard since winning endorsement to get his head around the workings of Brisbane City Council, a local government colossus with a budget bigger than Tasmania.

His campaign to date has been workmanlike and arguably more professional than his predecessors, and the Quinn administration acknowledges that the election is shaping up as a close contest. Predictably, Brisbane's roads will be the principal battleground. The Liberals have proposed a string of tunnels which form a triangular network called TransApex around inner Brisbane. Question marks remain over Newman's ability to deliver on these tunnels. Whoever triumphs will have a mammoth task over the next four years to manage the city's growth without destroying what makes Brisbane a special place to live.

With a state election also due early in the new year, Campbell and his team moved their operations out of the Liberal Party headquarters and into a commercial building at 10 Downing Street in Spring Hill, a property owned by Lisa's father, Frank Monsour. The campaign team worked around the clock to prepare the office. On one of those late nights Campbell crawled through the dirt underneath the building to lay cables for a computer network. As a leader, he knew the importance of getting his hands dirty on tasks he wasn't expected to perform. He was also a computer and electronics nerd, a hobby and interest he first developed as a teenager. Lesley Jenkin described him as an "IT expert", with any computer problems "fixed by Campbell in a wink".

Networking the campaign headquarters was nothing new for Campbell. He was always building and wiring up connected systems of second-hand computer parts and unseen cables in his own home, and winding down on weekends by shopping at school fetes and community boot sales for scraps of technology he could refashion and rebuild.

A double dose of elections

In a shock move on 13 January 2004, Premier Peter Beattie called a snap election. It was set down for 7 February, the earliest date in the calendar Queenslanders had ever voted in a state election. At a time when he needed all the media space he could possibly attract, Campbell and his team were sent into the background while the state election played out on the front pages and nightly news bulletins.

The judgement call to stage such an early election worked for Premier Beattie. His Government was comfortably returned, losing just three seats from the high of its 66-seat haul back in 2001. Nationals leader Lawrence Springborg caused a post-election stir within conservative ranks by telling the media he wanted the National and Liberal parties to merge: "I've always supported the ultimate objective of having one strong, focused conservative party, not only within Queensland but also Australia-wide."[32]

With the state election done and dusted, the focus returned to the 27 March Local Government poll. In mid-February, about five weeks out from the upcoming election, a bombshell landed in Campbell's campaign bunker. The Liberal Party had drafted in renowned political pollster Toby Ralph to conduct some late stage research on how Campbell and the candidates were tracking. Ralph, a marketing and political veteran who worked on all of John Howard's Prime Ministerial campaigns, remembered the significant challenges facing the Liberal campaign so close to election day:

> I've worked on almost 50 elections across three continents and although the 2004 Brisbane City Council election was among the smallest, it was one of the most interesting. I was funded to conduct research and recommend a communications strategy by a private donor, so flew in to find that the local Party Machine was being ignored. Instead some politically savvy locals – Bob Tucker and Graham Young – were central to the effort. I've dealt with hundreds of politicians – Presidents, Prime Ministers, Premiers, Ministers and so on, normally I'm ambivalent but Campbell was unusual in that I liked him. This is a bad sign,

because when I like a politician it's rare that the public will in the longer term. I like – or respect – politicians that have genuine purpose, but that means they throw themselves at that task and often lose public support along the way. Newman buzzed with purpose, he might have wanted to get elected, but he wanted to get elected so he could get on with doing something. This is rare.

In qualitative research involving interviews with over 70 voters across the city, Ralph discovered the public had incredibly low awareness of Campbell and the Liberal team. The team was going to lose if they continued on their current course. The Ralph report rocked the campaign. Despite nearly two years of hard work, fundraising and policy releases, the research found Campbell's name recognition was so low he had little to no chance of victory. Ralph's findings were backed a week later by a 28 February poll in *The Courier-Mail* under the headline "Newman distant second in poll":

> Labor incumbent Tim Quinn is on track to win the Lord Mayoralty at the Brisbane City Council election on March 27. With four weeks to go until Brisbane's 600,000 voters go to the polls, Cr Quinn's support is at a healthy 45 percent and Mr Newman's 29 percent. Mr Newman said the poll showed his team had a lot of work to do in the next month. 'We have to get out there and tell the people of Brisbane about what we want to do, and that they really do have a choice this time. They can go along with a complacent, tired and arrogant administration, or they can go for a new dynamic, energetic team'.

Ralph urged them to adopt a high-risk "crash though or crash" strategy, while Quirk described the team's chances as "100 to 1 and drifting". He later told *The Australian*:[33]

> I remember sitting in a room and the researcher was telling us where we stood with four weeks to go. The message was:

> 'you can run a safe campaign and lose honourably, or go high-risk with the potential to pull it off. But you could lose more seats'.
>
> I looked at Campbell and in his eyes you could see his view was 'just charge!'. So we did.

Cr Geraldine Knapp recalled the shockwaves the polling results had on the campaign team:

> That news from Toby's research and *The Courier-Mail* poll was devastating. With all of the work Campbell had done we were still no closer to winning. It showed that we as sitting councillors would've kept our council wards, but Campbell wasn't cutting it. That's when the Can Do thing really came to the fore. We had to go out and do stunts and get the jingle going and do all sorts of crazy things.
>
> There was a great big hole somewhere near the dry dock on the Brisbane River foreshore. We had hardhats with 'Can Do' on it. Campbell jumps in and I thought 'bloody hell we're going to lose the mayoral candidate!'

Using advice from Ralph's findings, Ben Myers steered the campaign in this dramatically different direction. They threw the rule book out the window.

In a frenzy of campaign stunts, Can Do Campbell and his team fixed potholes, trimmed grass on overgrown council land and ran a pseudo-bus service for Kuraby residents – complete with printed timetables and orange cones as bus stops – to show up the Quinn Council's shortcomings on public transport.

Footage of the stunts on the nightly news stole the thunder from the Labor campaign.

In a one-two punch combination, the team commissioned a series of attack ads featuring themes recommended by Ralph's research, painting Quinn as complacent, lazy and arrogant.

Importantly, FM radio picked up on the energy of the campaign, reaching an audience Campbell's team had never been able to penetrate. Cr Geraldine Knapp had fond memories of the campaign:

> It was a terrific time in the lead up the election. It was fun, it was terrific, all those new people coming in and out to help, young people who worked for nothing at Downing St. After two failed Lord Mayoral candidates and very ordinary campaigns, it was fantastic to be part of a very thoughtful, very skilled and strategic campaign. It was fabulous. Everyone came in and worked their arses off.

With less than a week to go before polling day, the issue of flooding again struck a major blow on the Quinn-Labor campaign. Flooding, it appeared, was going to be a common theme of Campbell's political career.

The Courier-Mail front page on 18 March read:

> Reports on unsafe dam kept secret: Brisbane City Council failed for a decade to warn residents in Brisbane's western suburbs they faced catastrophic and sudden flooding if a dam at Brookfield collapsed. The report by Brisbane Water, a subsidiary of the council, is a fresh embarrassment for Lord Mayor Quinn and his civic administration which goes to the polls next week. Brisbane Lord Mayoral candidate Campbell Newman said that by hiding the reports the council for 10 years had risked lives.

Polling Day

On the morning of the election on 27 March 2004, Campbell was exhausted but strangely elated. There was nothing more the Liberal campaign team could do. They had given it everything in the bid to snatch a miraculous victory from the jaws of defeat, predicted by polling just a few weeks earlier. Campbell's two-year gamble was now in the hands of Brisbane voters.

When the results started rolling in later that evening, success in the council wards was mixed. The Liberals ended up gaining just three seats, meaning Labor would keep its majority on council with 17 wards to the Liberal Party's 9. The race for Lord Mayor was tight, but by about 8pm the result became clear. Campbell had won over 47 percent of the primary vote, compared to Quinn's 40.5 percent. On a two-party preferred basis, the Liberal Party was in front 52.5 percent to Labor's 47.5 percent.

Campbell and Lisa could hardly believe it, much less their campaign team. Campbell Newman was now the Lord Mayor of the southern hemisphere's largest local government administration, accountable to more than 600,000 voters. In his election night victory speech he said:

> I fully appreciate the great responsibilities that are now placed upon me. I will work for the people of this city, I will work for all of the people of Brisbane and I intend to serve them for the next four years faithfully and to the very best of my abilities.

The celebrations at his election night party didn't last very long. Judging by the strong results for Labor in the council wards, he was about to walk into a political vipers' nest. Campbell would later describe his first few months in Brisbane's City Hall as the worst period of his political life.

5

KING OF A DIVIDED CASTLE

2004-2008: First term as Lord Mayor of Brisbane

The light and shade of Campbell Newman's first term as Brisbane Lord Mayor was captured by two front page headlines published in the days after his 2004 election win. On News Limited's free weekly newspaper *City News*, Campbell was pictured standing with a wide smile and arms akimbo, looking over a 3D model of Brisbane's skyline. The headline read:

> King Of The Castle:
> Newman's reign begins

In the same week, the front page headline of *The-Courier-Mail* gravely proclaimed:

> Labor rejects mandate

The article under that headline read: "The Brisbane City Council appeared to be headed for chaos last night after the Labor Party's most senior councillor disputed Lord Mayor-elect Campbell Newman's right to govern."

That was the new dichotomy of a fractious political landscape Campbell had walked into. As the first Liberal Lord Mayor since Sallyanne Atkinson was ousted by Labor's Jim Soorley back in 1991, he should've been elated. Instead, he was the new Lord Mayor with a minority on council, the first configuration of its kind since the creation of Greater Brisbane as a local government authority in 1925. When the counting of votes was completed, Labor had picked up a resounding 17 of the city's 26 wards, pitting the majority of councillors against the conservative leader. No-one really knew how it was all going to work. Labor was gutted and bitter at losing its hold on the Lord Mayor's office. Campbell just wanted to get on with it, but within days of the election result, there were already suggestions the Beattie Government might need to step in to sack the council, install an administrator and start again with a fresh election. Premier Peter Beattie told *The Courier-Mail* at the time:

> It's a bit like making Wally Lewis the captain of the NSW State of Origin team. But the people are the boss and they've expressed a view, now we all have to make it work.

On top of the partisan warfare being waged in the immediate wake of the election, Campbell also had to bat away an incident involving his brother-in-law Seb Monsour. Late into Campbell's election victory party at the Grand Chancellor Hotel, Seb and a friend had stolen away from the event to check on rumours the Labor Party was shredding confidential documents at the offices of Brisbane Water, where Seb was a manager at the time. It was a scene one reporter later likened to the Watergate scandal. A few days after the election, CCTV footage emerged showing Seb and his mate entering the building. A dossier on the incident was promptly written up by Soorley's former chief of staff and handed to council chief executive Jude Munro. Naturally, Seb's late-night escapade promptly made its way onto the front page of The *Courier-Mail*. A helpful adviser to Labor's interim council leader Maureen Hayes had handed out copies of the confidential council dossier to journalists. Seb was soon cleared of any criminal wrongdoing, and the focus returned to the whirlwind of running a divided council.

Just days into the job, living up to the "Can Do" persona he had won the election with was proving to be more difficult than Campbell – and any of his team – had imagined.

I'm the boss

Within a week of moving into City Hall, Campbell took aim at existing political staffers, particularly those who worked for the former Lord Mayor. In comments he later attributed to naivety in dealing with the media, a story in *The Courier-Mail* ran under the headline "Work with me or face the sack: Newman demands loyalty of top staff":

> If people want to get on board and come with us, that is great, but if people don't want to get with the program, their job is not safe.

On the same day the story was published, negotiating teams from the new Liberal and Labor caucuses met for the first time in a bid to make sense of the new Council. Meanwhile, Campbell met for the first time with Council CEO Jude Munro, an experienced council administrator first appointed to the top job by former Lord Mayor Soorley in 2000. Munro had the unenviable task of keeping this new fractured Council on something resembling an even keel.

Two pivotal members of his election campaign team, Ben Myers and Greg Bowden, were brought into the Lord Mayor's office as strategy and economic development advisors, while Lisa set about ramping up the long dormant mayoral fundraising efforts. In a profile piece a few days after the election, Lisa told *The Courier-Mail* she wanted to "put the heart back in City Hall and the suburbs":

> When I grew up, Brisbane was a capital city with capital city facilities, but a country town with a community feeling and I want that for my kids.

On 30 March, while his negotiating team of Graham Quirk, Carol Cashman and Michael Caltabiano attempted to hammer out a power-sharing arrangement with Labor councillors, Campbell went line-dancing with a senior's group inside City Hall, where one participant told him: "It's always lonely at the top." As the new leader of a gridlocked council, it already appeared that way to Campbell. Labor still didn't have a permanent leader in place, and the negotiating task he had delegated had stalled. Quirk remembered the Labor team as being "like stunned mullets":

> They were just in a stunned situation with this whole concept of having a Lord Mayor from a non-Labor side while they had the numbers. Half the time they would leave the negotiating table. They just didn't want a bar of it.

When they finally got their act together, Labor Councillor David Hinchliffe was chosen as their leader, an appointment Campbell described as "the light at the end of the tunnel". The long-serving councillor, first elected in 1988, was viewed as a "circuit breaker" in the negotiations between the two sides. But Campbell had spoken too soon.

While there was a certain commonality in key policy initiatives, the sticking point remained the makeup of Civic Cabinet. Campbell needed support at the Cabinet table, but Labor had the final say on which councillors would be allowed into the fold. For its part, the media loved the new drama at City Hall. In a classic 'gotcha' trap for a new politician, Campbell was asked by TV reporter Lane Calcutt to respond to comments made by Hinchliffe, who had just declared he was the real "boss" of the council. Campbell took the bait, saying he was the "boss" because he'd just been elected the Lord Mayor with a clear mandate. The TV crew cut up his sentence, and that night ran the story with a grab from Campbell, stating: "I'm the boss". The three-word grab became a meme the Labor Opposition and media dined out on for months afterwards. Hinchliffe later joked in an article in *The Courier-Mail* that his family gave him an over-sized fake medallion for his birthday, with the words "I'm The Boss" emblazoned across it. Underneath the jibes, however, Hinchliffe's comments carried some weight. Labor was threatening to use its majority on council to scuttle some of Campbell's TransApex projects, despite conditional support for the tunnel and bridge plan from Premier Beattie. Indeed, the Premier's early support for the TransApex program after they had met for the first time on 7 April – ten days after the council election – was the start of one of Campbell's most important, and unusual, political partnerships.

Campbell and the Premier knew they needed to work together to tackle the future needs of the rapidly growing south-east Queensland region. Population growth forecasts at the time suggested more than one million people would move to the area over the next 20 years. Early in Campbell's term as Lord Mayor, he and Beattie would occasionally hold private meetings atop Eildon Hill, usually at dawn. Beattie took his morning walk from his home in Wilston while Campbell arrived there on his run from nearby Windsor. On top of Eildon Hill, with its 360-degree views of Brisbane, they could see the rooftops of both their homes. Free of advisors and the media, the pair would negotiate and agree on plans for Brisbane's future.

Walking the leadership tightrope

A day after his 7 April meeting with Beattie, Campbell was paid a visit by Rupert Murdoch and his son Lachlan, along with New Limited executive Jerry Harris. Campbell and the billionaire media proprietor got along well, and Murdoch was impressed by the new mayor's attitude to politics and his enthusiasm for economic development. Campbell's handwritten meeting note from the time read:

> Quick discussion on the future of Brisbane infrastructure, urban planning, openness and city governance.

Those priorities would drive his tenure over the next four years. But before he delivered on infrastructure, planning and good governance, he took a moment to focus on symbolism. A week after his meeting with Murdoch, Campbell was climbing the Story Bridge to deliver his first election promise. He was there to raise the Australian and Queensland flags over the city for the first time in more than a decade. The emblematic gesture, with its notion of national heritage and pride, became a recurring theme throughout Campbell's political career. Like his parents, he was a student of history and defender of heritage. To this day, his bookshelves remain dominated by non-fiction tomes.

The smiles and thumbs up gestures for the cameras as he unfurled the flags high above Brisbane's skyline betrayed the increasingly bitter post-election battle still raging between his Liberal team and the Labor majority back at City Hall. Labor was flexing its muscle ahead of the first council meeting in mid-April. After all of the negotiations between the two sides, Campbell and Graham Quirk were the only Liberal councillors allowed in the seven-member Civic Cabinet. Confusion reigned when Labor appeared unsure whether Hinchliffe would be Deputy Mayor or Leader of the Opposition. He ended up being an awkward, adaptable combination of both. In a somewhat surreal twist to the tense situation, Hinchliffe's office was linked by a mutual door to Campbell's office, and they regularly received each other's phone calls. Campbell's staffers soon solved the issue of the mutual door by placing a heavy piece of furniture across it to prevent it being opened.

When the new council prepared to enter the chamber for their inaugural meeting in mid-April, Campbell had already set a cracking pace. His day began before dawn for an 8km run and finished late at night. He only paused for a brief moment of reflection and celebration when he addressed his first council meeting. With the Lord Mayoral chains around his neck, its gold medallions representing every Brisbane mayor since the city was formed in 1859, he took to the podium for his maiden speech on 16 April. His mother Jocelyn, wife Lisa and their two girls looked on as he thanked voters and outlined his priorities and commitments over the next four years. He felt the "weight of responsibility as well as the gold around my shoulders today", hugged his loved ones, shook the hands of his colleagues, and got back to work.

Political partnership of convenience

Relations between Campbell and Hinchliffe appeared to improve in the weeks after the first council meeting. The Deputy Mayor talked about his burgeoning respect for Campbell in an interview with *The Courier-Mail*, saying he was "not a doctrinaire Liberal".

> I respect him. He just wants to get on and do it. From what I've observed 'Can Do' fits his character profile. We have to bury the hatchet – not in each other's backs – and start working as a team.

By this time, Civic Cabinet was meeting weekly. Invariably, Campbell and Graham Quirk were manoeuvring and negotiating to avoid being overruled:

> It settled into a pattern where I had a certain policy agenda I'd been elected on and the Labor Party in Cabinet agreed to get on with most of those things. There were certainly a lot of fights, but we managed to get the key policies and projects through and that's all that mattered to the people of Brisbane. It was hard for everybody. There was no manual.

As the only other Liberal councillor in Cabinet, Graham Quirk had vivid memories of the theatrical antics inside the Cabinet and on the floor of the chamber:

> Every day when we walked into Cabinet we knew we didn't have the numbers so it became a bit of a theatre. To impose our will, well, let's say an actor's equity ticket would have been easily obtained. There were a lot of turbulent meetings where we saw some walkouts occur on both sides. It's not a period of time I would want to go back to.

For the most part, Campbell let his councillors do battle with Labor down in the trenches and on the floor of the Chamber. He knew he had to rise above it. The expectations to deliver on his promises were high. Brisbane voters wanted him to fulfill his Can Do election promises of future-proofing the traffic network, revitalising local parklands and making their streets safer. As they sat in traffic jams or faced the daily school run, they had no time for political bunfights.

Budgets and family adjustments

The first Budget of Campbell's Lord Mayoral career was a $1.4 billion set of accounts handed down with a line ball surplus of $296,000, the first of seven consecutive balanced or surplus city budgets delivered under Campbell's watch. In just over two months since the election, his fellow councillors – in particular Quirk, Nicholls and Caltabiano – had completed a comprehensive budget review. It left an antagonistic Labor majority little room to argue for its spending priorities without proposing savings of its own. In his speech, he called it a "Budget for the suburbs". The savings they found attracted backlash from Labor, which threatened to use its power in Civic Cabinet and on the floor of council to amend the Budget. While they grumbled about minor spending cuts, the punters and business community liked what they saw. Campbell and his team's steadfast approach to spending and his handling of the Labor majority was drawing praise. A prominent Brisbane lawyer wrote to him on 22 June 2004:

> A quick note of personal support in your dealings with the current political machinations of Labor. I sense the electorate believes you have accommodated them enough. You are of fine mind and purpose and to quote Dean Rusk (of the Cuban missile crisis) 'We're eye-ball to eye-ball and I think the other fellow just blinked'. One can be confident that you will not be the first to blink.

While Campbell grew in stature as he walked through the firestorm of politics at City Hall and the media's glare, the Newman family unit was making its own dramatic adjustments. Lisa knew what she was getting into, but she never wanted to be in the media spotlight. She was a reluctant interviewee. Meanwhile, their daughters Rebecca and Sarah became accustomed to seeing less of their father. Campbell had travelled extensively during his years with Grainco and as a management consultant, but the demands on his time as the new Lord Mayor were relentless. A handwritten card by Rebecca titled "Dad's birthday poem" for his 41st birthday touched on the family's new paradigm:

> You always say you love me, and I know that you do. I hope that you know; that I love you too. So don't go feeling guilty about being Lord Mayor. We have a lot of fun, me and 'Sare Bear'. So one more time, before we go away, to my dear Daddy, Happy Birthday!

Campbell grabbed moments with the girls when he could. Sometimes they'd do their homework on the floor of their father's office at City Hall. The time he spent away from his young daughters during his time in politics remained one of his greatest regrets. Personal correspondence from his early months in the role revealed Campbell was in a reflective mood as he transitioned into the new role. In one email to a former army superior he noted:

> I always think back fondly to my time working for you at 20 Division ESS. A bit like school days – they now feel like the best time of my life.

In another exchange, this time with a former colleague from Grainco, Campbell wrote:

> In regards to the situation I now find myself in, it is certainly difficult and the most challenging thing that I have ever done but I am determined to make it work. I very much take on board what you said about putting time aside for family –

like (one of our former colleagues) I put a heck of a lot of my time into Grainco and pushed family aside. That's why Lisa, the girls and I are doing this job together.

Federal dealings

His first Budget had proven to be something of a political watershed for Campbell by funding the basic services of council while allocating record spending on capital works. The handing down of the Budget less than three months after taking office showed he was getting on with the job, despite the partisan games by both sides on council. He gained kudos for juggling big ticket infrastructure items – normally the domain of a state government – with the everyday suburban duties of a Council. Always a stickler for getting the basics right, Campbell would often phone in potholes or footpaths that needed to be fixed. His working partnership with Council CEO Jude Munro was solidifying and the strange bedfellow arrangement with Labor was seemingly working. At the same time, planning and design work began on the multi-billion dollar TransApex program. With talk of the 2004 federal election in the air, Campbell flew to Canberra twice in the space of a few months to lobby the Howard Government for funding, and used a parochial Brisbane media to talk up the need for a Commonwealth contribution. While the TransApex program needed significant funding from the Queensland Government, Campbell also wanted $400 million from federal coffers to kickstart the suite of projects. *The Courier-Mail* editorialised about the situation on 1 September, urging the Lord Mayor to "get his federal colleagues engaged in the project, or risk seeing all that energy surrounding TransApex dissipate."

Campbell was unexpectedly handed a captive audience of Howard Government Ministers and MPs later that same month when he was invited to be master of ceremonies at the federal Coalition's 2004 election campaign launch. It would be his first foray onto the national political stage. Long-term Newman family friend and Prime Minister John Howard had called the election at a media conference on 29 August, asking voters who they trusted to keep the economy strong, interest rates low and the fight against international terrorism on track. Prime Minister Howard had been under siege from Labor leader Mark Latham, who at this stage was still functioning as a viable alternative as the nation's leader. Labor had led the Coalition in most polls published in the week after the election was called. But, as is often the case in election campaigns, external events intervened. On 9 September, a terrorist attack struck the Australian embassy in Jakarta. All campaigning was put on hold for two days out of respect for victims of the Jakarta incident. At the same time, the nation paused to honour the memory of those lost in the 11 September attacks of 2001. As expected, the mood of the campaign shifted in the Coalition's favour.

When the official campaign launch was held in front of 500 people at Brisbane City Hall on 26 September, Prime Minister Howard's re-election was back on track. Campbell gave his opening speech everything he had; his voice buoyant and booming, arms gesticulating for emphasis, his sentences geared towards soliciting applause at every turn:

> As one of Australia's capital city Lord Mayors, I have a very good feel for the aspirations of the people of this great nation. The consistent thing that they tell me is that to preserve their lifestyle, to secure their future, they want to see the return of the Coalition Government led by John Howard and John Anderson. On election day, Australia has a clear choice. Either a leap into the vast unknown with 'L-Plate Latham', or to stick with a team that has given Australia eight years of unparalleled economic growth, stability and security.

Shortly after the Coalition's campaign launch, Latham's performance began to unravel, from the infamous aggressive handshake with Howard outside a radio station studio to the impetuous Tasmanian forest policy launch alongside Greens Leader Bob Brown. When the dust settled on the night of the 9 October election, the Coalition had increased its majority, enshrining John Howard in political history as Australia's second longest serving Prime Minister.

Tunnels and water

In just eight months since coming to office, two of the issues that defined Campbell's political career had already emerged: infrastructure and water. Getting his TransApex election promise off the ground had dominated his personal agenda since the March election. He had to negotiate the projects through a hostile Civic Cabinet, find council money in the Budget to progress the planning studies, seek commitments from state and federal governments and develop public-private partnership arrangements worth hundreds of millions of dollars at a time.

In the latter half of 2004, the issue of water, and more specifically flooding, was emerging as the second defining tenet of his time in City Hall. South-East Queensland was in the tightening grip of a long dry spell. Water levels in the region's dams were low and experts were calling it the worst drought in 100 years. Warnings about the need for more storage infrastructure had fallen on deaf political ears.

Over the weekend of 6-7 November, the long dry burst in dramatic fashion. In the 48 hour period to 9am, 8 November, the south east corner of Queensland was lashed with rainfall totals of up to 365 mm. The heaviest rain bucketed down between Brisbane and Coolangatta in a weather band stretching from the coast to places 30km inland. Two children were killed on that weekend, drowned inside their family car after it was swept off a flooded causeway near Biggenden in the North Burnett region, some 300 km north-west of Brisbane. Campbell visited one of the worst hit suburbs, Rocklea in Brisbane's south, shortly after the rains began easing on the Sunday afternoon. It was the third time in a decade the local residents were forced to mop up and clean out their flooded houses. They asked the Lord Mayor if the council would buy back their homes. Within weeks, their pleas formed part of a study by a new Taskforce on Suburban Flooding, launched by Campbell to investigate ways of making Brisbane more flood proof.

"I hate politics"

As 2005 began, Campbell was earning his reputation as an "anti-politician". In an extended article in *The Courier-Mail*, he said his job as Lord Mayor was "no fun":

> Most of my opponents have been long-term career politicians, and I find politics an anathema. I hate it, I hate politics. I hate what it brings out in people, and I hate the games my political opponents play every day of the week.

To rise above the daily trench warfare of council politics, Campbell continued to devote much of his time and energy to the delivery of the traffic and transport policy Moving Brisbane, including the TransApex program. The first TransApex project to be rolled out was the North-South Bypass Tunnel – later named the Clem Jones Tunnel in honour of the former Brisbane Lord Mayor. The proposed tunnel was a four-lane, 4.7-kilometre link drilled 60 metres under the Brisbane River between Woolloongabba in the south and Bowen Hills in the north, providing a direct link through to the airport. It was first floated as a concept in 2001 by former Mayor Jim Soorley, but never progressed beyond some desktop studies. Just a few weeks shy of his first year anniversary as Lord Mayor, Campbell announced the official start of the project on 28 February.

He was joined at the announcement by Premier Beattie after

Treasury approved a low-interest loan of up to $450 million to the council for the project. Most of the funds for the project would eventually come from the private sector in a public-private partnership deal. The North-South Bypass Tunnel was the first element of a package deemed to be the biggest city road project ever built in Australia.[34] Beattie's appearance at the media conference alongside Campbell provided a rare positive distraction for the Premier in 2005. His Government was beset by scandals and administrative bungles for much of the year. A few days after the tunnel announcement, Beattie's Indigenous Policy Minister Liddy Clark stood down from the Cabinet after a series of incidents involving her office, such as the so-called "Winegate" affair involving a staffer caught with a bottle of red wine on a dry Indigenous community in Cape York. Three weeks after Clark's resignation, questions about a scandal unlike any other in Queensland's history were being asked of the Government on the floor of Parliament.

Just before 11am on 22 March, about 20 minutes into Question Time, the Shadow Minister for Health Stuart Copeland rose to his feet to ask Health Minister Gordon Nuttall about Bundaberg Hospital surgeon Jayant Patel. In response, Nuttall said:

> I am not aware of the issues raised by the Honourable member. I am more than happy, as the Minister responsible, to investigate those matters.

Some three months later, Nuttall was forced to resign as Health Minister over the Patel scandal, fuelled by the award-winning reportage of journalist Hedley Thomas. Premier Beattie took over the Health portfolio but kept Nuttall in the Cabinet, shifting him to the role of Primary Industries and Fisheries Minister. In the same month as Nuttall's resignation as Health Minister, Beattie's Deputy and Treasurer Terry Mackenroth, as well as Labor MP and Speaker Ray Hollis, both announced their intention to quit Parliament.

Mackenroth's departure from the state seat of Chatsworth opened a window that one of Campbell's right-hand men on council had long been waiting for. Michael Caltabiano, councillor for the Chandler ward and Queensland Liberal Party president, announced he would contest the state seat for the party at the 20 August by-election, a contest he went on to win by a slim margin. Rising Liberal star Adrian Schrinner in turn replaced him on Campbell's council team by winning the by-election on 10 September.

Even before Caltabiano was sworn in as the new state member for Chatsworth, his election caused waves in the Liberal caucus with speculation he would attempt to seize the party's leadership from Bob Quinn. Bruce Flegg was also tipped as a potential leader to replace Quinn in the now seven-member Liberal caucus, which also featured John-Paul Langbroek, Mark McArdle, Jann Stuckey and Terry Rogers. No such challenge occurred, and Quinn remained at the helm for the time being, with Flegg elevated to Deputy Leader. At the same time, Nationals leader Lawrence Springborg had 15 MPs in his caucus, wielding twice as much power as the Liberal cohort. Springborg had hoped to have locked in an official merger of the conservative parties in Queensland by now. Quinn and senior Liberals continued to block the move. Months earlier, in March 2005, Springborg had convened a "peace summit" between the two conservative parties. Prime Minister Howard and Deputy Prime Minister Anderson also attended. The meeting was deemed a disaster. Flegg was later quoted as dismissing Springborg as a "farmer from the Darling Downs" while Quinn upset the apple cart with a plan to convince candidates from The Nationals to instead run for the Liberal Party.

With politics at a state level resembling something of a tragicomic circus, Campbell was touted as a potential state or federal MP. It was a move he ruled out, again and again. In an article in *The Courier-Mail* on 29 May, he revealed his intention to return to the private sector after "fixing the transport and traffic issues I promised to deal with":

I'm just not interested in state or federal politics. I don't think I'm going to change.

Hush, Newman

Commentary on his popularity and speculation about his future were of little interest to Campbell at this time. Working closely with his colleagues, particularly Graham Quirk and Tim Nicholls, Campbell was focused on preparing and delivering his second Budget. Released on 8 June 2005, its centrepiece was a $544 million package for transport and traffic infrastructure, an increase of more than 23 percent on the previous year.

In the same month, Campbell was profiled in *Civil Engineers Australia* magazine. The wide-ranging article revealed his "children and their antics" made him laugh and his fitness regime involved running a total of around 40kms a week. He also said "people who put politics over outcomes" annoyed him and one of his weaknesses was "taking things too much to heart and getting emotional about issues".

Despite a range of hurdles, his work on the TransApex infrastructure package ramped up in the second half of 2005. In August, Campbell was joined at another TransApex media conference by Premier Beattie, cementing their close working relationship. They announced a $21 million planning and feasibility study for the proposed Airport Link Tunnel, the second major road infrastructure project in the TransApex network. Like their last joint media conference on TransApex back in February, the event proved to be a welcome diversion for the Premier.

At around the same time, Gordon Nuttall was forced to step down from Cabinet while the CMC investigated claims he had lied to a Parliamentary Estimates Committee about his knowledge of problems with overseas-trained doctors such as Patel. In glowing terms that annoyed some players in their respective political camps, Campbell and Premier Beattie highlighted their bipartisan partnership at the media conference. Later in November, they headlined a business and investment roadshow to Sydney. The *Australian Financial Review* ran a story titled: "Bipartisan schmooze from Brissy".[35]

The powerful combination of Campbell's popularity, tenacity and working partnership with the Premier grated with some of his federal colleagues. A front page story of *The Courier-Mail* at the time declared: "Libs try to hush Newman on roads". Anonymous comments from conservative federal MPs in Queensland revealed they were fed up with Campbell's "constant badgering" of the Howard Government for a funding contribution of $400 million for his TransApex program. Their calls on him to quieten down only fired him up. He was relentless in his push to deliver the projects, announcing studies into the Hale St Bridge (later named the Go Between Bridge) project, another part of TransApex, in the face of staunch opposition from Labor councillors and a local protest group.

Meanwhile, Graham Quirk put dozens of new, environmentally friendly buses into the council fleet to replace old diesel buses and thousands of residents took part in the formulation of the CityShape plan designed to guide the city's growth over the next 20 years. The Taskforce on Suburban Flooding handed down its final report at this time, noting that "up to 11,000 residential buildings may be prone to flooding" and "climate change is occurring and its impact on sea levels and storm events are yet to be fully determined". A key recommendation of the report included a voluntary buyback scheme of homes in flood-prone zones, following through on the request made directly to Campbell by distressed homeowners caught up in the flash-flooding events of November the previous year.

All of this progress and action in the face of daily political warfare had widened Campbell's appeal. Shortly after the comprehensive flooding report was handed down and its recommendations adopted, a small piece in *The Courier-Mail* on 27 August reported "a bunch of influential Liberal lawyers" wanted Campbell to run in a "head-to-head" battle with Peter Beattie in the Premier's seat of Brisbane Central. The same article reported the lawyers "also hope to entice Can Do's charming wife Lisa Newman to contest a state seat'." Lisa's connection with community groups and increasing charity fundraising efforts were widely admired across Brisbane. The group of lawyers, or anyone else for that matter, never did approach Lisa to gauge her interest in public office.

Bomb scare

The morning of 14 November began like most other weekdays for Campbell. A run before dawn, breakfast at home with Lisa and the girls, then off to City Hall for media briefings followed by meetings and functions. But by lunchtime his schedule was thrown into a most unexpected chaos with one of the most intense events of his 18 month reign so far. Just before midday, a 46-year-old truck driver from south Brisbane named Rodney Watson had phoned in a bomb threat. Speaking on a public payphone in suburban Brisbane, he told police of his plans to attack the city's bus and train network. A week earlier, 18 suspected terrorists had been arrested in separate raids in Sydney and Melbourne. Police took the threat seriously and mobilised immediately. Within minutes of receiving notice of the threat, Campbell was in conversation with Premier Beattie, Police Minister Judy Spence and Police Commissioner Bob Atkinson.

Campbell and Premier Beattie took no chances and decided to shut down the city's vast bus and train network for 90 minutes. Around 2pm, the Police received a second threatening call from Watson. As police zeroed in on Watson using fingerprint evidence collected at various payphones, Campbell was standing outside the entrance to the Myer Centre bus interchange on Adelaide St in Brisbane's CBD, not far from City Hall. Beattie too was at a nearby major transport hub, both of them portraying a sense of normality and calm to ease the confusion among nervous commuters. Police caught Watson late the following day after he had made a third bomb threat.

Some commuters and commentators decried Campbell and Premier Beattie's decision to shut down the transport network. But his performance during the Brisbane bomb hoax created new media speculation about Campbell's political future. Crikey reporter Martin Hirst wrote of a "growing whisper" that "Can Do Campbell could be the next Liberal Premier of Queensland". Despite being an unknown quantity just 20 months earlier, Campbell was increasingly being talked up for higher office.

Lisa's star also continued to rise, despite her ongoing reticence to feature in the media. In an end of year interview with *City News*, she talked about her passion for charity work, including the Abused Child Trust. The journalist noted that Lisa was "close to tears when she shares the experience of meeting a room full of abused children, some just five years old". The interview was Lisa's final media duty of the year before she prepared the family for its much-needed Christmas break. That year they were going camping at Moreton Island, one of their favourite holiday destinations.

As the Newman family looked forward to an overdue holiday, Premier Beattie's annus horribilis wasn't over yet. In December he was forced to reshuffle his Cabinet for the fourth time in nine months when the CMC handed down the results of its 15-week investigation into Gordon Nuttall. The CMC report released on 7 December recommended Nuttall be charged under section 57 of Queensland's Criminal Code for lying to a Parliamentary committee over the issue of overseas trained doctors during that year's Budget Estimate Hearings. To save Nuttall from prosecution, Premier Beattie took the extraordinary step of recalling Parliament from its summer break to consider the matter. In a vote on 9 December, Labor's massive majority decided Nuttall wouldn't face criminal charges. Instead, he

Meeting with Rupert Murdoch shortly after winning the Lord Mayoralty in 2004 and, below, Lisa shaves her head for charity in 2005

Matching 'can-do's are a cut above

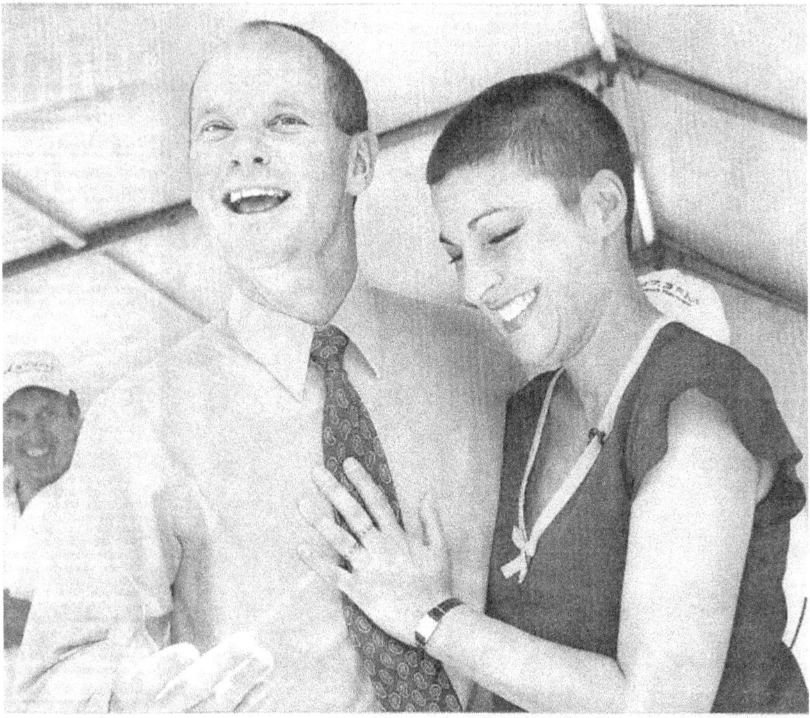

CLOSE shave... Campbell and Lisa Newman in sync hairstyles and Mrs Newman, *below*, before her No.1 trim.   Main picture: **Nathan Richter**

Citizenship ceremony as Lord Mayor in 2006 and, below, with Peter Beattie at Chinese New Year celebrations in 2007

would face potential fines administered by the Parliament. Six months later in May 2006 the Beattie Government passed the Criminal Code Amendment Bill, which decriminalised lying to Parliament. Speaking after the passing of the amendment bill, Opposition Leader Springborg declared "the lying season" was open. Labor's blatant move to protect Nuttall and effectively condone lying in Parliament was a "disgrace" the conservative side of politics vowed to correct when it was returned to power in the future.

2006: A big, busy year

A Roy Morgan poll released in early 2006 showed Campbell's approach to politics was making him one of Australia's most popular capital city Mayors. The survey found 58 percent of local residents thought the Brisbane City Council was doing a good job, while 63 percent approved of Campbell's performance, an increase of 8 percent over the same poll a year earlier. Responses to direct questions about Campbell focused on his ability to get things done in line with his election commitments. In a reflection of the occasional public fights with his Labor opposition on council – which had significantly cooled off compared to the tumultuous events of 2004 – one respondent said: "He is too caught up in personal issues".

The overwhelmingly positive sentiments in the poll were echoed in an email sent at this time by Brisbane resident Len Johnson to Campbell's mother, Jocelyn. As a long-term friend of the Newman family, Johnson wrote that Campbell was "doing exceptionally well":

> It's nice to have a city leader who displays quiet common sense and a general aura of good management and competence. A great change from past city leaders who were more interested in overdone public appearances and ideologies than urban management. He presents extremely well and makes sensible long-term proposals such as (those on) water. A big attaboy. I like him.[36]

Larry and Lisa

The nation's focus shifted to the far north of Queensland in March 2006 when Tropical Cyclone Larry tore through Innisfail and surrounding areas. Campbell's one time former superior in the army Peter Cosgrove was enlisted to oversee the clean-up, which would end up costing an estimated $1.5 billion.

While the Beattie Government was dealing with the cyclone's aftermath and the fallout from the Nuttall controversy, Campbell was on a roll. Against the odds, his TransApex vision was starting to become a reality. In the two years since he was elected, he had overcome the unprecedented situation of running a minority Council while dealing with a sceptical media and reluctant funding partners at a state and federal level. The Council had recently awarded a contract to a private consortium to build the North-South Bypass Tunnel (Clem Jones Tunnel). Construction or planning of most of the other TransApex projects was also underway.

Apart from progress on TransApex and delivery of other 2004 election commitments, Lisa's involvement in Campbell's mayoral career was emerging as one of the keys to his success. By April 2006, Lisa's charity work became so demanding she had a desk set up in the corner of Campbell's office. *The Courier-Mail* reported in April 2006:

> For many married couples, going to work each day is the perfect excuse to get away from each other. But not Brisbane's Lord Mayor and Lady Mayoress, who say sharing an office is the perfect arrangement. For her part, Mrs Newman, who also works one day a week as a nurse, says having her desk next to her husband's has its advantages. 'I am in and out irregularly, so we are like ships passing in the night. But every so often I can slip a note on his desk as I'm leaving saying, "Lord Mayor to babysit on Saturday night as wife has charity engagement to attend".[37]

A few days later, Campbell was included in *The Courier-Mail's* "A List", a feature article on the "people who will shape the future of the state". Fellow inclusions on the list included Bruce Flegg, Noel Pearson, Lawrence Springborg, Andrew Fraser, Paul de Jersey, Bill Ludwig, Anna Bligh, Kevin Rudd, Santo Santoro and Springborg's principal adviser Jake Smith.

Third Budget and state shenanigans

Out of the blue on 29 May 2006, Lawrence Springborg announced what appeared to be a major breakthrough for the conservative side of politics in Queensland:

> The Coalition has listened to the overwhelming voice of Queenslanders who want a single, strong, united alternative to the Labor Government, and the two parties have today determined to work towards that goal. The great winner from this will be the people of Queensland, who will have a single, united non-Labor party to address their issues.

Two days later, the merger deal was dead. Media reports suggested the federal wings of the parties had squashed it shortly after Springborg's public announcement. The on-again, off-again merger saga fed into Premier Beattie's rhetoric about disunity between the two conservative parties, punctuated by his adoption of an old political maxim: "if they can't govern themselves, how can they govern Queensland?"

Despite the embarrassing setback, Springborg vowed to push on with his vision of a united conservative force. Rather than earlier ambitions of a national pact, he focused his efforts solely on a Queensland deal. During this period, Campbell was re-endorsed as the Liberal Party's mayoral candidate for the 2008 election.

Less than three weeks later on 14 June he handed down his third Budget as Lord Mayor. The $620 million worth of funding for capital works was the highest spend on infrastructure in Brisbane City Council's 80-year history, while $142 million for public transport countered criticism he was too focused on building roads and tunnels. Labor's deputy mayor David Hinchliffe attempted to add a rise in water charges (brought on by ongoing drought conditions) to the general rates rise of 2.75 percent, demanding Campbell resign for breaking an election promise that he wouldn't raise rates above inflation. Campbell's response was blunt:

> I have delivered the lowest rate increases this city has seen in the last 20 years, and they are in line with inflation.[38]

Despite the best efforts of the Council's Labor Opposition to stir up attention in the media, the presiding focus at this time was on state politics. Speculation was mounting Premier Peter Beattie was going to call an early election. While he was running a Government described as "lurching between lethargy and crisis",[39] Beattie was still expected to win. The mix of his personal popularity and the perceived division of the conservative Opposition was enough to overcome Labor's failings. Indeed, it was an extraordinary period in Queensland state politics. Since being re-elected for its third term in 2004, the Beattie Government had been through an astonishing six ministerial reshuffles, three by-election losses and ongoing controversies over Jayant Patel, water management and underspending on services and infrastructure. One of Beattie's saving graces – apart from his willingness to front up to the media with regular acts of contrition – was the economy. Throughout 2004 and 2005, one-third of all new jobs created in Australia occurred in Queensland, pushing the state's unemployment rate to its lowest level in decades.

For its part, the Liberal Party was doing its best to lose the election before it was even called. Bruce Flegg toppled Bob Quinn in a leadership spill on 7 August. To capitalise on the public display of instability, Beattie confirmed the rumours of an early election by visiting Government House on 15 August. The Queensland election would be held on 9 September 2006. As expected within Liberal circles, Councillor Tim Nicholls announced he would contest the state seat of Clayfield at the election, taking on fallen former minister Liddy Clark.

The conservatives started the race disastrously. At the first media conference of the campaign, Springborg and Flegg were unable to provide a clear answer about who would be Premier if the Liberal-National coalition won. Things went downhill from there. Despite a solid performance by Springborg in the campaign, the dynamic with Flegg was a train wreck for the conservative's chances. The media labelled them the "Fumble Twins". After a horror term of government, Labor cruised to victory, only losing four seats. Nicholls picked up the seat of Clayfield while his former Council colleague Michael Caltabiano had his Parliamentary career cut short after losing to Labor in the seat of Chatsworth. Along with conservative newcomers Nicholls, Glen Elmes, Steve Dickson and David Gibson, Labor's Kate Jones was elected in the seat of Ashgrove.

A week after the election, Jeff Seeney replaced Springborg as Nationals Leader, and Fiona Simpson became his deputy. Nicholls was urged by some to challenge Flegg for the Liberal leadership, but the new state MP didn't have the numbers among the Liberal caucus of eight MPs.

Frustration creeps in

The public didn't see it, but two and a half years of almost daily guerilla warfare in the Labor dominated council was grinding Campbell down. Tensions between the two sides flared up again in the second half of 2006 over ongoing delays in progressing the Hale St Link Bridge (Go Between Bridge), the latest TransApex project. The media was also applying increased pressure. Relations with *The Courier-Mail* were deteriorating, while Mark Ludlow from the *Australian Financial Review* wrote in June 2006:

Cr Newman's honeymoon appears to be on the wane. The worst drought in a century has drained the city's dam levels to below 30 percent and increased rates in the (2006) budget. Brisbane City Council may be big but it needs state and federal government funding to achieve his dream of an orbital road for the city. The building of two tunnels would be a worthy legacy for most politicians, but Newman's problem may be that he dreamed too big.[40]

Campbell commented to the media that working with a majority Labor Opposition was like "being in a bad reality TV show, we're all trapped in this bunker together and we have to make it work." He told *The Courier-Mail* in November 2006:

> I've said to them 'if you want me out of this place, the quickest way is to support me to do what I've said and I'm out of here'. I have no interest in being a career politician'.[41]

A feature article on the current state of City Hall politics appeared in the same edition of the paper. Anonymous Labor sources confirmed the party had given up hope of winning the next Brisbane council election, due to be held on 15 March 2008:

> 'Campbell is unassailable', says a senior Labor figure. 'The undercurrent in our party is we have no hope in hell of beating him and it could be a bloodbath for some councillors'.[42]

The feature article also included a recent quote from Premier Beattie publicly backing Campbell for re-election:

> Having a Liberal Lord Mayor with whom we can work and a Labor majority at the council is a great outcome and I urge the people of Brisbane to keep the balance, keep it exactly as it is.[43]

A new political paradigm in '07

As Campbell entered the final full year of his first term in 2007, politics was about to be dramatically and comprehensively realigned. At different points throughout the year, the Kevin07 campaign ended the three-decade Parliamentary career of John Howard and Labor would dominate the Australian political landscape from coast to coast. In Queensland, Peter Beattie resigned and handed over to his deputy Anna Bligh on 10 September. On the state Opposition benches, Mark McArdle replaced Flegg as Liberal leader, and Lawrence Springborg made a comeback at the helm of the Nationals. He didn't know it at the time, but the electoral events of this year would culminate to steer Campbell's future towards State Parliament, a career course Beattie had predicted more than a year earlier in a private conversation between the pair.

For now, Campbell's eyes were on the prize of gaining re-election as Lord Mayor in March 2008. The foundations for the next nine months of unofficial campaigning were laid in Council's 2007 Budget, released on 13 June. The council's $2.33 billion Budget delivered a $693,000 surplus and massive spending on initiatives to tackle the drought, improve public transport, and continue the suite of TransApex and other congestion-busting projects.

The success of that Budget – Campbell's fourth consecutive set of balanced or surplus accounts – yet again reignited calls for him to step up to the state realm. The radically altered political terrain across the nation added fuel to the speculation. By the time Rudd was sworn in as Prime Minister on 3 December 2007, Campbell was elevated to the unexpected position of most senior Liberal Party politician in the country.

Nick Bryant later wrote in *The Monthly* magazine:

> Crestfallen conservatives would have drawn little consolation from the potentially morale-boosting fact that Brisbane

City Council is the biggest local government fiefdom in the country, nor from the 617,000 registered voters who make up Australia's largest single electorate. No, the citywide power wielded by Campbell Newman was a sore reminder of the Liberals' nationwide powerlessness. Labor had a monopoly. The Liberals had a municipality. Alert to the comic potential, the Chaser team ambushed Newman at his suburban home on Sunday morning (after the November 24 federal election), presenting him with a selection of Liberal totems including a Wallabies tracksuit and a pair of fishnet stockings.[44]

Bipartisan breakdown

The new Queensland Labor Premier in that national political monopoly was taking an altogether different approach than her predecessor when it came to relations with Brisbane's Liberal Lord Mayor. From the moment she was elevated to the office of Premier on 13 September 2007, Anna Bligh's gloves were off. Their first major fight related to water assets. With drought conditions still prevailing, the then Beattie Government wanted to take control of the water infrastructure and systems owned by local government authorities. In response, a coalition of south-east Queensland mayors demanded billions of dollars in compensation. The takeover move was announced by Beattie just six weeks before his retirement, leaving the new Premier to wage a bitter battle with Campbell and his fellow Mayors. As chair of the Council of Mayors (SEQ), Australia's largest local government advocacy organisation representing 12 councils, Campbell pursued the issue relentlessly. In October 2007, the Council of Mayors funded a series of full-page newspaper advertisements and flyers with the provocative headline "The Great Water Swindle". The ads asked voters:

> Why should you suffer because the State Government failed to build new dams, or plan for population growth? Don't get

conned. It's your money and you deserve better. If you share our anger, help us get our message to Anna Bligh.

When the group of Mayors released an independent review into the water grid, the value of the combined assets amounted to $6 billion. In a Parliamentary speech, Bligh dismissed the reports and Campbell's views on the issue:

> The truth is that Campbell Newman cannot tell the truth. He is a man whose word means nothing. He is dishonest and he has lied about every page of that report.[45]

The attacks by Bligh at this time were launched in the context of the impending Council election. As Campbell ramped up his re-election campaign towards the end of the year and into 2008, Labor's frontbench responded with frequent tirades against him amid platitudes of support for Labor's new Lord Mayoral candidate and former cricketer Greg Rowell. Judging by internal polling in both camps, the attacks were falling on deaf ears. As those anonymous Labor officials had predicted in *The Courier-Mail* more than 12 months earlier, Campbell was soaring in the race to secure a second term as Lord Mayor.

Can Do more

Throughout his first term, from the council politicking and suburban flooding, to tunnel projects and his partnership with Beattie, the Can Do man had, for the most part, delivered. In acrimonious circumstances, he had rolled out most of his TransApex vision, reined in the budget deficits of previous Labor councils and gained a reputation as an "anti-politician". The slogan for his re-election campaign was "Can Do More". His personal brand was everywhere in early 2008; on billboards, TV ads, and radio spots. The campaign even had its own irritatingly catchy jingle:

> You and Campbell Newman
> need a Can Do Team,
> You and Campbell Newman need a Can Do Team,
> You and Campbell Newman, you and Campbell Newman,
> with you and Campbell Newman and his Can Do Team.

Just like in 2004, the issue of traffic congestion was front and centre in the 2008 election. Brisbane had become a victim of its own success in attracting thousands of new residents. Labor's Lord Mayoral candidate Greg Rowell attacked Campbell's apparent failure to address the issue of congestion.[46] But the voters seemed to be siding with Campbell, with pre-election opinion polls predicting a landslide win. A leader's debate staged a fortnight before the 15 March election was deemed an "easy win" for Campbell, and a Galaxy Poll published in *The Sunday-Mail* recorded his approval rating at 72 percent.

But just as his team geared up for the intense final stretch of the campaign, Lisa was struck down with a mystery virus. She collapsed at a campaign event on 1 March, and the next day her father Frank Monsour rushed her to hospital. The media discovered she was recovering in St Andrews Hospital when they started asking questions about her absence from the campaign. A week before election day, Campbell told *The Sunday-Mail*:

> On Sunday (2 March), I was off campaigning when I got a call from my father-in-law, who's an oral surgeon. He said he had grabbed her and admitted her to St Andrew's and she has been there ever since. We found out the next morning she had glandular fever. She had it before years ago as a young person in her 20s, but she's got it really bad. I've been putting off the official launch because I want her there, but it's getting to the point where I might have to fly solo or perhaps get my eldest daughter to represent her.

Campbell visited Lisa in hospital twice a day in between campaign stops. When the campaign launch was eventually held just four days before polling day, Lisa was sitting in the front row. She received the loudest cheer of the night. Campbell's "Can Do" team of 15 male and 11 female candidates was energised. No-one wanted a repeat of the 2004 election. In an interview with *City News* magazine two days later, Campbell promised an "explosion of activity" in his second term if voters re-elected him with a majority Liberal team on the council. He revealed he would not seek a third term if he was re-elected with a minority Liberal council. Campbell dreaded facing another four years with a belligerent Labor majority. In shades of what was to come in his future political career, the article touched on Labor accusations and media portrayals of Campbell's "dictator-like image":

> Staff maintain the dictator-like image often painted of their boss by his foes, a kick-back of his military years, couldn't be further from the truth. They use an overheard telephone conversation in which Newman was caught scolding his child with a warning he was close to 'getting his stroppy shoes on' as proof. Tired of the stigma, Newman has sent himself up in the past, reportedly making staffers learn The Ballad of Green Beret, which was sung as they marched single file past rival councillors toward the weekly council meeting.

The office high jinks, inspired by Campbell's love of Monty Python sketches, masked a more serious political undercurrent emanating from the Labor Party.

During the campaign, Campbell was forced to write to Prime Minister Kevin Rudd, calling for his help in stamping out "negative and undemocratic" election tactics by Labor's council team. Campbell's letter raised the issue of "a telephone poll conducted by the Labor Party which sought to push false and negative impressions of me in what could only be described as a personal attack". Campbell wrote to Rudd:

> As a man of principle, I am certain you would be disturbed by these allegations and the misleading tactics being deployed by the Queensland branch of the Labor Party. I formally request that you remind your party members about the importance of integrity, transparency and decency when participating in the democratic process.[47]

While Campbell was taken aback by Labor's style of campaigning, their tactics had zero impact. By the closing of the rolls on 15 March, voters had backed Campbell in a tidal wave of support. After the bittersweet victory of 2004, he romped home with over 60 percent of the primary vote as Lord Mayor and an all-important majority in council, securing 18 wards to Labor's 8.

Despite persistent speculation and calls for him to step up to the state realm, the new majority enabled him to focus on finishing what he had started four years earlier.

6

Outcomes

2008-2011: Second Term as Lord Mayor

Brisbane was booming in early 2008, despite early tremors foreshadowing the global financial crisis to come. For now, new residents were flocking to the south-east corner of Queensland in their thousands. In the four years since he was elected Lord Mayor, more than 100,000 extra people now called Brisbane home. The city's population reached 1.95 million people in June.[48] Rapid population growth, emerging links between Brisbane and Asia, more residential living in the CBD and new infrastructure projects combined to help transition Brisbane from its reputation as a big country town into a cosmopolitan metropolis.

Most of that growth had been managed by Labor-dominated councils and state Labor governments. Now, for the first time in 17 years, Brisbane City Council would be run by a Liberal Lord Mayor with a majority of conservative councillors. The political demons from his first term had been banished. Despite headwinds from his deteriorating relationship with the Bligh Government and the impending GFC, the years ahead would prove to be among the most fulfilling and constructive of his working life.

2008 Budget

Campbell laid out his second-term agenda in his 2008 Budget speech in June, his fifth as Lord Mayor. Having a majority in council meant he could finally roll out his TransApex plan without delay:

> We want to get on with the job of getting Brisbane moving rather than spending our time feathering our nest and building Local Government careers.

The blockbuster Budget featured a $917.4 million spend on capital works projects, a staggering amount for a Local Government authority. In what is believed to have been an Australian first for a Council, a Future Fund-style entity called the City of Brisbane Investment Corporation was established. The independent investment firm would buy and sell major property assets and recycle the capital into residential and commercial developments while paying a healthy dividend back to the council to help fund new projects and bolster services. Funding was also allocated to council's "2 Million Trees" program, aimed at developing wildlife corridors, boosting local bushland and "keeping Brisbane looking green".

Merger deal?

In the first half of 2008, the push to merge the Liberal and National Parties was gaining traction. A growing army of supporters were joining Lawrence Springborg in his mission to make the dream of a united conservative force a reality. If the Liberal and National Parties wanted to win Government in Queensland, they first had to win Brisbane. Changes to electorate zoning and boundaries in 1992 meant a party needed to win around 30 of Queensland's 89 seats in the greater Brisbane area if it was to have any hope of forming government. Following the 2006 election, the National-Liberal coalition held just two. Griffith University politics lecturer Paul Williams said at the time:

> Since the 1980s, non-Labor voters have awaited Brisbane's 'Great Liberal Revival' – a resurgence that promises to push the party's Parliamentary numbers past the Nationals' and,

therefore, into senior status within the Queensland Coalition. But, once again, this failed to occur.[49]

Labor's domination of Brisbane was one of many reasons for the ongoing push to merge the two conservative parties to avoid splitting the vote in urban areas. On the weekend of 26-27 July 2008 the sustained effort led by Springborg finally hit pay-dirt. Over 1,000 delegates from the Liberal and National Parties had gathered at the Sofitel Hotel in Brisbane's CBD to thrash out the future course of conservative politics. They were in two adjoining rooms separated by a retractable wall, the Libs on one side, the Nats on the other. After so many false starts and hurdles over many years, the moment had finally arrived. On the Sunday of the conference, the partition wall separating the two groups was pulled back in symbolic confirmation that the Liberal National Party had been officially formed. Under a shower of confetti and the blaring music of U2's hit song "Beautiful Day", Springborg was mobbed on his way into the pavilion. *The Gold Coast Bulletin* described the scene:

> Watching were luminaries from both former parties, former Deputy Prime Minister Doug Anthony, former Premiers Russell Cooper and Rob Borbidge and former Brisbane Lord Mayor Sallyanne Atkinson as well as federal and state politicians and councillors. John Bjelke-Petersen, son of former premier Sir Joh, was also in the crowd and said his father would have approved. Surfers Paradise MP John-Paul Langbroek said he felt like a kid at Christmas: 'It's an exciting day. It is the start of a new beginning'.[50]

Springborg, who had done so much to make the amalgamation happen, was named Leader of the Liberal National Party. Liberals leader Mark McArdle, another key driver behind the successful merger, was made Deputy Leader. An exalted Springborg told the new party faithful:

> We are putting the last piece of Menzies' Lego in place. We are finally fulfilling a dream which started over six decades ago.[51]

Voted in as LNP President at the gathering, Bruce McIver said the new party was "a hard-won article of faith". Gary Spence was elected LNP Vice President. In his launch address McIver said:

> It is the birth of a new era of sensible, pragmatic politics. Yesterday we decided history. Today we start making it. The new LNP has not been formulated to be a party in Opposition. It has been built, chiselled, and honed for one purpose only – to be in Government.[52]

Despite lingering discontent from some Liberal Party heavyweights, most notably the then Liberal state president and former Howard Government Minister Mal Brough, the amalgamation was viewed as a major breakthrough, and a potential precursor to a federal merger. Subsequent moves in that regard quickly fell over.

Water and tunnels dominate again

During his second term, Campbell continued to juggle the issues of water and infrastructure, the twin themes of his first term as Lord Mayor. The North-South Bypass Tunnel, now known as the Clem7, was in full swing in the second half of 2008. Giant tunneling machines nicknamed Florence and Matilda reached the halfway mark under the Brisbane River in early November. Other traffic infrastructure projects were announced at this time in a $1.2 billion package to construct 15 years' worth of roadworks in just four years, a program of works called the Road Action Plan.

But Campbell's focus dramatically shifted back to water and the weather in mid-November when a series of freakish storms lashed Brisbane and the south-east. The three-day weather event was described by the Bureau of Meteorology as a "succession of severe thunderstorms (that) brought widespread havoc to southeast Queensland."[53] Residents described the power of a storm supercell that hit on the Sunday afternoon of 16 November as being "like a big bomb going off". ABC Radio reported:

> Weemala Street in The Gap on Brisbane's north side is almost unrecognisable this morning. Homes are without roofs, a hot water service sits in the street, corrugated iron is wrapped around power lines and countless trees are down. Seventy-thousand homes are still without power, as the storms cut a path of destruction through Toowoomba, the Gold Coast, Brisbane and the Sunshine Coast.[54]

Speaking on a mobile phone as he stood on one of the worst hit streets at The Gap, Campbell told the ABC: "The damage is absolutely extraordinary – I've not seen anything like it before."

Campbell was down at the scene of the devastation every day for more than a week, marshalling the clean-up efforts and taking part in it himself. The state MP for the area, Kate Jones, was there too. She played the role of comforter, hugging distressed homeowners and sipping cups of tea in contrast to Campbell's Can Do style.

A month later, the weather was starting to play havoc further north in the state. By the end of January, tropical cyclones Charlotte and Ellie had ravaged the state's north-west region, with the flow-on impacts of rain and flooding impacting more than half the state.[55]

2009 Queensland election

As the State Government and regional councils were mopping up from the January flooding events, speculation was rife about when the next state election would be called, and whether Campbell might be one of the candidates. He still wasn't interested, but it didn't stop the approaches. Regardless of the will to recruit Campbell into the state fold, the LNP was gaining in confidence at the prospect of facing

Premier Bligh as she attempted to win Labor's fifth consecutive term. The Springborg-led LNP was shaping up well against a backdrop of Labor's ongoing crises in both health and water, along with resentment in regional areas over the Government's mass amalgamation of local councils. By now, the global economic downturn was also starting to bite in the state's economy, adding to the pressure on Bligh and her Cabinet. The conservatives were in with their best shot for over a decade.

In February 2009, just days before the state election was set to be called, the LNP received a surprise pre-campaign fillip. The Government's Economic and Fiscal Update on 20 February revised its forecast Budget bottom line from a $56 million surplus to an operating deficit of $1.6 billion. As a result, the state's credit rating was downgraded from AAA to AA+. In its report on the downgrade decision, credit ratings agency Standard and Poor's warned of Queensland's "projected deteriorating budgetary performance, which is a result of both declining revenues and structural operating expenditure". Two days later on Sunday, 22 February Premier Bligh used a three-minute YouTube video to announce a four-week campaign with the election to be held on 21 March 2009, six months earlier than expected.

The LNP needed an 8.3 percent swing to win government, a substantial but not unattainable margin. Labor ran with the slogan 'Keep Queensland strong', promising to create 100,000 new jobs over the next three years. Premier Bligh attacked the LNP's pledge to save $1 billion a year, which included plans to reduce the skyrocketing number of public servants and rein-in Labor's prolonged spending spree. The LNP countered with its 'Change for a better Queensland' campaign, blasting Labor for racking up $74 billion worth of state debt after a decade-long boom. They also highlighted the Government's mismanagement of water infrastructure projects such as the disastrous Gold Coast desalination plant at Tugun. Budget blowouts on several projects in south-east Queensland had already cost taxpayers hundreds of millions of dollars.[56]

Springborg spearheaded a solid campaign with Mark McArdle as his Deputy. But the bungling of critical service, infrastructure and budgetary issues by successive Labor Governments wasn't enough to get the LNP over the line. Despite recording a 3.68 percent swing in its favour and picking up an extra nine seats at the 21 March poll, the LNP's chances were again cruelled in Brisbane, where it won just six seats.

With Labor's win, Bligh became the first female Premier in Australian history elected in her own right. Apart from a brief interlude between February 1996 and June 1998 when the conservatives won office under the leadership of Rob Borbidge, the Labor Party had ruled in Queensland for the past two decades. Springborg resigned from the leadership of the LNP in the wake of the loss. Surfers Paradise MP John-Paul Langbroek stepped up in his place amid hopes his Liberal credentials would do for the party's prospects in south-east Queensland what the rural-based Springborg had been unable to achieve in three previous elections.

In the months immediately after its victory, the Bligh Government effectively sealed its own demise with two surprise decisions sprung on Queenslanders without warning. First, it scrapped the beloved 8 cents per litre fuel subsidy for motorists. Then, on 2 June, the Premier shocked Labor's base as well as the union movement by announcing plans to sell around $15 billion worth of state assets, including ports, forestry and railways. The privatisation plan made economic sense if only to plug some of the gaping black holes in the 2009 state Budget caused by the onset of the GFC and Labor's recent lack of fiscal restraint. The deceit of keeping the privatisation plan secret until after the election was a fatal move. Queenslanders weren't told of the

Government's privatisation plans before the election, and they felt betrayed. Worse still for Bligh, she could no longer rely on the union movement to help keep her in power.

2009 Council Budget

Despite handing down his 2009 Budget in the maelstrom of the GFC, Campbell was determined to push on with his big-ticket infrastructure projects. But in a reflection of the ongoing strife in the world's economy, that year's budget was the soberest set of accounts he had handed down since his first in 2004. Much had happened since the release of Campbell's Budget the previous year. In the United States, Lehman Brothers had filed for bankruptcy while insurance company AIG and mortgage agencies Fannie Mae and Freddie Mac were bailed out by the US Government. The Rudd Government had already announced its major stimulus packages, the first worth $10.4 billion in October 2008 and a second round worth an astonishing $42 billion in February 2009. In his 2009 Budget speech, Campbell said:

> Our challenge has been to develop a responsible budget that cuts costs and provides a stimulus for the Brisbane economy. This has not been an easy task. It is never easy to cut programs and it is always hard to prioritise some of the very worthwhile projects submitted for funding. However, strong financial management is about making tough decisions. Regardless of how the media reports this budget – or what political games and scare campaigns the Opposition might deploy – I know it will make a real and positive difference in these tough times. All I want from this job is the satisfaction that comes from getting the job done. This has certainly been the toughest budget I have had to deliver. The one clear message Brisbane residents keep giving me is that they want their elected representatives to make tough decisions. They want us to

With Ben Myers, Mark Brodie and Jane Prentice meeting the Mayor of Inchon Ahn Sang-soo in South Korea in 2009 and, below, at Brisbane City Council's Stylin' Up Festival in 2009

Kevin Newman confronts Joh-Bjelke Petersen in November 1976

With Stephen Conry and John Howard in his Sydney office circa 2009

deal with problems and be honest about the challenges – no matter how big or small – that confront our city.

Growing pains

A major article in the *Weekend Australian Magazine* on 5 December 2009 examined the growing pains and future prospects of Australia's east coast capital cities. Reporter Tom Dusevic highlighted the remarkable pace and degree of change in Brisbane over the past two decades:

> At the ragged end of the Joh dynasty, Brisbane was a scuzzy backwater. Tarted up for Expo (in 1988), but vacant and eerily wog-free, it was beery, listless and lonesome. Anyone with talent from north of the Tweed was drifting to Sydney, whether footballer, artist or banker. (Today) Brisbane is the Australian city that has changed most during the past two decades. And, very likely, the past two weeks. This transformation, as in Melbourne, is due to several decisions and many people. Officials such as strategic thinkers Glyn Davis and Terry Moran, the "Smart State" salesman Peter Beattie and Wayne Goss, who busted through in 1989. Then there are the quirks of history and chance. You learn to love Brisbane's adolescent bravado and deep insecurities, tolerate its insolence and marvel at its energy ... living on concrete, air-con and rum. As well, there is Lord Mayor Campbell Newman, a Liberal. The immediate past chairman of the Infrastructure Association of Queensland, Jeremy Prentice, said: 'He is there for the betterment of the city, he distances himself from internal politics and he works well across boundaries when it comes to infrastructure.'

The article quoted two anonymous business leaders who were scathing about the Bligh Government:

> 'Bligh is operating in a period of crisis politics, lurching from

one disaster to another,' one of the sources says. Another condemns Bligh for 'throwing money at problems like the water crisis to avoid criticism'. 'These sorts of decisions are piling up, they're made in haste. We need a more structured approach if Brisbane is to keep growing. Ports, roads, and homes are one thing, but the real worry is water, then energy, then maintenance.'

In response to the pressure, Premier Bligh convened a "Growth Summit" to map out a "sustainable" path forward for the south-east corner. Campbell would later describe it as an "Anti-Growth" Summit, with so many regulations, land use controls and planning restrictions flowing from the event it served as a proxy cap on population. Ross Elliot, former Property Council of Australia head and inaugural Brisbane Marketing CEO, noted at the time:

> It's become an industry joke that we now produce more plans than houses. But the inevitable consequence of this explosion of planning regulation – matched at the same time by the surreptitious introduction of exorbitant per lot housing levies under the guise of 'user pays' – was to drive up housing costs rapidly while drying up new supply.

City Hall, health payroll system collapsing

The positive reviews of Campbell's performance as Lord Mayor continued into 2010. In January, a column in *The Sunday Mail* by Darrell Giles pondered the need for a new Opposition Leader to take the LNP into the next election, due by the latest possible date of 16 June 2012. Under the headline "Out-of-box players needed for LNP win", Giles noted Campbell was shaping up as a popular choice for the role:

> The polls and public anger with Labor in Queensland point to an easy win for the Liberal National Party at the

next election. But history and the foot-shooting ability of the LNP would suggest anything but a romp home. While Premier Anna Bligh considers a Cabinet reshuffle, some LNP insiders believe drastic action is needed by the conservatives to overhaul the Labor majority. Delegates at last year's (2009) LNP State Convention were unstinting in their praise of Campbell Newman ... describing him as a leader and a fighter who wasn't prepared to just 'sit back and expect somebody else to do it.' One delegate told the audience Newman was a 'shining light we can all aspire to'.

Once again, Campbell wasn't interested. He had too much on his plate as Lord Mayor to consider switching to state politics. One of the biggest challenges at this time was the deteriorating condition of a building he had grown to love. In April 2010, Brisbane's iconic City Hall celebrated its 80th birthday. Described by a British journalist as "an Italianate building with a campanile-style clock tower",[57] the place was literally falling apart. Major repairs had been put on the backburner for years, but the grand old building could take it no more. The whole place was sinking and concrete cancer was rife. Water – one of the ever-present themes of Campbell's Lord Mayoralty – was leaking in from above and rising up from below. As far back as 2002, fears over potential fire risks within the building were tabled in reports to the council. Over time, flowing water had burrowed a tunnel underneath some rooms in the basement, causing the flooring to collapse in 2006. In what would become one of the biggest restoration projects in Australia's history, Campbell announced a three-year, $210 million project. Campbell told *The Courier-Mail* in early 2010:

> There were so many reports you could pile them up into a respectable mound. Over the years stuff started to come across my desk. By the time I got to late 2007, I realised we had a major, major problem. It was time to bite the bullet.

Despite the urgency of the repair job and the building's historical significance, Campbell faced a tough sell in convincing the public. A poll conducted by the council in late 2009 found 40 percent of people were open to the option of demolishing City Hall. But Campbell's passion for history and heritage overcame community ambivalence to the project. He told *The Courier Mail*:

> You look back at the way city leaders might have felt at the time they wanted to build City Hall and where they felt the city of Brisbane was going. That sense of optimism and excitement about this place would ring true with people today. Let's be true to their vision of Brisbane. Let's fix it up. Let's not have people saying in 50 or 100 years' time, 'What a terrible tragedy that they didn't have the gumption to go and save the City Hall'.

At the same time City Hall was crumbling, so too was the Bligh Government's credibility on the health and hospital system. In the same month City Hall celebrated its 80th birthday, a new payroll system was quietly unravelling. Nurses and health workers weren't getting paid on time, or at all. Others were underpaid or overpaid. The situation quickly descended into an unmitigated disaster, and Premier Bligh was forced to cut short a planned trade mission to Latin America to return home to address the growing crisis. As time dragged on without an apparent solution, and the cost to fix the escalating problem kept blowing out, Deputy Premier Paul Lucas was flat out clinging to his other job as Health Minister. Blame was instead sheeted home to senior health bureaucrats, with two Queensland Health executives from the Corporate Services Division sacked over the payroll bungle in June 2010.

A month later in July, the former Bundaberg Hospital surgeon Jayant Patel was found guilty of three charges of manslaughter and one count of grievous bodily harm and sentenced to seven years' jail. Both issues fed into the growing perception the health system was out of control under the stewardship of the Bligh Labor Government. The health portfolio was supposed to be one of Labor's strong suits. Instead, the administration of health and hospital services in Queensland was fast becoming a key driver in the Bligh Government's great undoing.

2010 Council Budget

Campbell liked Paul Lucas, and his friendship was almost as crucial as the working dynamic he enjoyed with Beattie. They were particularly close during Campbell's first term in that difficult and divided council and remained on friendly terms. Campbell used to joke that Lucas was his "case worker", dispensing advice on how to deal with Labor councillors. It was another stark contrast to Campbell's dealings with Premier Bligh. Graham Quirk said Beattie and Lucas were "genuine people to deal with":

> It became a bit of an ongoing joke between Campbell and Paul Lucas. Campbell would say 'Paul, you have to help me. You're my case worker'. It was a relationship based around being honest with each other. A person like Paul would tell you if he had a different view. You knew where they stood. You were never left in any doubt and that is the way a good working relationship was built. I found Peter and Paul both honorable to deal with.

Earlier in his mayoral career, Campbell had also formed a working relationship with the then Labor Treasurer Terry Mackenroth, who was "very helpful" during the early days of the divided council. Mackenroth also assisted with finance approvals for TransApex projects up until his retirement in 2009. Mackenroth was the last of the disciplined Queensland Labor Treasurers. Campbell said:

> Mackenroth was in my view a much better Treasurer than what came afterwards. The real explosion in public service

numbers and operating costs occurred after he left. We had a very cordial but direct and honest working relationship.

While Lucas was mired in the health payroll fiasco, Campbell and Graham Quirk were busy spruiking their 2010 Budget, their seventh together. Campbell described the $2.8 billion Budget, released on 9 June, as "workman-like". In the long shadow cast by the global financial crisis, the Budget pulled back on infrastructure spending and consolidated on the previous year's restrained set of accounts:

> Despite sharp falls in revenue, a significant slump in building and development activity; lower than expected population growth; major changes to our organisation as a consequence of water reform; the slashing of State Government grants, and some very large ongoing infrastructure commitments, this Council remains in a very strong financial position. Gone are the days of Labor's Grange swilling parties and administrative excesses. Gone are the days when the previous administration raised rates but failed to deliver any major projects. Gone are the days of previous administration Councillors jetting off overseas to watch migrating birds in their natural habitat. This Budget continues to deliver value for money. It's a Budget that confirms our commitment to delivering on the promises we made to residents in the 2008 election. Importantly, it's a Budget that will once again leave Brisbane City Council in a much stronger financial position.

The Budget quantified Campbell's efficiency drive at $190 million worth of operational savings across his two terms so far.

Departures

Apart from Graham Quirk and Ben Myers, one of the most important working relationships of Campbell's political career was coming to an end around the time the Budget was being released. Long-serving council chief executive Jude Munro had announced her resignation in June 2010 after a decade in the job. Campbell showered warm praise on Munro's legacy in his 2010 Budget speech, but an email exchange between the pair revealed how close they had become since the difficult and divided days of his first term in office. Munro wrote:

> Dear Lord Mayor, a fond farewell. Forgive me for not saying goodbye personally but it would be too emotional for me. I think you've been a terrific boss, and I've loved your leadership. You are, and will be remembered as one of the finest of our Lord Mayors. Thank you and au revoir, Jude.

Campbell replied:

> Jude, you have been fantastic! You have taught me a heck of a lot! As I said publicly, it's been the most important working relationship in my life. I will miss you heaps! Please stay in touch, your friend always, Cam.

At around the same time, an altogether different exit from the halls of public administration burst onto the front page of every major newspaper. In a backroom coup d'état on the night of 23 June 2010, Julia Gillard and Labor's infamous faceless men knifed Prime Minister Kevin Rudd. The following day Gillard was sworn in as Australia's 27th Prime Minister, with Wayne Swan elevated to Deputy Prime Minister. Just 23 days later the new Prime Minister called a snap election for 21 August in a bid to catch the Tony Abbott-led Opposition off guard. It resulted in the first hung Parliament since 1940. Following intense negotiations over 17 days with crossbench MPs Bob Katter, Tony Windsor and Rob Oakeshott, the Gillard Government was sworn in on 14 September.

Campbell may have secured the luxury of a majority on council, but his dealings with the two other levels of government, both of them Labor, would prove virtually impossible. The fruitful days of political partnerships with Peter Beattie and John Howard were a distant, bittersweet memory.

Delivery on TransApex

The tangible benefits and outcomes from those early productive relationships were increasingly on show in Brisbane throughout 2010. Campbell opened the Go-Between Bridge to traffic on 5 July 2010, the first new inner-city road bridge over the Brisbane River in 40 years. With the Clem7 tunnel opened a few months earlier, the TransApex plan he had developed with Graham Quirk back in 2002 was being rolled out.

The scale and nature of change in Brisbane's traffic, public transport and road networks since the changing of the mayoral guard in 2004 should not be underestimated. When Campbell was first elected, Brisbane motorists had the use of one bypass corridor to avoid the CBD. At the same time, the city's buses were ageing and run down. Despite Brisbane's sweltering summers, only 25 percent of the fleet was air-conditioned. By this stage of his tenure as Lord Mayor, work was either underway or completed on three tunnels – Clem Jones (Clem7), Airport Link and Legacy Way – as well as the Go-Between Bridge and Eleanor Schonell Bridge (formerly known as Green Bridge). Every bus in the fleet was now air-conditioned, with an additional 740 new buses added to the network and two new bus depots built to cope with the extra capacity since 2004. To round out the original Moving Brisbane policy first devised in 2002, the car and bus transport upgrades were complemented with seven new City Cat ferries and three new ferry terminals, as well as expanded networks of bicycle and walking paths. The total package was worth more than $10 billion, the largest of its kind in Australia.

An infrastructure package of this magnitude was bound to draw fire from critics, and concerns over tolls and patronage emerged early in the life of the Clem7 and the Go-Between Bridge in particular. Mark Ludlow wrote in the *Australian Financial Review* on 6 July 2010:

> Mr Newman yesterday dismissed the suggestion that money-conscious Brisbane motorists didn't like paying tolls. 'It's also the economic times – people are watching their money very closely,' he said. 'I don't want people to pay tolls at all but it's the only way we're going to be able to get these projects going given the federal and state governments don't make the appropriate level of investment.

The Go-Between Bridge provided a focal point for Campbell's frustrations over construction delays caused by political obstructionism and layers of red tape across levels of government, mostly on a state level. Once construction finally got underway in July 2008, the Go-Between Bridge took less than two years to build and came in $42 million under budget. But it took four years of argument and obstruction in his first term just to start construction, adding to the final cost significantly.

Campbell's focus on his TransApex vision led to inevitable claims he was too fixated on vehicular infrastructure, putting cars ahead of pedestrians and cyclists, and the environment. To the surprise of those critics, he launched Australia's second public bike hire scheme in October 2010, a few months after Melbourne's Bike Share program. The CityCycle bike hire program came on the back of a $100 million spend in the current council term to build better cycling infrastructure. Peak cycling groups applauded the measures, but mandatory helmet laws proved a dampener for the CityCycle scheme.

In a broader sense, CityCycle was another example of Campbell's modus operandi as Lord Mayor. Fuelled by his background in army logistics and his work for Grainco, Campbell believed in building infrastructure ahead of the demand curve. He had seen the impact of the state Labor Government's failure to plan for growth and build infrastructure to keep pace with increasing population in the southeast corner of the state. Campbell believed Brisbane would grow into projects like the TransApex tunnels and river crossings, as well as the CityCycle scheme, over time:

> I never wanted to build things that last for one electoral cycle over the next three or four years. I wanted to build infrastructure and projects that last for the next 50 years, the next 100 years.

Graham Quirk said the projects were "for the long term" and called them "100-year life assets and projects designed to provide for growth."

Brisbane voters didn't appear to care much at all about political bunfights, delays to infrastructure or the historical costings of TransApex projects. After more than six years in the top job, Campbell was voted one of the world's best mayors of 2010 in an annual competition run by the German think-thank City Mayors' Foundation. The poll ranked Campbell as the fifth-best mayor in the world, crediting him for having "great intellect and a can-do attitude". It was a gratifying way to end 2010, but the glow of global recognition vanished in a flash when the spectre of flooding rose yet again, this time with a fury not seen since the 1970s.

Brisbane floods

At the end of 2010, Lisa Newman was trying to work out a Christmas and New Year holiday destination, and considered heading overseas. Campbell insisted they stay much closer to home. His fear of the upcoming storm season was so great he wanted to be within driving distance of Brisbane. For weeks, the forecasts of inclement weather weighed heavily on his shoulders.

On 4 October the Bureau of Meteorology issued a media release urging Queensland residents to "prepare early not only for cyclones but also for floods as we have already experienced record September rainfalls across the state". Campbell was concerned enough to issue his own warning, telling residents in flood-risk zones to prepare for the worst. In a story featured in *The Courier-Mail* under the headline "Brisbane suburbs most at risk of flooding as Campbell Newman warns of repeat of 1974", he said "no amount of concrete or steel or flood mitigation works will stop flooding in those parts of town".[58]

Some thought Campbell's dire predictions were unnecessarily alarmist, and the Labor Opposition on council went on the attack. Council Opposition Leader Shayne Sutton said:

> Campbell Newman's statements about the potential flooding were alarmist and clearly made off his own bat without taking any notice of the agencies which are best equipped to provide us with this information.[59]

The various public warnings and council's offering of free sandbags prompted mild bursts of panic in the community. When the storms arrived a few days later, the big floods Campbell warned about never eventuated. About 100mms of rain fell in a 48-hour period, enough to warrant water releases from an overflowing Wivenhoe Dam, located about 70kms north-west of Brisbane. Labor councillors lambasted Campbell, calling him "Chicken Little" for predicting the sky would fall in. Some in the media also accused him of hyperbole. Speaking to reporters from her week-long temporary base in Townsville, Premier Anna Bligh weighed in with thinly veiled criticism.[60] Despite the public backlash, Campbell was undeterred.

For weeks he had been poring over statistics from the Bureau of Meteorology, its website permanently open and constantly refreshing in the browser of his Blackberry phone. He absorbed it all; forecasts, historical data, dam levels, countless charts, tables, and maps. He read a book on Brisbane's topography and history of floods, which confirmed his fears. For a time, it seemed to be the only topic he spoke about. Regardless of the moderate rainfall after his first warnings back in early October, Campbell remained convinced Brisbane faced grave risks that summer storm season, more than at any time in recent decades. On 16 December 2010 he told Radio 4BC:

> My concern is that over the last 15 years we have had a very dry period and we are now seeing a return to the conditions that prevailed during the 60s and 70s. Since then we have had a lot of people [move to Brisbane] and they have chosen to live near this beautiful, idyllic little creek in suburbia. I'm afraid they don't know that it could turn into a raging torrent and it could actually threaten their property.

A few days later, Campbell, Lisa, their two daughters and other Monsour family members departed their Windsor home for a driving holiday to the Girraween National Park, south-west of Brisbane. It was the last extended family holiday they would take for many years. While they were away, torrential rain over a number of weeks had caused Wivenhoe Dam to fill to 188.5 percent of its supply capacity. Nearby Somerset Dam had filled to 189.7 percent. When they returned home to Brisbane on 9 January, the horror and destruction of the Queensland floods of 2011 would arrive within the next 72 hours.

By the Monday night of 10 January, the Toowoomba area about 125kms west of Brisbane resembled a scene of post-apocalyptic proportions. An inland tsunami had devastated the region, and the confirmed death toll rose to seven by nightfall. Dozens more residents were missing, and towns further inland in the path of the raging torrent were evacuated. Authorities were overwhelmed. Simultaneously they were dealing with the unfolding emergencies in the Toowoomba and Lockyer Valley regions while preparing for the worst in Ipswich and Brisbane. All that water still needed to get out to sea. As the floodwaters were rushing towards Brisbane, Campbell was finalising a four-phase action plan and working through details of a massive volunteer coordination effort, later dubbed "The Mud Army":

> We need to divide a very big job up into manageable chunks. We will be dividing the city up into five sectors for the recovery effort, and each sector will have someone in charge, and they'll have a team around them.[61]

By the Tuesday morning of 11 January, the floodwaters started to rise in low-lying suburbs across Brisbane. Later that afternoon, the raging waters broke the banks of the Brisbane River, submerging pedestrian walkways and ferry terminals for kilometres along its course. The entire area was declared a disaster zone while thousands of homes and businesses were evacuated. By the time the river peaked on 13 January, an estimated 15,000 homes and businesses and 160 roads had been inundated, and over half of the city's ferry terminals were severely damaged or swept away. When the floodwaters began receding on 14 January, Campbell was shoveling mud out of inundated homes alongside crestfallen residents. Across town, Lisa and their daughters were attending to distressed families at Evacuation Centres, set up to accommodate around 2000 people forced to flee their homes.

In the weeks after the floods, the accusations of fear-mongering levelled against him months earlier were replaced with widespread praise for his "calm and steady" leadership during the crisis. It gave him no comfort or satisfaction. His anger at repeated government failings in planning and mitigation overwhelmed him.

The floods clean-up was still in train by the time Campbell attended a funeral for a work colleague's husband at the Albert St Uniting Church on the morning of 2 February. Exactly 60 days later, he was the Premier-in-waiting.

7

THE COST OF VICTORY

April 2011-24 March 2012:
Queensland election campaign

Lisa Newman couldn't bring herself to get out of bed. Trapped in a dark cloud of anger and anxiety, she was crying and fearful, needing to go grocery shopping but lacking the energy and will to venture outside. It was late 2011 and Lisa felt like her family was under siege in their own home, perched atop a steep dog-legged street in the Brisbane suburb of Windsor. At irregular intervals, the media was staking out their home. A couple of doors away on the same street, news reporters had on occasion confronted her ageing parents.

On the day she couldn't get up to face the morning, *The Australian* was running another story featuring the latest allegation against her family.[62] It had stirred up the Pavlovian response of other media outlets, and Lisa suspected camera crews and photographers were waiting across the street yet again that morning. She was too afraid of being spotted or snapped by a photographer if she peered through the windows to check if the media pack was there.

The thought of going to the supermarket had become a loathsome idea. The last time Lisa was at the Ashgrove Woolworths she was abused by a woman who jumped into her personal space and called her a "rich bitch". For months, Labor's attacks and the media coverage it generated had escalated exponentially. Labor's campaign team led by operatives like Jackie Trad and Eamonn Fitzpatrick had done their research. They knew Campbell's family was his weak point. He had a hard exterior. But contrary to the public perception Labor was busily crafting around him, Campbell was a soft touch when it came to his wife, children, and extended family. Labor's sole purpose during the campaign was to keep digging and poking at that vulnerable spot until he cracked.

They didn't care – and still don't – that the intrusive media coverage of the Newman and Monsour families had somehow granted certain people the implicit right to behave like animals. Like the time an older woman wearing a "Keep Kate" t-shirt – a supporter of Campbell's Labor opponent Kate Jones – yelled abuse at one of the Newman girls. Or the occasion when their eldest daughter Rebecca came home in tears after being on the receiving end of a particularly foul-mouthed tirade while out campaigning for her father. At the time she told her mum: "I'm sick and tired of feeling like I'm less of a human being to people when I put this ("Can Do" campaign) t-shirt on."

Lisa's seven years of charity work as Lady Mayoress, her efforts to fundraise over $4 million for local organisations and causes,[63] her decades of nursing and an impeccable reputation in the community all seemed to count for naught. The insinuations of impropriety against the Newman and Monsour families – which would later prove to be completely fabricated – were demoralising and demeaning. Having agreed to leave politics before the 2012 mayoral election, all of this dirt and smear being shoveled on to their doorstep wasn't part of the Newman family's plan. Lisa was looking forward to getting her husband back. Now he was further away than ever before. On reflection, she described this campaign as one of the worst experiences of her life:

> In my eyes our time at City Hall and the campaigns we were involved in, they were the best times and the closest times of our relationship. I look back on it as almost the happiest time in our marriage because I felt like we were this incredible team. I loved being there at City Hall, I loved how happy

Campbell was serving the community, and I loved being with the people we worked with, they were like family. Compared to that, the 2011-2012 state campaign was the worst. The absolute worst. I could not believe that human beings could be so unjust and lie so much for their own gain. It got to a stage where I did not want to leave the house. I was terrified about going to the supermarket. Once the Labor Party started having a go at me, it was almost like everyone in the general public felt like it was a free-for-all. People would scream and yell at me, they'd come up and abuse me, abuse our teenage girls. I felt traumatised. I didn't want to leave the house. I felt like I hadn't signed up to this. We were just devastated.

Frank Monsour

Lisa's parents were also being dragged through the mud. As respected elders of the Brisbane community, Frank Monsour and his wife of nearly 50 years Elizabeth were blindsided by Labor's campaign and the media's reporting of it. Labor had manufactured a series of allegations that Frank had materially benefited from decisions his son-in-law made as Lord Mayor and featured the accusations in their campaign attack ads. Based entirely on methods of insinuation and inference, much of the creative material was largely dreamed up by Labor's self-styled advertising guru Dee Madigan.

Just a few months into Campbell's bid to be Premier, the campaign of smear started to take its toll on Frank's health, with family noting he looked increasingly "ashen-faced". He turned 73 in May 2011, about a month after Campbell's preselection in the seat of Ashgrove. Elizabeth's health, already waning and fragile, also deteriorated at this time.

For Frank, a reserved and honourable man, it was a period of great personal pain. He had lived by a set of abiding morals and principles driven by his deep Catholic faith and "old-world" values inherited from his family roots in Lebanon. As a renowned and respected Oral and Maxillofacial Surgeon, he had been the Clinical Professor in the Department of Surgery at the University of Queensland and a key member of the Surgeon General's Office at the Australian Defence Force. For his work in surgical education and training as well as broader service to the community, he was made a Member of the Order of Australia in 2008. For his long service as an officer in the Army Reserve, he was awarded a Reserve Force Decoration.

He knew full well how brutal politics could be. But this was something else. This was unprecedented in Australian political history. These attacks on "Papa" Monsour were tearing shreds from the family's collective heart.

Lisa blamed herself for the stress and damage her family was suffering. For her entire adult life as a nurse practitioner, she had been the family's protector and helper. Now she was a mess. She didn't know how to make it stop:

> In late 2011, when we were in the throes of it, I was really upset. I was crying. I just couldn't get out of bed this one particular day. I was crying and crying. I'd just had it. Cam came in and sat down and said he was prepared to pull out. I was crying and just said 'no' ... evil can't prevail. People can't win in this fashion. They have to win because they're the best for the job, not because they sit there saying horrible things about the opposition. So that's when I said no matter what we were just going to have to deal with it. But it was terribly traumatic. I withdrew from my family. I felt that I was to blame for their suffering as well. I felt like a pariah.

At times, the campaign pushed Lisa and her relationship with Campbell to low ebbs. She considered seeking professional help but was afraid any visit to a psychiatrist or psychologist would inevitably end up in the media.

Reporting the dirt

Seeing the impact on his family, and with no way to combat it, Campbell was increasingly incensed at particular stories running with factual errors and the media's apparent lack of scrutiny of source material provided by Labor. While it was easier said than done, the LNP's campaign director James McGrath wanted Campbell to ignore the media's treatment of stories about him. McGrath had worked for London Mayor Boris Johnson. Brisbane journos had nothing on Fleet Street hacks. McGrath also wondered if there was an element of payback at play from individual journalists who had been at war with Campbell and his media team during his time at City Hall.

Regardless of the advice from McGrath and his media adviser Kylie Lindsay, Campbell's views on the media had reached new dimensions of loathing by the end of 2011. He was disgusted by the ethics of some journalists, who he believed had repeatedly failed to question and filter the dirt Labor was delivering. Privately he described *The Australian's* Queensland reporter Michael McKenna as "the tool of the Australian Labor Party during this campaign". Other reporters such as Channel 7's Patrick Condren, Channel 9's Spencer Jolly, and Steven Wardill from *The Courier-Mail* all fed off each other in the Brisbane media bubble. They worked in an unofficial pattern commonplace in the modern media landscape. Print journalists McKenna and Wardill would write up stories with all sorts of allegations in the morning newspapers, social media would fan the fire during the day, and TV reporters Condren and Jolly would re-broadcast the same story on the nightly news. And they'd do it all again day after day. That vicious and unyielding media cycle left little room for policy debate, and the same level of blood-thirsty scrutiny didn't seem to apply to the Labor Party.

The sources of the allegations – people like Labor's Jackie Trad and Eamonn Fitzpatrick – were never scrutinised or exposed for their actions, particularly later in the campaign when their claims were dismissed as baseless by authorities. Specifically, Campbell wondered why the media didn't put the tactics and background of Labor's Jackie Trad under the microscope at any point. To be fair to the reporters, Trad's background was something of a closely guarded mystery.

Jackie Trad

Jacklyn "Jackie" Trad had always operated in the political shadows with a driving ambition to become a Member of Parliament. By the time the 2011-12 state campaign was in motion, the then 39-year-old's entire working life reflected those aspirations. Like so many Labor apparatchiks of the modern era, Trad had little-to-no experience in the private sector. Her career shifted back and forth between university studies, the offices of Labor MPs and Ministers, unions and the Labor Party itself.

Her friendship with Premier Bligh stretched back nearly a decade. Trad was 12 years Bligh's junior, but they hit it off as fellow travellers in Queensland Labor's Left faction. When Bligh was first elected to the Queensland Parliament in 1995, Trad was her campaign director, and upon victory was hired as her electorate officer. Similarly, when Bligh was made a Minister in June 1998 Trad duly followed her, working in Bligh's ministerial office as an adviser.

Trad liked to talk up her assertion that she had lived in Bligh's South Brisbane electorate and surrounding areas for most of her life. It would help her credibility with local voters when she was tapped to replace her mentor in the seat. But Trad's movements appear to have dropped off the public radar for a period starting from around the year 2000. It was around this time that Trad left Bligh's office to live in Sydney.

Whilst there is no evidence or suggestion of any wrong doing, it is not known whether Trad had (or still has) any relevant information which may have assisted authorities in addressing the controversial issue of branch stacking as raised in The Sunday Mail on 10 December 2000. That article read:

"The Criminal Justice Commission has interviewed a Labor Party national executive member over branch stacking allegations in a near-Brisbane electorate. Investigators spoke to a woman and two other Queensland Left faction members after an anonymous letter claimed three Brisbane residents had leased a home in Narangba in the state seat of Kallangur held by the Labor Left's Ken Hayward."

There is certainly no suggestion at all that Trad was one of the Labor identities mentioned in the above The Sunday Mail article.

When Trad was living in Sydney, she worked for Labor MPs and Ministers in the Carr Government, and completed a Master's degree in public policy at the University of Sydney in 2003. Soon after, she returned to Brisbane to work for the Labor Party as a grassroots organiser and campaigner.

After the Bligh Government had suffered a 4.67 percent swing against it at the 2009 election, a broom swept through Labor's campaign headquarters. With support from old friends and new "comrades" in the Left faction, Trad was elevated to Assistant Secretary. That cumulative 15 years' experience in Labor offices and union campaigns fuelled her work on the 2011-12 state election. Jackie Trad refused the author's repeated requests for an interview.

Trad's team

Trad and her boss, Queensland Labor secretary Anthony Chisolm, were ably assisted in the campaign against Campbell and his extended family by Labor adviser Eamonn Fitzpatrick. Brought up from Sydney in September 2011 to work in Anna Bligh's office, Fitzpatrick's reputation for peddling Labor's new style of intensely personal political attacks preceded him. He was often seen in a side room at the Premier's office on level 15 at the Executive Building on George

St in Brisbane, scribbling away at a whiteboard full of Newman and Monsour family connections and allegations.

Fitzpatrick was a little-known journalist before entering the public relations industry in 1998, working first as a media advisor for NSW Police. Two years later, he jumped from that relatively low-level apolitical department job over into the highly-charged world of political spin-doctoring, spending more than six years in the offices of NSW Labor Ministers. In mid-2007, Fitzpatrick went straight from those ministerial offices into the lucrative arms of leftwing lobbying firm Hawker Britton, co-founded in 1997 by Labor luminary Bruce Hawker. When Fitzpatrick joined the company, Hawker was running strategy on the Kevin07 federal election campaign. While so many of his ilk inevitably make the leap into politics, Fitzpatrick always seemed reluctant to step up and face the public's glare as a Member of Parliament.

From the moment he arrived in Bligh's office, Fitzpatrick worked side-by-side with Trad and Dee Madigan, an old friend, as well as Labor state secretary Chisolm. Their interlinking efforts combined the resources of Labor's Peel St headquarters and the Premier's office with Madigan's creative flair bringing their campaign dreams to life. All four of them appeared to have no qualms about targeting Lisa and the Newman and Monsour families. Madigan apparently saw no hypocrisy in her stance as a progressive and a feminist at the same time she was making Lisa's life hell. Working as a pack, Trad, Chisholm, Fitzpatrick and Madigan concocted the most intrusive campaign in Australian political history. Trad, Fitzpatrick, and Madigan all refused to participate in interviews for this book, and Chisholm could not be contacted.

In his only comment in response to questions put to him, Fitzpatrick said it was unfair for political staff members – such as he was – to be targeted or singled out for attention and scrutiny. He was adamant someone in his position should be left out of the public spotlight. Fitzpatrick didn't answer questions about whether he believed this same courtesy and boundary should be extended to the family members of politicians.

Campbell's long-time collaborator and future chief of staff Ben Myers, who became involved in the campaign in mid-2011, couldn't believe what the Labor Party and a compliant media were engaged in:

> It was absolutely disconcerting from a political perspective that a campaign like this could get traction, and it was heartbreaking to see what it was doing to Campbell and Lisa and their family. The emotional issues were huge. There's Campbell, who is confronting this stuff during the day and confronting it with the family at night. He just had nowhere to go, other than to fight. I remember having a go at *The Courier-Mail* journalist Steven Wardill over one fabricated, misinformed story in particular that he had written. Wardill was unrepentant. Not even a basic examination of the facts could have led him to the conclusions that he wrote, but because he was told it, he wrote it. Through laziness and some inherent bias the media didn't do its job. The Labor Party was working the angles very hard, and the media just took the stories at face value and ran with them.[65]

Campbell had faced scrutiny from the media and the Labor Party since 2002 when he first put his hand up for public office. Despite running in two elections and living in the public eye as the leader of Australia's largest local government authority over the past nine years, he had never experienced anything like this.

Labor realised it needed to throw everything at him, and then some. The Bligh Government was a tired, disgraced administration seeking its ninth consecutive election win, and it had to beat one of the most popular political leaders of any Australian jurisdiction to get there. Labor's dirt unit needed to drag him down, and fast. They tried to do it with a multi-pronged attack. At various times they targeted his army career, his tenure as Lord Mayor, his historical attachment to his chosen electorate of Ashgrove, his wife, father-in-law, brother-in-law, business associates, and his mother's property interests.

The Ashgrove connection

The attempt to discredit his run in the seat of Ashgrove by muddying his long association with the area was particularly galling. He was labeled a blow-in and the media repeated the lie that he was a candidate parachuted in by party heavyweights. Sitting MP Kate Jones called him a "carpetbagger",[66] tagging him as a fraudulent and opportunistic outsider. The truth, of course, wasn't allowed to get in the way of a good smear campaign. In reality, Campbell and Lisa had deep connections to Ashgrove. They had met and married there, their daughter Rebecca was christened there, and they had bought their

First day of campaigning on 4 April 2011 after being preselected in Ashgrove the day before. Pic credit: Robert Cavallucci

first house in the electorate. The smear campaign about Ashgrove was one of the mounting reasons Campbell "detests" the Labor Party. He had forged relationships across the party divide as Lord Mayor because the players involved such as Beattie, Lucas, and Mackenroth were upfront and honest in their dealings with him. This new breed of Labor was poisonous and fixated on personal attacks:

> At its most basic level, Labor sought to smear us when we had a complete and total association with the area. But they keep saying the smear over and over, and journalists keep repeating it. You've got reporters like Steven Wardill swallowing the Labor Party lines without a second thought. Wardill got our street wrong, and in his snarky way wrote that we never lived in Ashgrove. There were other examples where Wardill wrote about property interests that proved to be incorrect. And then Wardill kept repeating some of those errors in subsequent stories. People like him who are happy hiding behind a computer keyboard never have what it takes to be a Lord Mayor or Premier, and yet they pass judgement and make flippant, dismissive comments about others who do put themselves out there and give it a shot.

Like the Labor Party's chief campaign operatives Trad, Fitzpatrick and Madigan, Steven Wardill refused to answer a range of questions for this book. He would only confirm that a correction was printed for the error about the location of the Newman's previous address in Ashgrove.

Leadership style

Apart from casting doubt over the Newman family's connection to the electorate he had chosen to run in, the Labor Party and the media also took delight in misrepresenting his army career and approach to leadership. They manufactured an image of Campbell as a hardened and dictatorial military man, a command-and-control style of manager who ordered his staff around with shouted demands. Later, he would be described as "Little Hitler", and *The Courier-Mail's* cartoonist Sean Leahy had Campbell's caricature dressed up to look like a Nazi SS soldier, complete with a red armband featuring two crossed bananas in the style of a swastika.

Staff who had worked closely with Campbell over a number of years knew otherwise. There was no doubt Campbell was tough, blunt and often demanding. He set the performance bar very high and would call or email staff at any point from pre-dawn to midnight seven days a week. But he never asked his colleagues or staff to do something he wouldn't, or to work any harder than he did. The fact he had a remarkably stable roster of dedicated staff through various careers spoke volumes about the relationship Campbell had with them. Some of them, such as his assistant Richard Ang and secretary Lesley Jenkin, worked for him closely on and off for more than a decade. Campbell also attracted a close-knit group of bright young professionals who worked with him across different jobs over a number of years, such as Kylie Lindsay, Carly Blaik, Diane Balke, Chris Ireland, Katherine Hornbuckle, Mitch Grayson, Kate Winter, Colin Chua, Francis Quinlivan and others. Ben Myers, of course, would work side-by-side with Campbell for most of his 13-year political career. But if anyone was qualified to describe Campbell's leadership style, it was his mother Jocelyn. In an interview with *The Australian* back in March 2011 she said:

> He will be firm with anyone who is working under him, but he'll be fair to anyone who's trying to do the right thing. He is quite often ahead of the people who work for him because he thinks ahead. He'd be cross if he asked and told someone to do a job and they hadn't done it, or done it badly. Then he's cross. He wants things to be done properly. He's not lazy and he doesn't expect others to be lazy.[67]

Robert Cavallucci, who would go on to win the state seat of Brisbane Central and be appointed an Assistant Minister, recalled:

> I think the media's portrayal of Campbell had more to do with his relationship with the reporters, rather than who he actually is as a person. I always found him approachable on any issue. He was neither a bully nor a dictator. If you had an issue, one of the things he loved was 'war rooming' through it. But what he couldn't stand – and this I guess is where MP's and others fell foul of him – was laziness and incompetence. You had to go to him with three or four well thought out ideas and not just roll up with the expectation he was going to solve the world's problems for you. His expectations of us were high, but they were a lot higher of himself.

In a perceptive piece published in *The Courier-Mail*, senior lecturer in the School of Humanities at Griffith University Dr Paul Williams wrote that much of the commentary about Campbell's leadership was not credible because no journalist had "bothered to ask this new breed of conservative politician to define his own leadership style".[68]

Digging into the Duntroon days

While Campbell had grown accustomed to misconceptions about his leadership style, it was his time at Duntroon some 30 years earlier that provided the first sign of what was to come in the relentless and personally intrusive campaign ahead. In mid-2011, *The Australian's* Sean Parnell lodged a Freedom of Information request seeking all of Campbell's Duntroon records. The Department of Defence obliged, and released everything they had on Campbell, including his medical records. *The Australian* published the full suite of files on its website, later removing most of the personal family information.

Parnell's "exclusive" story ran on the front page under the headline "How Can't-do Campbell Newman earned his army stripes", focusing on a few paragraphs from a report about the then 20-year-old cadet. The 47-year-old Campbell could hardly believe it, labeling the style of reporting "intrusive, irrelevant and puerile". He'd had plenty of negative media coverage in his mayoral career, but this was below the belt. Campbell said he was "gob-smacked" when he picked up the paper to see his training records from Duntroon splashed on the front page of the national broadsheet:

> How would the reporter Sean Parnell feel if someone published all sorts of his personal details on the internet? It confirmed in my mind that there needs to be a debate in this country about media ethics. A serious debate. I really believe it's critical.

The story denigrating his time at Duntroon also fired up Campbell's anger about the hypocrisy of the Left and sections of the media when it came to the treatment of those who had served in the military. On the one hand, they celebrated soldiers and basked in the glow of commemorative occasions such as ANZAC and Remembrance Day. But when it suited their narrative, they used derogatory and negative military stereotypes to pigeonhole Campbell's apparent persona and style. Journalist Nick Bryant described Labor's tactic of targeting Campbell's army career as the "A Few Good Men" strategy:

> Labor, which believes Newman has the most crystalline of glass jaws, will keep pressing the dictatorial line, knowing that it needles him. The aim seems to be to provoke Newman into an angry eruption that transforms 'Can Do Campbell' into Krakatoa Campbell. Perhaps we should call it the A Few Good Men strategy, after the movie in which a tightly coiled colonel played by Jack Nicholson explodes under hostile cross-examination.[69]

Campbell's web

The Australian's attempt to colour in Campbell's military background with editorial crayons in its June 2011 story was just the beginning of an all-out personal onslaught that would assail the Newman family for the next nine months.

While the deep search into his youth as an army cadet and the subsequent front page story was unsettling, it was relatively mild compared to the next brutal phase of the smear campaign.

After *The Australian's* Duntroon story, Labor and an obliging media started honing in on Lisa and her family. They linked the family's business dealings, campaign donations and various family interests to spin the lines of "Campbell's intricate web". Internet ads appeared with Campbell's face on the body of a spider crawling back and forth across the top of the browser page. A TV commercial created by Dee Madigan suggested nefarious links between Lisa, her father, her brother Seb and a mutual friend. The so-called "tangled web" involved a land deal, a council decision and a company bidding for flood recovery work. Journalist Dennis Atkins, writing in *The Courier-Mail*, explained:

> (Anthony) Chisholm knew he had to counter the LNP's one big strategic risk – running Newman in Ashgrove from outside the Parliament. The only option was to tear Newman down; to sow seeds of doubt in enough voting minds in the leafy and hilly streets in Brisbane's inner-north west. This was the dodgy-deals card which was parlayed into Campbell's Web. A complex series of business entities linked to the family of Newman's wife Lisa and occasionally intersecting with decisions taken by the Brisbane City Council which the LNP leader led for seven years, provided the raw material. Dee Madigan, the self-styled ad chick from Sydney who handled the party's creative work, asked Bligh's chief of staff Nicole Scurrah to set down a simple explanation of these businesses and deals. Scurrah gave Madigan a single piece of paper with

names and lines linking them. Madigan immediately saw an ad and Campbell's Web was born.[70]

By the end of 2011, Labor appeared to virtually give up on the act of governing. The only thing that mattered for them now was winning the next election. That meant tearing down Campbell and his family at every opportunity.

Labor's attacks knew no bounds and, at times, they descended into high farce. They lampooned the fact he wasn't born in Queensland and went so far as to accuse him of being paid by a company involved in a "tax minimisation scheme to avoid paying the flood levy".[71] Labor Treasurer Andrew Fraser, a bitter and facile critic, took aim at what he dubbed the "Newman Nation". In what began as a speech to Parliament about the Queensland-India Council, Fraser speculated that trade and investment from the subcontinent would be funneled into the coffers of "Newman nation" if the LNP were elected, instead of the state of Queensland.[72] Another Labor Minister predicted the imminent extinction of the Fleay's barred frog under a future LNP Government because of Campbell's supposed desire to introduce his scorched earth environmental policies.[73]

Through the darkness of the campaign, though, there were innumerable moments of light and comedy. Like the Minister's ridiculous comment about that poor frog, or the time Campbell phoned Lisa to tell her "one last time" that he loved her before he boarded a dodgy-looking light aircraft in North Queensland. Campbell's media officer Kylie Lindsay, one of his closest advisers, said the intensity of the campaign and the far-flung road trips across the state created friendships that would last a lifetime:

> It felt like we worked seven days a week, 24 hours a day. All we could do was get up each morning and put one foot in front of the other and keep going. There was nothing left in the tank by the end of it. We became a family. We nearly

died on several occasions due to the driving of some MPs and candidates. We nearly ended up driving into a creek after going down the wrong dirt road. It was a hard campaign. But we laughed a lot.

The most insightful portrayal of Campbell in all the media coverage during the campaign came from award-winning journalist Trent Dalton. After his road trip with Campbell through central Queensland in mid-October 2011, Dalton later wrote in *The Courier Mail's QWeekend* magazine:

> Look at this man. Late forties going on late teens. This morning at five o'clock on the pacing track at Eagle Farm racecourse, a female jockey tells him he's hot. Newman says he knows a good optometrist. He's 48 but doesn't age. He doesn't stop. And he doesn't lie. He told me so. I believe him because I know there could not be anything remotely sinful about a man who uses the term 'gee-whiz!'

Dalton had spent more time with Campbell than mere fiery confrontations at media conferences and was able to paint a more rounded, accurate picture. Other journalists like Sarah Vogler, Nick Bryant, Lane Calcutt and Des Houghton also developed a better understanding of the man who would be Premier.

As if Labor's muck-raking wasn't enough, pockets of trouble raining down on Campbell were self-inflicted. Shortly after announcing his candidacy he declared all existing LNP policy was "null and void", putting his new colleague's noses out of joint. He let fly at Labor over its "State Of Origin" jibes, fuelling their claims he had a "glass jaw", and he caused internal LNP ructions when he declared his support for gay marriage in an interview on Sky News. There were occasions he threatened to resign from the campaign, and some of his team clashed bitterly with officials at LNP headquarters.

Through it all though, he kept traversing the state and spent an inordinate amount of time in regional and rural Queensland to shake the perception he was a Brisbane-centric leader. Given the margin and polling in Ashgrove, he also had to spend more time in his chosen electorate than any other Premier or Opposition Leader in living memory.

Many voters didn't know it at the time, but he also released policies, including plans to reduce the cost of living, empower local governments and tackle crime.

Ashgrove polls

From the beginning of his bold bid to be Premier, the major parties and the media were obsessed with polls in his seat of Ashgrove. While the true sense of significance may not have registered with many of the media pack, Campbell's effort was historic in more ways than just his complex out-of-Parliament experiment. He was vying to be the first Brisbane-based Premier from the conservative side of politics since Digby Denham was elevated to that high office on 7 February 1911.

In May 2011, a Galaxy Poll showed Labor's primary vote tanking to just 30 percent, giving the LNP a two-party preferred margin of 61 percent to 39. A result like that would decimate Labor. But the internal polling from both major parties highlighted the disparity between the substantial statewide swing versus the line ball contest in Ashgrove.

While the LNP was set for an almost certain victory under Campbell's leadership, the situation in Ashgrove was precarious. Campbell was predicted to win, but only just. Kate Jones was so concerned about retaining Ashgrove she stood down from the Bligh Cabinet on 19 June to focus exclusively on keeping her seat. Together with the grass roots "Keep Kate" campaign and the relentless attacks on the Newman and Monsour families in the second half of 2011, her decision to stand down from the Cabinet appeared to be paying off. Campbell's lead in Ashgrove was being trimmed back the longer the campaign went on.

Daily questions about Ashgrove and who would be Premier if he didn't win, plus the attacks on his integrity and his family's financial interests, made it virtually impossible to find clear air to discuss and debate policy. About the only area of public policy gaining some attention at the time was the LNP's intentions for the public service. In the 2009 state election, the newly merged LNP pledged to rein in Labor's ballooning deficits by reducing the public service through natural attrition. To great effect, former Premier Anna Bligh attacked the Opposition over the policy. Labor campaigned on a slogan of "jobs, not job cuts" and claimed the LNP would need to sack 12,000 public servants to meet its stated three percent efficiency dividend target. As part of its promise to create 100,000 jobs over the term, the re-elected Bligh Government continued the exponential trend of growing the bureaucracy, a pattern first established under the Beattie Government. The bureaucracy had ballooned from around 140,000 staff in 2002 to 204,000 in 2011, with growth in both public sector wages and employment higher in Queensland than any other state over the past decade.

In a rerun of its 2009 attack on the then Opposition Leader Lawrence Springborg, Labor predicted a Newman LNP Government would "slash and burn" the public service. In a media conference at Parliament House in mid-2011, Campbell denied a future LNP Government would make cuts to Queensland's public service:

> Labor over the last two weeks have thrown all sorts of mud at me. What I'm saying is that the public service has nothing to fear from me.

It was a comment he would later regret ever making.

Katter

In June 2011, maverick federal MP Bob Katter threw a curveball into the campaign with the announcement he was forming his own party to contest dozens of seats in the state election. James Packer donated $250,000 to the party, and he gained some early traction in regional areas of the state. But for all his bluster about winning "dozens of seats" in the election, Katter was a mere distraction. Later in the campaign, Katter ran a TV ad condemning Campbell's support for gay marriage. The ads were a disgrace. Among widespread condemnation, Malcolm Turnbull labelled them "a shocker":

> It is homophobic. It's designed to do Anna Bligh's work in undermining Campbell Newman.[74]

Katter's antic aside, the more important political development during this period was Labor's sinking ship. In September 2011, Deputy Premier Paul Lucas was one of seven Labor MPs to announce they would not contest the next election. The mass exodus came as the most recent Galaxy poll put Campbell well ahead as preferred Premier on 55 percent compared to Bligh on 38 percent. Labor's attacks on Campbell ramped up in equal and opposite measure to the Government's deteriorating electoral fortunes.

By October 2011, Campbell had had enough. During his time as Lord Mayor he had gone above and beyond all relevant financial disclosure requirements. Since becoming the LNP leader in March he had declared even more information, and so too had Lisa, even though they weren't required to do so by law. Short of giving out his bank account details to a salivating media, there was nothing left for him to declare. But the Labor dirt unit was relentless and utterly thorough.

The most recent attack focused on two units at Port Douglas owned by a holding company run by Campbell's mum Jocelyn Newman. Campbell was a shareholder of the company that owned the units, an interest he had earlier declared on the council's public register of interest. The inclusion of his mum in the campaign in this regard came at a sharply difficult time for Campbell and his sister Kate. As early as 2007, Jocelyn began displaying early symptoms of

Alzheimer's disease. During what would be her final overseas trip in mid-2010 – she insisted on taking the holiday despite protests by Campbell and Kate – Jocelyn's health deteriorated further. By the time her name was dragged into the campaign fray over the ownership of the Port Douglas units, Jocelyn – who had turned 74 in July that year – was increasingly unwell. Treasurer Fraser wasn't to know, of course, and dutifully referred the matter of the Port Douglas units to the CMC. Once again, a baseless allegation fuelled another day's media coverage. The CMC dismissed Fraser's vexatious and frivolous complaint in short shrift, but the episode sparked the only major outburst from Campbell during the 12-month campaign. On the back of so many similar incursions since his preselection in April, Campbell let loose in his daily media conference, held on the Gold Coast on 5 October:

> Queensland is run today by drunks, punks and desperadoes headed by Anna Bligh with her dirt unit. This is just more of the same 'summer of sleaze'. Anna Bligh's dirt unit went after my wife, went after my brother-in-law, went after my father-in-law and now they're going after my mum. Come on Anna Bligh – haven't you got something better to do like actually sort out the economy of Queensland?'

In the same month, Campbell's walk along the campaign moral high ground momentarily faltered when it was revealed the LNP paid a former Labor Party official to compile information on Government MPs and Ministers. The benign material was never going to be used in the media and Campbell had nothing to do with the exercise – campaign director James McGrath had commissioned the research – but it was not a good look after the LNP had spent months decrying Labor's gutter tactics. Labor, apparently without sarcasm, screamed blue murder at the revelations of the so-called "LNP dirt file".

Campbell called for a ceasefire of personal hostilities and pleaded for a focus on policy. No-one listened, least of all Labor. They could see their campaign of negativity was working in Ashgrove, as negative campaigns customarily do. Blips and dips were appearing in internal polling of Campbell's personal popularity. Doubts about his ability to win the seat of Ashgrove intensified. Election analyst and commentator William Bowe wrote during the campaign:

> Opinion polls continue to suggest that a sufficient swing (to the LNP) is more than likely, but there remains another wild card in the deck – the appalling risk the LNP has taken in pitting its prospective leader against Kate Jones in Ashgrove, which the popular incumbent holds with a margin of 7.1 percent, and the possibility that the wheels might fall off yet another conservative Queensland election campaign if indications emerge that he might fall short.

Campbell's standard line in response to the daily speculation about his chances in Ashgrove was always the same: "If I don't win Ashgrove, the LNP won't win government". The line wasn't technically correct, of course. The LNP needed a uniform swing of 4.6 percent to win majority government, compared to the 7.1 percent Campbell required to win Ashgrove. But the rehearsed line repeated ad infinitum was all he could do to bat away the ever-present question clouding his political future.

The run home to 24 March

Campaign hostilities were briefly halted over Christmas and into January 2012 when remembrance ceremonies were held for victims of the deadly 2011 floods. On 13 January, Treasurer Andrew Fraser released his mid-year Budget review, flagging significant public service staff reductions to curb rising costs and offset revenue write-downs. The Bligh Government had introduced a voluntary separation program to cut 3500 public servants in 2010 and extended that program to remove an extra 1500 staff in this mid-year review.

At the time, more than 9000 public servants across all departments expressed an interest in accepting a redundancy payout. When asked what the total loss of 5000 government workers would mean to service delivery, Fraser said: "It will have nil impact."

Meanwhile, everyone just wanted to know when the election would be held. Speculation had bubbled away ever since Campbell announced he was running for Premier nearly 12 months earlier. It had been a long and gruelling unofficial campaign.

The final hurdle in Premier Bligh naming the election date was the Commission of Inquiry report into the 2011 floods. The report was due to be handed down on 17 January 2012, but in a dramatic twist the Inquiry chair Justice Catherine Holmes requested an extension of time. Justice Holmes wanted to investigate newspaper reports alleging discrepancies in the accounts of events by three engineers working at Wivenhoe Dam as well as claims of a conflict of interest involving one of her own deputy commissioners.

The delay allowed for one more sitting of Parliament just five weeks before the expected election. Bligh used those last sitting days of her Parliamentary career in a most unedifying way. Media reports on 15 February suggested the FBI was investigating Seb Monsour for improperly obtaining US Defence Force technology and using it to spruik for government contract work in the Brisbane floods recovery effort. Bligh seized on the allegations and launched two vitriolic sprays at the Newman and Monsour families when Parliament began that morning. Under the cloak of Parliamentary privilege, Bligh read out Campbell and Lisa's home address and made the extraordinary prediction that Campbell would end up in jail. She told Parliament:

> When Gordon Nuttall happened, we referred him to the CMC. Mr Speaker, I gave evidence against him in court. I never laughed about it. Those people are behind jail and Campbell Newman will end up there as well.[75]

Bligh later defended her comments by saying she was "passionate". The 2011 floods report was released the following day on 16 February. The 650-page report contained 177 recommendations, including that the CMC investigates three engineers from Wivenhoe Dam. The report also concluded the 2010-11 floods "took a state more accustomed to drought by surprise" and noted concern about the "apparent inertia of government when the possibility (of pre-emptively lowering the dam level) was raised (in late 2010)."

On 19 February, Bligh visited Queensland Governor Penelope Wensley to announce the election would be held on 24 March. The chosen date was the same day Queensland's council elections had long been scheduled for, forcing mayors and candidates to postpone their own fate for a month. A Galaxy poll at the start of the campaign found Campbell's support had dropped six percentage points since August 2011. He and Bligh were neck and neck on issues of trust and "being in touch with Queenslanders", while Bligh's only lead over Campbell was on the point of "listening".

The Premier embarked on the "Bligh Blitz" of 50 seats at the start of the campaign, but her plan was almost derailed shortly after it began with renewed speculation of a federal Labor leadership spill. Julia Gillard and Kevin Rudd were waging their latest bitter public battle for the office of Prime Minister, a fight Gillard won in the 27 February ballot.

Media attention in Queensland was allowed to return to the state campaign, with all eyes on the fight for Ashgrove. The statewide result in favour of the LNP was long assured. The only contest left in the state campaign was between Campbell Newman and Kate Jones. Privately, Campbell believed it was a battle he wouldn't win.

Service above self

Just after dawn on 7 March, Campbell was running along the beachfront Strand in Townsville. A handful of reporters, advisors and protective officers from Queensland Police followed him. He was also joined by the LNP's candidate for the seat of Mundingburra David Crisafulli, the city's former deputy mayor and one of the few candidates capable of keeping pace with the notoriously speedy Premier-in-waiting. Locals out for their morning exercise nodded and waved as the pack hurtled by. The campaign was at its midway point and every minute was planned out and accounted for. When they finished the run, Crisafulli had no time to return home to get changed out of his jogging gear. So they returned to Campbell's hotel room on nearby Palmer St. They prepared for a frenetic day of campaigning and announcements in Townsville, starting with a series of local radio interviews. As he stepped out from the hotel's bathroom after a shave, Campbell made an extraordinary, unsolicited confession to Crisafulli, who remembered the event vividly:

> Campbell walks out and just says 'well, the polling shows that I'm probably cooked in Ashgrove … I don't think I'll get there… In fact, I'm sure I won't get there. But we're going to win across the state. I've achieved exactly what I needed to achieve and that was to get rid of the worst State Government we've ever had'. In that moment, that one second in time, I realised I was dealing with someone special. To me, that was a defining moment. I remember going home and pondering his comments at the end of that manic day. I said to myself… that's what they mean when they talk about service above self. I genuinely thought he was gone. And I didn't know who was going to be Premier. But I remember the gesture, the honesty, the raw emotion in it. There was no bullshit in it. He thought he was tanked. I just thought to myself…here's a guy who was willing to give up the Mayoralty of the biggest council in the nation to do a kamikaze mission on a disgraceful Government. That to me was the ultimate sacrifice. I'll remember that moment until the day I die.

When Campbell made this very private concession speech, he

couldn't have known Labor's campaign would implode in the most spectacular fashion two days later. It happened when AAP reporter Larine Statham wouldn't budge in her questioning of Bligh at a campaign stop in Caboolture. Tired of hearing the Premier brush off questions about the substance of her allegations against the Newman family, Statham persisted with her questions. She asked again and again what evidence Bligh had to back up her litany of claims about the Newman and Monsour families. Bligh floundered, and like sharks finally smelling blood the media pack circled in, pushing Bligh to provide evidence of Labor's laundry list of allegations. Bligh's eventual, reluctant answer changed the course of the entire campaign. She told the reporters:

> Right now, all I have is questions. I don't have enough answers from Mr Newman or enough material.

With the election just ten days away, this was a monumental admission. After nearly 12 months of histrionics, allegations and smear, her confession of a lack of evidence provided the penultimate turning point in Labor's final act. The dramatic end occurred just two days later. On the afternoon of 16 March, the Crime and Misconduct Commission issued a written statement clearing Campbell of any and all allegations Labor had thrown at him. It took just seven words in the CMC statement to smash the final nail into Labor's campaign coffin: "There is no evidence of official misconduct".

With just over a week to go until polling day, Labor could do nothing but sit by and plan for its own funeral. Trad, Madigan, Fitzpatrick, and Chisolm had become the architects of a disastrous campaign. Their obsession with damaging Campbell and his family and their lack of foresight as to the public's reaction to that campaign had signed Labor's death warrant.

In the final days before the election, Labor tried to change the narrative of its campaign, practically urging voters to show it some mercy and avoid giving the LNP "too big a majority". It was all too late. The swing was on to a degree not even the most positive polls had predicted.

On 24 March 2012, Campbell Newman won the seat of Ashgrove and led the LNP to the biggest electoral landslide in Australia's political history, securing 78 of the 89 seats in the Queensland Parliament. Labor was reduced to just seven seats, with two Katter Party MPs and two Independents making up the balance of seats.

Like his unconventional, improbable bid to become Lord Mayor of Brisbane as an unknown political debutante back in 2004, Campbell had done it. He was elected the 38th Premier of Queensland. In a powerful speech on election night, the new Premier promised to govern with "dignity, grace and humility".

Behind closed doors at the Newman household, the historic victory came at a high cost to Campbell and Lisa. The relentless campaign of smear, innuendo and negativity had damaged their relationship and their health. During their years as young parents, and then as Lord Mayor and Mayoress of Brisbane, they had enjoyed a remarkably symbiotic relationship. They had been incredibly affectionate and loving, a dynamic team in perpetual forward motion. But they were nearly torn asunder by the state campaign.

It also changed Campbell's outlook and persona. Indeed, the toll this campaign took on his demeanor would linger long into his term as Premier. He hated what Labor and the media had done to his wife, their children, his extended family, his reputation. It affected him and his thoughts on politics and service, and it altered the team dynamic he and Lisa had enjoyed and thrived on for so many years. From the day he was sworn in as Premier, whenever he was prickly in Parliament or abrasive in front of the media pack, he was thinking of Labor and the journalists and what they had done during that campaign. On reflection, Campbell said:

It hurt me. I had a wife who was absolutely traumatised, really traumatised, and her family was dragged through the mud, all of it lies. I was hurt and I was affected by it. It affected my demeanor. I behaved differently in Parliament for about two years after that. I was extremely angry and bitter and it came through. It came through in my interactions in the chamber. The person who is the real victor, the one who deserves the credit for all this, is Jackie Trad.

Labor may have lost the battle in 2012. But the damage they did in that campaign may have helped them win the war in the long run.

8

POLICY VERSUS POLITICS – PART ONE

2012-2015: Queensland Premier

Time was not on Premier Campbell Newman's side. It was Sunday 25 March, day one of the Newman LNP Government. Some of the state's top bureaucrats were gathered to deliver the incoming government brief to the new Premier, Treasurer and Deputy Premier. The first paragraph of Treasury's brief read:

> Queensland's fiscal position and outlook is unsustainable, and restoration is an urgent priority for this term of government.

Their advice confirmed what Campbell, Deputy Premier Jeff Seeney and Treasurer Tim Nicholls already knew – Queensland was in serious financial strife. Recurrent expenditure had to be reined in, and fast. There were too many public servants in the bloated bureaucracy. State debt was forecast to blow out to $100 billion unless drastic and immediate remedial action was taken. The loss of the state's triple AAA credit rating in 2009 compounded the problem, with interest repayments running at an estimated $450,000 an hour.

Labor and the unions disputed the debt figures, naturally, but didn't object to concerns about the massive escalation in the over-sized public service. Even the Bligh Government had attempted to reduce numbers by around 5000 workers in their final term. Regardless, the boffins at Treasury were unequivocal in their advice to the new leadership team. Their sombre briefing would define and consume much of the Government's work over the next three years. The

Premier, his Deputy and the Treasurer left the meetings with a plan already in mind. To fix the problem, they first had to diagnose it.

Within days of winning office, they launched a Commission Of Audit into the state's finances. Simultaneously, they began rolling out the First 100 Day Action Plan featuring 58 specific items across all portfolios. Both concepts were featured in the LNP's internal plan for transition to Government, developed over the past 12 months by a tight circle of advisers. Campbell was aware from the beginning that his new Government would face an uphill battle selling a message of drastic reform and spending restraint. The general public wasn't fully cognisant of the scale of the problem, as if Labor's profligate spending over recent years had lulled the public into a false sense of comfort. Queenslanders had no prevailing sense of economic doom or a "banana republic" moment to prepare them for the changes and challenges ahead. Campbell reflected:

> I don't think Queenslanders saw the state's finances in the terms we were aware of. The man and woman in the street haven't felt or seen it the way the briefings described. When Jeff Kennett was elected in 1992, there was a recession on in Victoria, it was biting hard, there were collapses of institutions, and it got really bad, it got to a crisis point. The body politic in Queensland had never seen it in those terms.

The man chosen to head the Government's Commission of Audit came from a recommendation spearheaded by Nicholls. On 29 March, five days after the election, former Federal Treasurer Peter Costello was appointed to chair the Commission. Campbell endorsed the appointment of Costello, but later wished he hadn't. Costello was eminently qualified for the job, as were his fellow Commissioners Doug McTaggart, a former Under Treasurer of Queensland, and Sandra Harding, the Vice-Chancellor of James Cook University. But Costello's political baggage gave the Labor Opposition too much

With Deputy Premier Jeff Seeney and Treasurer Tim Nicholls at their swearing in with Queensland Governor Penelope Wensley on 26 March 2012

material to work with. No matter how vital the Commission's work would be, opponents painted it as a purely political exercise, a mere ruse to provide the Newman Government with cover to prosecute its austerity drive. With hindsight, Campbell said:

> It would've been better to go with someone else. That's not a negative reflection on Peter Costello, but we needed to explain to Queenslanders how bad things were in the state because of what Labor had done when they were in power. But by

using Costello, unfortunately the Labor Party, unions and the media were able to claim it was a political exercise, which is completely untrue. We had a former Under Treasurer and a leading Vice Chancellor, but Labor and the unions were able to effectively marginalise the exercise. That's one of the things I regret. I take responsibility for it as the Premier. If I could turn back time, I'd pick a different person.

The appointment of Costello was the first blip on a political radar the new leadership team wasn't paying careful enough attention to. On a policy level, such decisions were sound and necessary. The intention was honourable. But too often the politics of those decisions would miss the mark and bring electoral grief to Campbell's door.

A few days later on 3 April, the first conservative Cabinet in nearly 20 years was sworn in by Queensland Governor Penelope Wensley. Campbell was pleased with the spread of geographical representation and experience in his Cabinet but lamented the lack of women he was able to include. Jann Stuckey, Tracy Davis and Ros Bates were the only females in the 19-member Ministry. Campbell later said:

> I was never happy with the number of women that we had in the Cabinet, but we just didn't have the experience in the team to do otherwise. That's why we had some up-and-coming female candidates as Assistant Ministers, people like Lisa France, Deb Frecklington and Saxon Rice, to give them the opportunity to work their way up into Cabinet.

On the same day the first LNP Cabinet was being sworn in, word started to spread of the Government's decision to axe the Queensland Premier's Literary Awards. Following the appointment of Costello, it was the second instance of sound policy trumping smart politics. It saved taxpayers a sum of $244,000 – a figure the Left believed was paltry. The flowing tap of grants, cheques and funding had been turned on for so long the Left had lost perspective on the value of public dollars.

The Courier-Mail reporter Matthew Condon typified the Left's response, as though the Premier himself had driven a fascist-branded stake through Condon's delicate literary heart. Abandoning any notion of journalistic balance with his distinctly ostentatious prose in full flight, Condon predicted the axing of the awards would send Queensland back to the "dark ages". Condon called the literary awards an "irreplaceable treasure" that "speak to children dreaming of a career in books and writing".[76] In response to the backlash, Campbell explained at the time:

> There is an old saying: if you look after pennies, well the pounds they take care of themselves. You get a $2.8 billion deficit by being wasteful and reckless in spending a dollar at a time. That is how it happens. So we are going to make sure that we save $100,000 here, $50,000 there, $20,000 there, a quarter of a million dollars etcetera, so we can close this budget deficit, this great big yawning hole we have been given by Anna Bligh and Labor.

Condon and the Left didn't seem to mind that many of the award finalists and winners weren't from Queensland and, in many cases, the top cash prizes were being scooped up by authors who were already so successful they often didn't bother turning up to the awards night to collect their cheques.

Broadly, the decision reflected the LNP's ethos about the type of services and costs a government should be involved in. At a time when every public dollar counted, the Newman Government believed the money would be better spent on essential services such as health, police and schools. Why couldn't corporate sponsorship help fund the awards, as it did immediately after the public funding was cut?

Regardless of the Government's rationale and broader community support for the decision, Campbell had killed one of the Left's darlings. In a climate of necessary cost-cutting the decision was made for the right reasons. But the ideological battlelines had now been drawn. The inner-city chattering class across the nation, together with their fellow travellers in the media, had a totemic cause to latch on to. They were all very upset. They tweeted furiously, launched online petitions and formed a committee to revive the awards. On reflection, Campbell said:

> That was a bad political decision, which I have to take responsibility for. I don't think it actually hurt us at all at the time out in the general population, most people didn't give two hoots about a literary prize, but the Left did. It became emblematic of us as a Government, it was one of those important causes to the Left in the community who chatter and carry on and network, it was like a rallying flag for them. It was just another excuse for the Left to engage in their usual negative personal labelling of people and political teams. It was a free kick for them to help them create their narrative. I'm quite happy to justify why the decision was made but was it a good political decision? No, it wasn't.

Another issue soon supplanted the literary awards in the eye of the state's media. On 17 April, a fortnight after Cabinet was sworn in and the awards were axed, new Police Minister David Gibson was forced to resign over a series of issues related to his driving record. Gibson was the first casualty in the new Government. Half a dozen more Ministers or MPs would fall or jump over the next 12 months.

Action

For the time being, the punters didn't seem to mind the loss of both the book awards and a Cabinet Minister. Polling conducted during the first three months of the Government's tenure showed the LNP was maintaining its election-winning dominance, sitting at around 60 percent to Labor's 40 percent on a two-party preferred basis.

With his Cabinet in place and work on the first LNP Budget progressing, the Government marked its first 100 days in office on 3 July by ticking off all 58 items contained in its Action Plan. A national park was handed back to traditional owners, a strategic assessment of the Great Barrier Reef began and legislation was introduced to address crime, reduce the cost of living and reinstate a stand-alone Department of Agriculture, axed under a previous Labor Government. Following through on a commitment to slash red tape, nearly one major project was approved for every business day of the Newman Government's first three months in office. The literary awards weren't the only program to get the chop. The Government saved $3 million a year by cutting public funding to political parties, with the LNP itself losing out to the tune of around $2 million, causing a rift with party bosses. Taxpayer-funded corporate boxes at sporting events and all government advertising were also axed. In just a few months, the Newman Government had so far found $186.5 million in savings.

In a brief respite from the focus on the state's acute budgetary woes, the 100 Day Action Plan featured a landmark Commission of Inquiry into Queensland's troubled child protection system. Launched on 29 June, the Inquiry followed through on an election commitment and was set up to "chart a road map for the state's child protection system for the next decade." The Honourable Tim Carmody QC, a former police officer who rose through the legal ranks to become a Queensland Crime Commissioner and Family Court Judge, was appointed to chair the Commission. His final report was due within 12 months. With all of that work underway, Campbell was interviewed by the ABC to mark his Government's first 100 days in office:

> You actually have to get into it and get into it quickly. A three-year term doesn't give you a lot of time, doesn't give

you much time at all, and if you don't get stuck in during the first six months and make the necessary changes you won't actually get reform and deliver on the things you promised to do for Queensland.

On the same day, he told the *Brisbane Times*:

> Why does the public service think that it shouldn't change? I believe that we need to, in a very careful way, restructure the public service to ensure that it is efficient and that it delivers for Queenslanders. What we need to do is find new, cutting-edge ways to deliver services and to cut down on waste and inefficiency, in particular in the back office.

When he reached the 100-day milestone, Campbell had been working for 20 months with only two brief breaks in between, a 2011 Christmas visit to see his mum and sister's family, and a few days with Lisa and the girls around Gayndah and Monto in September 2011. He had made it through the Brisbane flood disaster, the long and brutal election campaign and his first three months as Premier of Queensland. Looking back however, Campbell believed he wouldn't have made it through if it weren't for his army training, including his formative years at Duntroon. His morning run became a metaphor for his leadership as Premier. An interchangeable roster of Ministers and staffers would join him for the dawn run, usually around 8kms. Few of them could keep up.

In the second half of 2012, Campbell continued to set the unprecedented pace of change. After nearly two decades of Labor in power, there was a lot to do. A former public servant in Campbell's office, a decidedly non-political staffer who had worked for previous Labor Premiers, recalled:

> Every Monday morning when Campbell's diary was read out I was exhausted just listening to it. I don't think people

comprehended how full on his schedule really was. I don't know how he ever did it without collapsing in a heap. Every time someone complains to me about how busy they are I roll my eyes and say 'try being the Premier of Queensland for a day'. When someone complains to me that they don't have time to exercise then I say 'Campbell ran every day and he was Premier of Queensland. If he can make the time then so can you'. The volume of correspondence he signed was also phenomenal. Up until January 2014 I think he signed nearly every response. Some people he even called personally. There was a man who wrote to him complaining that no-one from Queensland Health would meet with him. I think he had a labour hire company. So Campbell called him and assured him that someone would meet with him. I'm not sure if any other Premier would do that.

In a revealing post-retirement interview with *The Courier-Mail's* Des Houghton, the Queensland Government's former chief of security Barry Seeley described Campbell as a man on a mission. Seeley, who worked in government security for nearly three decades, had served in the same battalion as Campbell's dad Kevin in Vietnam in 1967. For many years, Seeley stood guard at the Executive Building on George St in the Brisbane CBD, the epicentre of Queensland political power. When asked to describe Campbell, Seeley told Houghton:

> What amazes me is Campbell's workload and the pace he is going at it. His hours are incredibly long. He is here early in the morning and still here late at night. The number of visitors he has to his office is more than double the number to previous Premiers.

As noted by a variety of staff members who had worked with Campbell, he was a demanding boss. But he gave more to his job than he ever asked of others in theirs.

A boiler room of combustibles

Having served in the Queensland Parliament since 2004, Newman Government Minister Jann Stuckey described the LNP's extraordinary 71-seat majority in the 2012 Parliament as an "unnatural situation". Stuckey believed the scale of the victory clouded the Government's performance from its very beginning. There were so many competing demands to meet, not least of which were nearly 60 LNP backbenchers, most of them first-timers. The Newman Government Cabinet also had to deal with the unnaturally high expectations from LNP branch members who had fought for a conservative victory for so long. When the relentless pressure from unions, various vested interest groups and a hostile media were thrown into the mix, Stuckey's description of an "unnatural situation" was valid. According to Stuckey:

> Winning Government with a record majority after almost twenty years in Opposition presented incredibly high expectations and challenges. These would impact the way we carried out our duties in the Parliament, affect the pace of much-needed reform for Queensland's economic future and see us try to satisfy the aspirations of party members and constituents. It really was a boiler room of combustibles.

Perhaps the greatest threat to the Government's ability to meet the competing demands it faced was the immense and urgent fiscal repair task it had inherited from successive Labor administrations. From the start, Labor's legacy of debt and deficits dominated the Government's time in office. As the advice from Treasury unambiguously highlighted on that first day of the Newman Government after the election, recurrent expenditure had spiraled out of control. On 15 June 2012, the Commission of Audit's interim report found recurrent expenditure in Queensland increased by a cumulative 127 percent between 2000-01 and 2010-11, compared to an average increase of 92 percent in the other states. Successive Labor Governments had been borrowing simply to keep the lights on.

The explosion of growth in the public sector head count had become the main drag on the Budget's bottom line, with employee related costs in 2010-11 reaching $20 billion, accounting for 46 percent of total recurrent expenses. The growth rate of employee expenses had increased by around 8.7 percent per annum between 2000-01 and 2010-11, compared with an average rate of growth of 7.1 percent per annum in other states. There was little doubt a large part of that problem was due to Anna Bligh's thought bubble during the 2009 election campaign that a re-elected Labor Government would create 100,000 jobs in its next term. An analysis of state budget papers by *The Weekend Australian* found one in every four of the 100,000 new jobs Bligh had promised were generated in the bureaucracy. The newspaper's report, published a fortnight before the 2012 election, also revealed the jump in government staff numbers was "double the rate of Victoria's, which has a million more residents than Queensland yet employs only 15,000 more public servants".

For the average Queensland taxpayer, the combination of those thousands of additional public servants and all of that increased expenditure wasn't translating into improvements in frontline services. Hospital surgical lists and emergency department waiting times were increasing, the educational performance of students was flat-lining or declining and crime in some parts of the state was considered out of control, from bikie gangs on the Gold Coast to youth crime in North Queensland.

The Newman Government's four-person razor gang – the Cabinet Budget Review Committee featuring the leadership trio alongside a member of the Cabinet on a rotational basis – worked towards a target of reducing the state's bureaucracy by up to 20,000 public servants, a figure suggested in the work of the Commission Of Audit. Campbell's 2011 comment on the campaign trail that public servants had "nothing to fear" from an LNP Government quickly became a favourite line of attack by the unions. Campbell later reflected:

> The payroll has to be paid day in, day out, you can't avoid it like putting off a capital project a year or two. And we were literally borrowing to fund the payroll. We had to bring the head count down. And we set about to do it. But that was poorly handled by myself, poorly handled by the Government.

Nervous backbenchers questioned why the head count couldn't be reduced by natural attrition to avoid the mounting political backlash. The move was considered by the leadership team but quickly rejected. The rate of separation from the public service had dropped in recent years as the jobs market cooled off during the global financial crisis and gradual slow-down in mining. Relying on natural attrition would be insufficient for the urgent nature of the budget repair task at hand. The reduction in the public service had to happen quickly to stabilise the Budget's ongoing blow-outs in recurrent expenditure. The Commission of Audit's interim report noted:

> It is disturbing to report that, in recent years, the Government of Queensland embarked on an unsustainable level of spending which has jeopardised the financial position of the state.
>
> Urgent fiscal repair is necessary just to stabilise debt which will continue growing in the absence of corrective measures. After that, the state will need a very large program of debt repayment to recover its AAA rating.
>
> The revenue options open to the State are limited. As a result, most of the effort will have to be taken on the expenditure side, by implementing savings. The magnitude of the task is substantially larger than previously recognised because the

former Government has built in unrealistically optimistic Budget assumptions that have masked the magnitude of the underlying structural problems.

First Budget of the Newman Government

Released on 11 September 2012, the Government's first Budget identified $3.5 billion worth of expenditure savings over the forward estimates. Health and education budgets were increased, and a fund was created to clear the school maintenance backlog at every public school in the state. Speaking on the Budget's release, Tim Nicholls said:

> This afternoon we reset the clock and we break from the addiction to debt and deficit that characterised Queensland's finances under Labor. We will stabilise debt at $81.7 billion in 2014-15, ensuring debt will no longer reach $100 billion in 2018-19, as it would have done under a Labor Government. The cost of interest payments in 2012-13 will be $174 million less under the Newman Government and $500 million less in 2015-16. This will save $1.3 billion over four years.

A Government that burst out of the electoral wilderness to secure victory with 78 MPs in an 89 seat Parliament was inevitably bound to attract some internal trouble. It started shortly after the 2012 Budget. In the six months after its release, the Government lost three MPs to minor parties and two Ministers from the Cabinet. Another MP Scott Driscoll became embroiled in a controversy that would later see him exit the Parliament.

The revolt by three MPs – one to the Katter Party and two to Palmer United – was markedly less than media and political commentators had predicted. After a sustained campaign examining their performance (and in some instances their private lives) by *The Courier-Mail*, Ministers Bruce Flegg and Ros Bates resigned from the Cabinet for what turned out to be relatively minor transgressions.

The LNP Member for Redcliffe Scott Driscoll was another matter altogether. From day one, Driscoll failed to form any meaningful connections with most, if not all, of his LNP colleagues in the Parliament. By the time he resigned after a seven-month investigation into his pecuniary interests alongside claims he had misled the House, an Ethics Committee report ultimately found him guilty on 49 counts of contempt of Parliament. Campbell believed Driscoll should never have been pre-selected in the first place, but rejected suggestions he stood by the MP for too long. Others close to Campbell weren't so sure. Some believed certain MPs or Ministers should've been cut loose when they were causing untold political damage. To his detriment, loyalty overrode political expediency. The then Member for Brisbane Central and Assistant Minister Robert Cavallucci, whose electorate shared a border with Campbell's seat of Ashgrove, said:

> Campbell is extraordinarily loyal. It is probably his greatest strength and greatest weakness. Sometimes his loyalty was misplaced and resulted in holding onto people and policies that were damaging him badly. He wore the political cost and in some cases that loyalty was not reciprocated.

For the most part though, it was a leadership trait his backbenchers applauded. The Government's youngest MP, Neil Symes, said he saw a side of Campbell "the media would never write about":

> If there was ever an issue in your local patch or the need for advice, Campbell would always return your call to work out the issue. He would also regularly ring to just see how I was going, and how the electorate was going. Campbell epitomised true leadership. He was someone who sacrificed his own political career for the betterment of Queenslanders.[77]

A final diversion from the Government's attempt to sell a positive message in the second half of 2012 arrived in the form of Michael Caltabiano, Campbell's former colleague on council. Caltabiano was initially considered for the role of Campbell's chief of staff. Both men were headstrong, fiercely independent and forthright in manner, as well as sharing a mutual background in engineering. On the face of it, the pairing would likely have been a disaster. When Ben Myers was instead chosen to head up Campbell's office, Caltabiano was offered the position of Director-General of the Department of Transport and Main Roads. The appointment proved to be a mistake.

At a Budget Estimates Hearing on 18 October 2012, Caltabiano stumbled over a response to questions about his involvement with the lobbying firm Entree Vous, a company established by Cabinet Minister Ros Bates before her arrival in Parliament. Caltabiano was later accused of misleading the committee about the circumstances of the departmental appointment of Ben Gommers, the son of Ms Bates. Gommers had worked at Entrée Vous at the same time Caltabiano was listed as a managing partner of the firm. *The Courier-Mail's* relentless pursuit of Gommers caused an immense personal toll

Addressing the party faithful in March 2013. Pic credit: Dominika Lis

on the then 27-year-old's health. Gommers was in fact well qualified for the role he was selected for in the department, but perception is a cruel beast in politics, and the media coverage dogged the Government for months. Gommers later resigned, and Caltabiano, who had already clashed with his Minister Scott Emerson, was stood down on full pay after he was referred to the Crime and Misconduct Commission and the Parliament's Ethics Committee in late 2012. With the saga still raging through to February 2013, Campbell sacked Caltabiano, who was later cleared of any wrong-doing by both the CMC and the Parliamentary Committee.

At year's end, the mood in the electorate had turned against the Government. The austerity measures and the cull of public servants, the loss of MPs and Ministers, the union marches and social media campaigns, the Driscoll affair and the Caltabiano sacking were interlocking and aggregating to damage the Government's early fortunes.

Letting go

Beneath the surface of his breakneck style of governing and the delivery of all items in the Government's Action Plans, Campbell couldn't shake off the bitterness he felt over the attacks on his family during the 2011-12 campaign. That lingering resentment first boiled over onto the floor of Parliament when Jackie Trad won a by-election back in April, a month after the general election.

Despite previously promising to stay in office regardless of the election outcome,[78] Anna Bligh announced her resignation from the seat of South Brisbane the day after her election drubbing. As a paid Labor Party apparatchik who had worked for the unions and former Labor ministers, Trad embodied the modern caricature of a Labor candidate for higher office. She was always destined for her old friend's seat in the Parliament. With little scrutiny of her personal and professional past, Trad won the South Brisbane by-election on 28

April 2012. She did it courtesy of preferences from the Greens, which had secured 19.4 percent of the primary vote. Trad polled just 32.9 percent, compared to the LNP's 38 percent.

With one of the key players responsible for the campaign of smear against his family now sitting in the green leather chairs of the Parliamentary chamber directly across from him, Campbell could hardly contain his disdain. He reflected later:

> It hurt me. Because I'd been through that, because I had a wife who was absolutely traumatised by it, I was affected by it and it affected my demeanour. I behaved differently in Parliament for the first two years, I was extremely angry and bitter and it came through. It came through in my interactions in the chamber. It wasn't until 2014 that I got over it and dealt with it.

Lisa also felt the impact of that vicious campaign for nearly 12 months after the election. This is the dark side of life as an elected representative. People are quick to judge politicians. But only those individuals and their families who've put their hands up and won a seat on a Council or in Parliament can truly know the personal toll it can take:

> If people are wondering what happened to the 'Can Do' from City Hall, well, I think a big part of it was that we weren't the same old strong unit we were when Cam was Lord Mayor. It took me a long time after the election to recover. The time I started to recover was in early 2013, and the turning point for me was when I started sitting in the public gallery at the Parliamentary chamber. I would sit up in the balcony, and I wasn't hiding away anymore. I took up crocheting, and the reason was that I was so stressed, so depressed, that I started thinking I had to find something that used to make me feel calm. Life was so simple back in the 1980s and '90s, and I remembered it was so nice to sit down and knit and crochet

and sew. That's when I thought I needed something to be calm, peaceful, to be happy. As 2013 progressed, I just got over what happened during the campaign and Cam and I started reconnecting and enjoying the role.

Campbell's jaded outlook toward his opponents merged with the tough decisions his Government was making. It didn't help that he shouldered virtually all of the blame for the Government's austerity drive since the election win.

Political partnership

Almost by default Campbell became the face of the public service job cuts, taking most of the hits for the Government in the media and Parliament. Indeed, the lack of a political partnership that was "greater than the sum of its parts" dogged him throughout his tenure as Premier.

Deputy Premier Jeff Seeney, a seasoned Parliamentarian, and Treasurer Tim Nicholls, his former Council colleague, provided a reliable sounding board for Campbell. In an unusual political dynamic, the trio steered the LNP Government with stable, purposeful leadership. They got along well on a personal level and shared a commonality of vision about what they needed to do to "get Queensland back on track". Despite their diversity of backgrounds and some philosophical differences, perhaps they were too alike. While former Ministers described Cabinet discussions as robust and constructive, the leadership trio would always meet beforehand to agree on the main decisions. Campbell himself was out-voted and over-ruled on occasion, but there was never any doubt the three of them were in charge.

In one sense, the triumvirate leadership structure had an inadvertent consequence. Howard had Costello, Hawke had Keating, Peter Beattie had Terry Mackenroth, and Jeff Kennett and

Alan Stockdale transformed Victoria. But Campbell was new to the Parliament, and he didn't have the benefit of time to build alliances and cultivate a true political partnership like those of governments past. Given the dominant themes of economic management, budget repair and the downsizing of the public service the new Premier needed a loyal lieutenant, a gutsy Treasurer possessing equal measures of eloquence, empathy and media panache. When it came to the administration of his department Nicholls was unquestionably an outstanding Treasurer. But during this period of upheaval and change, Campbell also needed him to act as a kind of wingman to explain the hard decisions and absorb the heat of enemy fire. In many ways, the Government's fortunes relied on Nicholls quarantining Campbell from the daily doses of tough medicine it was prescribing. Nicholls was making the tough calls behind the scenes, but didn't do enough in a supporting role when the cameras were switched on. A formalised team dynamic with Nicholls as the public face of austerity, allowing Campbell to focus on the Government's unmatched record of early action, was never formally discussed by the leadership team. It should've been.

Some political pundits, LNP MPs and Campbell loyalists believed that Nicholls was in some way engineering the Premier's demise from the start, with a view to taking over the top job when Campbell lost his seat of Ashgrove at the next election. Let Campbell take the hits and make the tough calls, the theory went, and when he was booted out as a oncer, the job as Premier would be up for grabs. Campbell heard the talk but never gave it much thought. He was too focused on what needed to be done. Campbell believed in what his Government was doing, he was resolute they were making tough decisions for the right reasons and he never ran away from them.

When it came to public statements about the fiscal repair efforts, Campbell sometimes led from the front with his chin in the air. Part of his success as Lord Mayor was his reputation as an anti-politician.

While most of his ilk carefully smoothed out their language and thought twice before uttering every sentence, Campbell didn't. It wasn't in his nature. Witness his answer to a question in Parliament on 23 August about Clive Palmer's plan to fund counselling services for public servants who had lost their jobs. Campbell provided a reasoned response, except for a single line:

> The people who are the victims at the moment are public servants who have been employed by the people opposite when there was not enough money to pay their salaries. Unfortunately, we are the ones who are cleaning up Anna Bligh's mess. It is Anna Bligh's legacy. We get the pooper scooper out every day of the week. We have to make these tough decisions. We know there is fear and anxiety and we are sorry about that. It will end as soon as possible.

As one would expect, the "pooper scooper" comment was magnified and repeated ad nauseam in social and mainstream media, becoming a meme for Campbell's perceived disdain for public servants. He didn't think that way at all, but details and nuance don't matter in today's political and media climate. There were times Campbell needed to retreat out of the trenches, but his instinct to stand firm and confront whatever came his way took precedence.

With the cost-cutting and public service downsizing sucking the oxygen out of everything else the Government was doing, the general public was never really aware of what its new Government was actually achieving. Underneath the media and public radar, the Government was in fact delivering an unparalleled level of activity and outcomes. Throughout the term, an action plan was released every six months, starting with its 100-day plan. Hundreds of specific tasks were identified and all of them were delivered. At the same time, broader overhauls in health, education and the police service were recording measurable improvements in service delivery.

From the beginning of its term, the Government's greatest achievements flowed from reforms and increased spending in the public health and hospital system. Queensland Health – described as a "basketcase" by Anna Bligh just a few months before the 2012 election – was transformed under Health Minister Lawrence Springborg. The 8,000-plus head count in the department's top-heavy head office in Brisbane was massively reduced to free up funds for emergency departments and surgical waiting lists. The introduction of local hospital boards – part of the Government's philosophy to empower communities and regions with local decision making – was a pivotal reform. The work of hospital boards was a concept the former Health Minister Paul Lucas ridiculed in 2010. He preferred a centralised control-and-command model, a "strong national framework"[79] as he called it. Now, the boards were helping to deliver some of the best emergency and surgical performances in the nation.

Similarly, a policy allowing for the creation of Independent public schools provided unprecedented school autonomy while the massive maintenance backlog at Queensland schools was cleared with a $150 million spend. Hundreds of police were recruited, trained and deployed as part of a policy to put an extra 1100 police on the beat across the three-year term. Industry plans were developed for mining, tourism, construction and agriculture, key sectors identified by the Government as the state's "four economic pillars". The building and construction industry watchdog was replaced with a new body after years of complaints and dysfunction. An overhaul of the worker's compensation laws resulted in an average 15 percent reduction in WorkCover premiums for businesses and the payroll tax exemption threshold was raised. A 10-year, $10 billion action plan to upgrade the Bruce Highway from Brisbane to Cairns was developed and funded and planning for another major road project, the $1.6 billion Toowoomba Second Range Crossing, was underway.

In the final Galaxy Poll of the year, primary support for the

Newman Government had dropped 5 percent since the election. While it still enjoyed a commanding two-party preferred lead of 56 percent to 44 over Labor, the gloss of its euphoric victory nine months earlier was long gone. No-one within the leadership team was surprised. The historic victory of March 2012 was a high watermark. Support for the LNP was going to recede irrespective of how well the Government performed.

In an end-of-year review column on 15 December, *The Courier-Mail's* Steve Wardill declared Campbell remained "the LNP's stand-out asset". Wardill made the bold and bizarre prediction that a "mid-year (2013) election cannot be totally ruled out". No such thing was ever considered or discussed. There was still so much work left to do.

9

POLICY VERSUS POLITICS – PART TWO

2012-2015: Queensland Premier

Like so many Queensland summers, 2013 began with a severe weather event. The Bureau of Meteorology began tracking a tropical low in the Gulf of Carpentaria on 17 January. In subsequent days, the system dissipated before reorganising and strengthening into what authorities named Tropical Cyclone Oswald on 21 January. When it struck the coast and made landfall as a category one system in Cape York, Oswald caused minor damage. But as Oswald started heading south, pushed along by a strong monsoonal trough to its north, authorities feared the worst. The memories of the 2011 floods were still raw.

On its winding 3000km path down through Queensland to New South Wales, Oswald dumped extraordinary volumes of rain across the length and breadth of the state. On 25 January, with Oswald getting closer to Brisbane, Campbell insisted on the pre-emptive release of water from Wivenhoe Dam. The move was applauded by water experts and engineers, with one telling *The Courier-Mail*: "It's a pity 'paralysis by analysis' did not allow similar decisive action in January 2011."

By the time Oswald petered out in the Tasman Sea on 29 January, more than 390,000 homes had lost power and nearly a quarter of all state-controlled roads across 57 local government areas were affected. The total cost was estimated at $2.5 billion. Bundaberg and surrounding areas were among the hardest hit communities, with thousands of people evacuated and properties damaged. The clean-up and repair job spawned the Government's new "recovery and resilience" philosophy, led by Minister David Crisafulli.

In a break from the past, the LNP Government took a longer term, strategic view of natural disaster recovery. Instead of replacing bridges and infrastructure to the same specifications that had just been damaged and inundated, the Government wanted to rebuild to a higher, stronger standard. Some of Campbell's skills derived from his various careers – the principles of project management, maintaining calm in the midst of a crisis and an orderly delegation of tasks – helped him enormously during the extraordinary Oswald weather event. Former Premier Anna Bligh mastered the art of set speeches at media conferences during natural disasters, and people were comforted by her performance and reassurances. Campbell preferred to be at ground zero, marshalling resources, driving his Cabinet to act and overseeing the detail of the recovery efforts. His appearances at media conferences couldn't match Bligh, but the Newman Government's management of Oswald was exemplary.

The mission to rebuild Bundaberg and other damaged towns was among the quickest and most practical in Queensland's history. Minister Crisafulli later noted that in less than 18 months the recovery effort had reached the halfway point with about $56 million worth of work completed, compared to the former Labor Government which took "18 months just to issue tenders."

Commission of Audit final report

While the reconstruction of Bundaberg was happening at an unprecedented pace, a repair task of a different kind was presented to the Government on 30 April 2013. The release of the Commission of Audit's final report laid out the immense challenge to fix the mess the Government had inherited while at the same time rendering the job of selling a positive message even harder than it already was.

Speaking on the release of the final report, Costello painted a grim picture in an interview with the *Australian Financial Review*.

> Queensland has a problem: its credit rating has been downgraded, it's paying higher and higher interest costs, and something has got to happen. If it doesn't change, it's just going to get worse and worse, and if Queensland won't get back to AAA, the risk is that the state will be downgraded further. There is no easy answer here. The money has gone out and the money has been spent and somebody has got to clear up the mess.[80]

The Government pledged to enact around 75 percent of the report's 155 recommendations. At the time, Campbell told the media there was "a heck of a lot of political risk in this for the Government":

> I am concerned about what we are proposing because it is going to be a tough sell. Why would a Premier and a political team put up things that are difficult and unpalatable and unpopular if we weren't fair dinkum about doing the right thing? We are doing what is right.

The Commission's three-volume final report received praise and scorn in equal measure. Labor called it a "pre-ordained, manufactured, made-to-order report from Peter Costello for the Newman Government". Unions let forth cries of impending doom, corralling their troops for protests and social media campaigns. In a somewhat more measured appraisal, Brisbane economist and former state and federal treasury official Gene Tunney described the Commission's final report as "an impressive guide to the reform of the Queensland Government over the rest of the decade":

> With solid analysis of policy issues across the wide range of public services in Queensland, and strong arguments in support of greater outsourcing and privatisation, the report will have a long shelf life. I have no doubt the report will one

day be cited as instrumental in the inevitable privatisation of Energex and Ergon, which unfortunately the Government in its response has rejected for now, even though sales proceeds would pay off a big chunk of state debt, as Commission head Peter Costello pointed out.[81]

The report's recommendation to sell electricity assets was the subject of heated debate within Cabinet and the party room. Some MPs deemed it necessary to help Queensland reclaim its AAA credit rating and bring the state into line with Victoria and South Australia, which had long since privatised their electricity assets. Others, including Campbell, viewed the sale of electricity assets as a bridge too far. Given the electoral poison of the Bligh Government's asset sales program and the inevitable campaign by the militant unions, many Government MPs were adamantly opposed to any sale of electricity assets.

In any case, it was hard to see how the LNP Government could manage to convince a majority of Queenslanders to abandon their long-held devotion to "the people's assets". Having already burnt so much political capital on tough decisions since coming to office, the Government would be doubling down on its chances of winning the next election.

Following an animated discussion between ministers in a Cabinet meeting on the Monday morning of 29 April, the Audit report was tabled for debate at the LNP's party room gathering later that afternoon, a day before its official release.

Government MPs were united on nearly all of the report's recommendations but the response hinged on the sale of certain assets, such as the electricity transmission network Powerlink. Midway through the marathon meeting, when support for the full sale of electricity assets seemed to be building, Campbell was exasperated at colleagues so willing to go down the path of a total package of asset sales. He stood up, slammed his fists on the table at the front of the room and said: "Are you fucking kidding me? Wake up and smell the coffee!"

The then MP for Morayfield Darren Grimwade, who intended to oppose any asset sales, remembered the scene well:

> It was nearly two hours into the meeting when the Premier rose to express his position. I can remember sitting there thinking 'what's Campbell going to say'? Is he going to back any suggestion of asset sales or not? It was at this time I remember Campbell standing up behind the front table where the leadership team sat, posing the question something like 'You want to go to an election with a policy to sell assets?' It was at this time I understood that the Premier shared the same concerns as myself in relation to selling assets. This outburst and expression of personal opinion on such a critical issue was one of only a handful of times I can remember the Premier expressing his personal view in the party room. After the longest party room meeting we ever had I remember walking out knowing that this man was going to be a strong leader who was willing to accept responsibility for decisions made by the Government even if that meant it was against his personal view. It was this courage and leadership character that I ultimately gained a true respect for.

Campbell's impassioned plea for a political reality check was enough to convince his colleagues to abandon the full suite of asset sales proposed by the Commission of Audit and backed by Tim Nicholls. After much internal debate, the Government eventually settled on a compromise strategy of long-term leases for around 12 percent of the state's publicly-owned assets, including some electricity assets, the Gladstone and Townsville ports, and a water distribution network.

But when the Government's second Budget was handed down a

month later on 4 June 2013, the issue of what to do with the state's assets was not included. That came later, with the launch of the Strong Choices consultation campaign in April 2014.

For now, the Government was busy selling the merits of its "no frills" 2013 Budget. Highlights included a 6.6 percent increase in the education budget (an extra $707 million), a 4.7 percent rise in the disability services budget (up $64 million), and 4.5 percent extra for health (a $533 million increase). The Budget also provided an update on the Government's reduction of the public service. After predicting up to 20,000 staff might be cut, the latest count was around 12,800 staff. Of those, 9200 took generous redundancies. Heeding the dire messages out of the Commission Of Audit's final report, general Government expenses in 2012-13 were estimated to be only 1.1 percent higher than in 2011-12. As Tim Nicholls noted:

> This is the lowest rate of expenses growth since the introduction of accrual accounting in the public sector in 1998-99 and contrasts with average rates of expenses growth of 8.9 percent over the decade to 2011-12.

Despite the sensible, disciplined set of accounts contained in the 2013 Budget, the union's relentless and well-funded campaign over public service job cuts was crowding out nearly all other reforms and achievements.

Rupert Murdoch weighs in

During its first 12 months in government, few critics were as harsh as *The Courier-Mail's* David Fagan. By the time the Newman Government was elected, Fagan had been at the helm of Brisbane's only daily newspaper for a decade. Despite presiding over dramatic circulation falls during his tenure, he wielded great influence and power. He had been a loyal foot soldier in Rupert Murdoch's media empire for three decades, working his way up from junior journalist at a rural paper to editor-in-chief of *The Courier-Mail*. His partner, the radio broadcaster Madonna King, wrote a weekly opinion column for Saturday's edition of the paper.

In June 2012, three months after the LNP won in a landslide, Fagan was elevated to the role of editorial director of News Limited's operations in Queensland. His new job involved transitioning the company's newsrooms from its old print model to a digital, online future. He also worked with the bean counters at News Limited's Holt St headquarters in Sydney to oversee the sacking of hundreds of reporters and sub-editors, among other staff, across the company's Queensland publications.

Over the years, Fagan had increasingly clashed with Campbell and his administration at City Hall. The paper's coverage of the 2011-12 campaign, when it seemed unwilling to question the source of the dirt it was receiving from Labor, put the pair on something of a permanent war footing. Surprisingly for a News Limited metro, the paper's coverage of the new LNP Government was relentlessly unforgiving and, for the most part, negative.

When he sat down at a meeting with Murdoch and other senior editorial executives from papers across Australia in April 2013, Fagan was in for a rude awakening. Campbell first met Rupert back in 2004, shortly after he had won the keys to City Hall. The global media baron appeared to have kept tabs on Campbell's career over the years, and seemed to be impressed with his work as Queensland Premier.

A number of News Corporation insiders have said that Murdoch made it clear he wasn't happy with *The Courier-Mail's* coverage of the LNP Government, and he let Fagan know about it at that April editor's meeting. Fagan was defensive, and told his boss the paper's coverage was a reflection of the Government's culling of 14,000 public servants. Murdoch reportedly leaned in and pointedly told

Fagan the Premier should've sacked many thousands more of them.

Within a couple of months of that meeting, Fagan's three decades at News Limited were suddenly over. Michael Crutcher, *The Courier-Mail's* editor who worked under Fagan and helped drive the daily editorial coverage at the time, also exited the company. In a benign statement announcing their departure in mid-June, the then News Limited CEO Kim Williams said:

> David has had a distinguished career and made a huge contribution to our company, to Australian journalism and to the people of Queensland. We announce this decision with great regret.

Later that year, on 1 November 2013, Murdoch invited the Premier and Lisa to sit at his table as his guests of honour at the media company's annual News Awards in Brisbane. During the speeches at the black-tie gala event, a number of positive references were made to the tough decisions being delivered by the Premier and his Government.

Fagan has denied such a meeting between the editors and Murdoch occurred back in April 2013.[82]

National Disability Insurance Scheme

Campbell's media team hoped the changing of the guard at *The Courier-Mail* would help generate some clear media air for its many achievements to be seen and heard. They were reducing crime, improving the performance of hospitals, giving schools more funding and independence, and producing long-term strategic plans for key economic sectors. But all of that was hard to sell in the midst of the restrictive fiscal environment the Government had inherited. And despite all of its gains on the Budget bottom line, the belt tightening had to continue in the face of intense pressure to open the state's cheque book. Somehow they had to fund increasing demand on existing services and programs, as well as new projects and initiatives.

A prime example during this period in 2013 was the National Disability Insurance Scheme. The campaign urging Queensland to sign up had been building and intensifying since mid-2012. NSW and Victorian Liberal governments jumped on board the Gillard Government program in July 2012. Given Queensland's ugly balance sheet, Campbell wanted clarity and certainty on the funding arrangements before signing any agreement.

Campbell was labelled "cold-hearted and callous" for his cautious approach, with a strident Federal Treasurer Wayne Swan accusing him of "playing with people's lives". In fact, Campbell had always supported the scheme. His reservations centred on the shambolic process of negotiation between the Commonwealth and the states:

> Julia Gillard was totally reckless and politically cynical in her approach to the NDIS. She proceeded to go headlong into that scheme without proper costings, without a proper funding mechanism, and without proper agreement from the states. Gillard and Shorten (the then Parliamentary Secretary for Disabilities) essentially announced it in the media and rolled over the top of everybody. Given the level of expenditure it was one of the most reckless things I've seen anyone do in politics. Yes we need a national scheme, yes everybody wanted to do it, but we saw a Prime Minister who used the issue as a political point-scoring exercise instead of sitting down and working through it with the states. (Former NSW Premier) Barry O'Farrell played a less than glorious role in the whole saga in that he essentially rolled over to her and hung the rest of the states out to dry.

The NDIS process and COAG meetings soured the relationship between Campbell and the Federal Labor Government. In terms of his relationship with state leaders during this period, he formed strong ties with Ted Baillieu in Victoria and Adam Giles in the Northern Territory and developed a working relationship with Labor's Jay Weatherill in South Australia. Colin Barnett, the Premier of Western Australia, was generally a lone wolf at COAG meetings. Privately, Campbell joked that O'Farrell was the "best Labor Premier that New South Wales ever had".

During the early stages of development in the NDIS process, Campbell floated a proposal for a federal levy on income taxes to help fund the scheme, and discussed it with other Premiers and Chief Ministers at a COAG dinner at the Lodge on 24 July 2012. Gillard immediately rejected the idea, in private and in the media. Ten months later, as she began to realise the scale of the funding challenge, Gillard would swallow her pride and adopt Campbell's suggestion. When asked by the media to reflect on Gillard's decision, Campbell said:

> This is too an important a day to reflect on that sort of commentary. My position has been consistent for the last year; NDIS is something that has never been undertaken in Australia. This is a bold, new important social initiative that brings a level of care and protection for people with disabilities and their families that have never been provided before in Australia's history. If you are going to do something like that, you either have to find new money through a tax or a levy and savings or a combination, so I did support a levy last year and I am going to support the Prime Minister on this today.

With the levy providing an extra $200 million contribution to Queensland, the Newman Government signed up to the NDIS on 8 May 2013. An adviser to Campbell during the negotiations said:

> Campbell was very concerned about the lack of detail and negotiations around the NDIS. One of the issues we had with rolling out the NDIS trial site was the 'honeypot effect' whereby if we had a trial site in a particular area then people

would move to that area to access services. We didn't have anything in place to cope with that if it occurred.

To Gonski, or not

Like the NDIS, the Gillard Government's process of education funding reform was condemned by Campbell and his Government. The deadline to sign a Gonski deal loomed large at the end of July 2013, just weeks after the NDIS agreement was signed. Campbell described the federal funding and policy package offered to Queensland schools as a "bucket of custard".

The Newman Government's submission to a Senate inquiry on the Gonski legislation outlined its opposition to the plan, calling it a "de facto Federal Government takeover of schooling". While all attention was on the Gonski reforms, Campbell and his Education Minister John-Paul Langbroek had already announced the LNP Government's own package of school reforms, including the granting of Independent status to public schools and the Great Teachers = Great Results policy, a four-year $535 million funding boost launched on 8 April 2013.

As pressure mounted over the Gonski reforms throughout the first half of 2013, Queensland historian and political commentator Ross Fitzgerald backed the Newman Government's reticence to sign up against a backdrop of "state and federal Labor's incompetence in further and higher education":

> In spite of the political costs, the Newman Government is engaged in a thorough analysis of the pros and cons of buying into a policy of this incompetent federal Labor Government. It is an approach that Queenslanders and most Australians should welcome as a necessary return to sound governance after Labor's reckless years.

On 12 July 2013, a few weeks after rejecting the Gillard Government's Gonski offer, Campbell met with Kevin Rudd, the newly re-installed Prime Minister. With a federal election due within the next few months, Rudd wanted the Gonski deals sewn up and out of the way before the official campaign began. The talks between the two Queensland-based leaders and their relevant Education Ministers John-Paul Langbroek and Bill Shorten were cordial, but an agreement remained out of reach at that stage.

The state-federal negotiations and processes over the NDIS and Gonski reforms heightened Campbell's resolve about the desperate need for reform of the federation. He would later call it one of the "biggest issues facing the nation":

> We need to clearly define which levels of government should deliver education in schools and universities, which level has responsibility for health services in hospitals, as well as who should provide the roads, rail, ports, electricity and water supplies that are essential to our future prosperity. There are far too many areas where federal and state responsibilities overlap and create waste, duplication and confusion. We've reached a situation where funding for vital services – like health, education and housing – is provided only if the services are delivered as the federal government sees fit and only if states agree to complex, onerous and expensive administrative requirements. States must have untied access to a sustainable revenue base that is sufficient to deliver on their responsibilities. All Australians are the losers in this because billions of dollars are wasted on unnecessary bureaucracy. I also believe that getting out of each other's way will not only mean more efficient government but more accountable government.

Clive Palmer

The concept of accountability and transparency – or the lack thereof – was a recurring theme used by Labor and its comrades on the Left to attack the LNP Government. They cast aspersions of corruption and accused the Government of secrecy in all manner of decisions. Campbell was routinely compared to Joh Bjelke-Petersen and, just like reporter Matthew Condon's fears over the axing of the literary awards, they predicted Queensland was headed back to the "dark old days". They even had clever t-shirts printed with the slogan "Here we Joh again".

The Left conveniently ignored the accountability measures introduced by the Newman Government. They didn't mention the relatively swift resignations of three LNP Ministers for what amounted to minor infractions, in stark contrast to the drawn out travails of former Labor Ministers like Gordon Nuttall or the contemporary blunders of Palaszczuk Government Minister Jo-Ann Miller. The Left and its associated commentariat declined to acknowledge the LNP reinstated the law that made it illegal to lie to Parliament, scrapped back in 2006 by the Beattie Government to protect Nuttall. They also brushed over the Newman Government's move to publicly release the diaries of Cabinet Ministers on a monthly basis. The policy that gave departmental public servants the responsibility to assess Right To Information applications, instead of ministerial staff as per Labor's previous policy, went completely unnoticed. Most of all, the Left's hypocrisy on the topic of openness and accountability in government was highlighted by the LNP administration's ongoing battle with Clive Palmer.

Before his falling out with the Liberal National Party, Palmer's close ties and substantial donations to the party were used against Campbell and his new government. According to the Left, the mining billionaire was going to be some kind of puppet master calling in favours and bending the Newman Government to his will.

But by the middle of 2013, that sentiment had flipped on its axis. Palmer had become a media darling with his incessant rants against the Newman Government.

As the enemy of their enemy, he also became a fair-weather friend of the Left. Reporters and the Labor Opposition lapped up his outrageous comments. By this point, the media had completely lost perspective on the reasons behind Palmer's outlandish attacks.

As a life member and generous donor of the LNP, Palmer had been on the side of conservative politics in Queensland ever since he joined the National Party in the mid-1970s. He had worked on campaigns for Joh Bjelke-Petersen and was instrumental in the formation of the LNP in 2008. Four decades of support vanished in an explosive burst of froth and fury when the Newman Government didn't automatically accede to Palmer's wishes.

The falling out had its roots in a meeting between Palmer and Deputy Premier Seeney in April 2012, shortly after the election. Essentially, Palmer wanted the new LNP Government to introduce specific legislation related to his plan to build a rail-line from his massive Waratah Coal mining project in Central Queensland's Galilee Basin to the Abbott Point coal terminal near the coastal town of Bowen. Accounts of that particular meeting differed, and it later became the subject of a Crime and Misconduct Commission investigation.

Palmer had hoped his private meeting with Campbell on 1 July 2012 would convince the Premier to over-rule Seeney's reluctance to introduce Palmer's suggested bill into Parliament. For months, Palmer had been chasing a meeting with Campbell, and the new Premier was running out of excuses to avoid him. Competition to develop the Galilee Basin was heating up in a multi-billion dollar game of extremely high stakes. A joint venture between Indian conglomerate GVK and Gina Rinehart's Hancock was considered the frontrunner to develop the first coal mine in the region, but Palmer wanted special consideration to build a rail line as part of his planned pit-to-port operation.

Having avoided meeting him for months, Campbell had no choice but to agree to a meeting on 1 July 2012. They were due to be in the same Melbourne hotel together – the Sofitel on Collins St – attending the Liberal Party's Federal Council Meeting. At the behest of party president Bruce McIver, Campbell reluctantly agreed to meet on one condition – they had to catch up for a talk in the most public way possible. Any hint of a secret meeting with a mining proponent seeking government support at this juncture of the Galilee Basin's development would be seriously damaging, particularly given it would be held at a Liberal Party function. Campbell suggested a breakfast meeting in the hotel's lobby restaurant but Palmer refused. Instead, they eventually met in Palmer's luxurious penthouse suite at the hotel. Ben Myers and McIver also attended. Campbell knew it was a mistake to agree to the meeting:

> I felt very uneasy about meeting with him. When we got into the meeting Palmer talked about the rail line from his mine to the coast. He also talked about a plan for his Coolum Resort, where he wanted very high buildings built almost on the sand dunes down at the beach. He showed us artist's impressions and a proposal for a monorail from the airport to his resort. There was no disagreement or any bad words spoken at the meeting. He wanted X, Y and Z to happen and I basically said 'well Clive, I love investment in the state but we have to follow due process, you have to go to council, you have to complete all of the steps and the requirements'. But he wanted to do it the way it used to be done, and I said 'you don't get to do that these days'.

All hell broke loose between the two camps after that meeting. Palmer went on a verbal rampage in the media, at various points calling Campbell a "little Hitler" who introduced "Nazi legislation" and a "crook" who was going to "jail". He also claimed Campbell didn't "make any decisions on what happens in the government" because the Premier was suffering from a "bi-polar condition". Palmer resigned his life membership of the LNP and launched legal action against the Queensland Government, as well as defamation proceedings against the Premier and his Deputy. In April 2013, Palmer announced the formation of his own political party with the dual purpose of making him the next Prime Minister of Australia and annihilating the Newman Government.

Campbell lamented the fact he didn't use taxpayer's money to sue Palmer for his defamatory comments early on in the dispute:

> I think the ongoing Palmer stuff was one of the biggest problems we had. Not particularly because of what he was saying in terms of the credibility of his allegations but because day after day after day he could say the most outrageous, wild things, and the media would report on it. His comments and the back and forth responses consumed so much air time we couldn't get our message out. I was told time and time again you can't sue, you won't win, you're a politician. But I regret that I didn't sue Clive Palmer using taxpayer resources, I do regret that. If I'd won, I would have put the money back into the system. I think in hindsight I was given poor political advice. If we'd taken legal action early in 2013 when he started making outrageous comments, it might have changed the whole tone. By not standing up to people like Palmer, we actually ceded civility, rationality and reasonableness and we bore the consequences of that. It was a big mistake.

Alan Jones

Another loud-mouthed juggernaut capable of usurping the media cycle and sidelining the Government's ability to get its message out was radio shock jock Alan Jones. Like Palmer, the falling out between the Newman Government and Jones originated in a private meeting in a penthouse suite.

For months leading up to their meeting, Jones had been riled up about coal seam gas and the potential loss of prime agricultural land in south-western Queensland. Chief among his concerns were a proposal to expand a massive open cut coal mine near his hometown of Acland and a coal-to-liquids project at Felton in the Darling Downs region. To calm his concerns, a meeting was arranged for mid-March 2012, after the then Premier Bligh had called the election.

Campbell and LNP president Bruce McIver flew down to meet with Jones at his multi-million dollar luxury apartment on the 6th floor of Bennelong Apartments at Circular Quay. The meeting with Jones on the Sunday morning of 11 March was arranged by Tony Abbott, the then Opposition Leader. Jones had been in Abbott's ear about CSG, and Abbott wanted Campbell to sit down with the broadcasting giant to address his concerns about the future of mining in Queensland. After introductions and brief pleasantries, Abbott left the meeting to allow a full and frank discussion to occur. By the end of the meeting, Jones felt he had secured a commitment from Campbell that a future Newman Government would not approve the proposed expansion of the coal mine near Acland. Campbell explained the background of his meeting with Jones:

> CSG was a political issue in New South Wales and Sydney, which is why Tony Abbott was rightly concerned about it. He was concerned about what Jones was saying about the issue so he asked me to meet with him. But it wasn't an issue with political bite in Queensland and it wasn't a political issue that would impact Abbott in Queensland. For the most part, the issues around agricultural land and CSG had really been sorted out here. Yes there were people concerned about it up here but they weren't in the majority and they really didn't have a case.

The LNP Member for Beaudesert Jon Krause credited Campbell's leadership for banning CSG mining in the picturesque Scenic Rim region in south-east Queensland.[83] With several proposals for CSG mines on the table, Campbell heeded the concerns of the local community and farmers to rule out any mines there. All of that was lost on or ignored by Alan Jones. He had his blinkers on, and ratings to chase. Campbell recalled the details of the meeting:

> So we're with Jones at his penthouse and he went on and on about CSG, he went on about Acland, he went on about Felton. The trouble with that meeting was that Jones felt he'd had certain commitments made and he hadn't. I just point to what we did. We did further work to sort out CSG with the Gasfields Commission and a whole lot of stuff to empower farmers. It wasn't an issue up here. It was fixed. We stopped the proposed coal-to-liquids project at Felton that Jones was concerned about. The early proposals for the expansion of the Acland Mine that Jones was worried about, which would have seen the township of Acland destroyed, didn't go ahead. It was massively scaled back. I think the meeting was a terrible mistake because it created this false set of expectations and put in Jones's mind that I wasn't to be trusted, that I had no integrity.

One of Jones's early on-air bombing raids against Campbell and the LNP happened in late 2012 over the Government's support for the $6 billion Alpha Coal mine project in the Galilee Basin, a partnership between Gina Rinehart and India's GVK Power & Infrastructure. The approval of the Rinehart-GVK bid was the same matter fuelling Clive Palmer's attacks on the Government around this time. Jones blasted the Newman Government for "selling out" to Indian developers and engaging in the "betrayal of ordinary Australians", and his attacks descended into defamatory, venomous tirades from that point on. Campbell reflected:

> I don't think he made one iota of difference in terms of what he was saying. Our MPs in the areas he was going on about

didn't feel much electoral impact on the ground. But what did he do? He made outrageous statements day after day and the media kept reporting on it. Every press conference I did I was being asked about what Clive Palmer had said or what Alan Jones was saying about me and the Government. They sucked the oxygen out of every press conference and we just couldn't get our message out. The media was more interested in reporting on what those two gentlemen were saying as opposed to the latest initiative or project we were launching in health or education.

The Palmer and Jones attacks fed into a broader narrative of the Government as a brawling, pugnacious administration. Campbell took full responsibility for the actions of his Government, regardless of his level of involvement in controversial decisions. Either way, Campbell's name was indelibly attached to the Government's declining popularity.

In mid-2013, when the fights with Palmer and Jones (among others) were at fever pitch, Campbell copped the brunt of the public's scorn over massive pay increases for state MPs in mid-2013. That was a policy change poorly managed by Deputy Premier Jeff Seeney while Campbell was on holidays in Vietnam with his family. But in the public's collective mind, Campbell was greedy and heartless for introducing such a pay rise at a time when he was sacking public servants. When he flew back into the eye of the storm, Campbell reversed the decision and established an Independent Remuneration Tribunal to develop a more transparent system for the salaries and entitlements of Queensland MPs. Regardless, Campbell remained the public face of that decision and most of the other damaging battles besetting his Government. Such is the burden of the leader.

The Queensland Plan

In order to counter the daily cut and thrust of political conflict engulfing the Government throughout 2013, Campbell's chief of staff Ben Myers knew they needed a positive, forward thinking project to lift them up and out of the trenches. As far back as 2012, Myers began working on an ambitious vision that would become known as the Queensland Plan.

In an age when politicians are rightly accused of focusing on short-term agendas aimed at winning the next election, the Queensland Plan would chart a course for the state's future over the next 30 years. The notion aligned with Campbell's approach to life and politics. His army and business careers had instilled the importance of mapping out a clear plan and strategy, for whatever challenge or project that had confronted him. Be it crossing the Tanami Desert as a young Army officer or developing the TransApex policy to address Brisbane's transport and traffic needs, Campbell relished the process of determining a particular course of action, and the certainty of sticking to it.

The Queensland Plan would be the most important and far-reaching planning exercise of his working life. The concept was launched in February 2013 by Campbell and his Environment Minister Andrew Powell, who led the Plan's development with a community consultation process that ran for 15 months.

Throughout 2013, hundreds of delegates from across Queensland attended Summits in Mackay and Brisbane, while thousands more participated in online forums, surveys, and business and community group workshops. Priority areas focused on education, the environment and economic diversity. Targets stretching out to 2044 were set, including doubling the population in the state's regional areas, achieving 100 percent literacy in primary schools and closing the life expectancy gap between Indigenous and non-Indigenous Queenslanders. Campbell was passionate about the process and the outcomes it promised to deliver. More than 80,000 Queenslanders had taken part in the plan's development. Legislation was later introduced in July 2014 to ensure it was implemented beyond mere words on a page. Labor described the Plan as "an absolute joke" while Campbell believed some MPs within LNP ranks were reticent to embrace it:

> One of the most disappointing things about long-term and strategic thinking is so many people in politics never get it. The Labor Party sought to politicise the Queensland Plan, which was the normal, shameful tactics they exhibit time and time again. It is very much a precious and important document for Queensland that no other state has. It received the endorsement of Queenslanders and should be retained. It was an important initiative.

Doctor's dispute

Under normal circumstances, the Queensland Plan would've been the type of long-term, bipartisan and consultative vision the community had long yearned for out of its political system. But just as the process was ramping up in mid-2013, the Government was considering a brave move to take on doctors and medical specialists. They were a vested interest group so powerful few governments anywhere in Australia had ever dared to confront them before. At the centre of the protracted acrimonious battle was a policy to transfer the state's 2,800 senior medical officers to individual contracts. The potential goodwill up for grabs during the Queensland Plan process was effectively sidelined by the raging dispute with doctors, as well as the fights with Palmer, Jones, the unions and others. Once again, it was a case of the Government pursuing a politically risky policy for the right reasons.

The contracts policy had its genesis in a 2012 report about the alleged rorting of taxpayer funds by a cohort of the state's doctors, who were accused of using public hospital facilities to treat private patients without refunding the Government, among other issues. Those generous arrangements for doctors stemmed from the time of the Beattie Government in around 2006. The then Labor Government had to find a way to meet the demands of senior medical officers seeking to boost their salaries. At the same time, it had to be careful not to upset the nurses and other medical staff who would want similar rises for their own pay packets if the doctors were seen to be given preferential treatment. So the chequebook was opened up and a policy called Right Of Private Practice introduced. The new policy avoided putting nurses offside because it wasn't viewed as a direct pay rise for doctors.

When the Newman Government decided to take the issue on, it was well known within medical circles that some of the state's doctors were rorting the system. Some would play golf and lodge a claim that they were at work. Others were racking up exorbitant overtime bills without actually doing the overtime. There was no flexibility in the system and it was impacting on patient care. There were patients who couldn't be discharged from hospitals on Friday, Saturday or Sunday because some doctors would work their salaried 40-hour week in the first four days, allowing them to either take a long weekend off or charge sky-high overtime for the remaining days, which hospitals couldn't always afford. By double-dipping in both the public and private hospital systems under the existing Right Of Private Practice provisions, there was a sense of entitlement in their work and salary arrangements.

Springborg commissioned the Auditor-General to further investigate the issue. When that report was handed down in July 2013 it found the existing private practice arrangements enjoyed by doctors had caused a loss to Queensland Health of more than $800 million over the past decade. This systemic rorting was second only to that other Queensland Health bungle inherited from Labor – the $1.25 billion health payroll scandal. Springborg was dealing with both issues simultaneously. An adviser to Campbell recalled a particularly caustic meeting between the Premier and senior medical officers in his Ashgrove electorate office, calling it "one of the most appalling meetings I witnessed":

They threatened to quit the public system and go to the private sector, which was a joke because the private hospitals wouldn't employ them as they wouldn't work on a weekend. These doctors had exceptional entitlements. They got 3.6 weeks of paid study leave, $20,000 professional development allowance and motor vehicle allowance of up to $24,500 per annum. Tasmania was the only other jurisdiction that also had this allowance. Some of these doctors were earning in excess of $1 million a year and behaving like union thugs.

Within Government circles, Springborg was considered the Cabinet's best performing Minister. His grasp of a portfolio once considered a poisoned chalice was remarkable. Systemic reforms under his watch delivered some of the nation's best frontline hospital results, with surgery, emergency departments and services all being transformed. But when it came to taking on doctors – that most trusted of professions – Springborg was on a hiding to nothing. The case for transitioning doctors onto individual contracts wasn't made as well as it could've been, and the conflict simmered for months from mid-2013.

It was early 2014 when the all-powerful cartel of specialists and doctors really ramped up their campaign against the contracts policy. They threatened to resign en masse and launched an emotive advertising and social media campaign. They claimed patients would die if over-worked and over-tired doctors were forced on to individual contracts and predicted a mass exodus of doctors from Queensland. In response, Queensland Health launched legal action to stop the doctor's associations and health unions "spreading misleading information" about the contracts. At the height of the dispute in early 2014, the Medical Journal of Australia wrote "Queensland doctors are now mired in one of the worst industrial disputes the Australian medical profession has ever seen, with the potential to cripple Queensland's public hospital system".

Campbell and Tony Abbott with Menzies statue in Canberra, 2013 and, below, LNP Government MPs at a government retreat in 2014

The furore had far-reaching consequences. In a major and lasting blow to the Government, Springborg's Assistant Minister for Health, the Member for Stafford Chris Davis, eventually resigned from Parliament over the issue. As a surgeon who had been Queensland president of the Australian Medical Association and state chair of the Royal Australasian College of Physicians, Dr Davis felt duty bound to side with his medical colleagues. He repeatedly breached Cabinet solidarity to speak out in the media against the Government's contract reforms, and left the Parliament in a blaze of publicity and stinging rebukes. Davis would later go on to be a champion for the union's ongoing campaign against the Newman Government. He also applied for membership of the Labor Party, which it rejected.

Much of the campaign by doctors against individual contracts was based on their own vested interests and used emotion and hyperbole to great effect. They used hypotheticals and misconceptions about the contract's clauses to spread fear and confusion. Regardless of the reality and the necessity for the reforms, the medical profession was always going to win the public PR battle.

For its part, Labor and the media inflamed the attacks on the Government. They ignored any sense of perspective they may have had about the origins of the rorting back in 2006 or the need for the reforms as outlined in the Auditor-General's report.

Eventually, Springborg and his director-general Ian Maynard reached a compromise deal with the doctors in mid-April 2014. Neither side really laid claim to a victory in public. But the reforms introduced as a result of the Government's policy meant the doctors could no longer double-dip, while the specific concerns raised by the Auditor-General in his 2013 report were addressed and corrected in subsequent contract arrangements. Campbell and his MPs were just glad to see the long-running and highly damaging issue put to bed. Like so many political scare campaigns and hypothetical worst-case scenarios during the Government's term, the dire consequences predicted by doctors and the unions never eventuated.

2013 federal election

In a stroke of fortunate timing for the Abbott-led Opposition, the doctors' dispute only ramped up after the federal election was held in September 2013. Still, the litany of controversies plaguing the Newman Government had already gifted the Labor Party a focal point of attack ahead of the federal battle. For months before the official start of the federal campaign on 4 August 2013, Labor and the unions attached Campbell's brand to Tony Abbott, painting the Queensland Premier as a mere warm-up act for a future Coalition Government in Canberra. They talked endlessly of job cuts and the slashing of services, regardless of the reality of increased spending or improvements in frontline services. Despite the Left's best efforts, the tactic didn't appear to be working. Research by the ABC's Vote Compass website published three weeks before the 7 September election found the recently reinstalled Prime Minister Kevin Rudd had "failed to establish any clear advantage with voters" in his home state of Queensland.[84]

In a remarkable return to politics, Peter Beattie added to the theatre of the national campaign with his bid for the outer Brisbane seat of Forde. His preselection was announced in an awkward media conference side by side with Rudd, an old and at times bitter foe. Meanwhile, Clive Palmer reached peak hyperbole with claims he would be the next Prime Minister. He also threatened to reveal evidence of "corruption" committed by the Newman Government if he was elected in the seat of Fairfax.

When the election was held on 7 September, the Coalition romped home in Queensland, picking up two extra seats for a total of 22 out of 30 seats on offer in the state. The Member for Brisbane Teresa Gambaro, who had privately expressed fears she would lose her seat as a result of the Newman Government's performance, cruised home to victory with a 3.1 percent primary vote swing in her favour. Beattie didn't succeed in Forde.

Palmer lost on the primary vote in Fairfax but ended up winning due to preferences from minor parties. His seat in the Federal Parliament became little more than a platform for revenge. A subsequent inquiry into the Newman Government established by Palmer's helpers in the Senate was a farce that cost taxpayers an estimated $100,000. The Left supported the need for the inquiry. Reporters like Matthew Condon, who were so upset about the axing of the literary prize 18 months earlier, had no compulsion to point out the cost of the Senate investigation could've funded their beloved book awards.

Shortly after the Abbott Government was elected, the Newman Government signed up to a revised education funding deal worth $884 million over the ensuing four years. It was $130 million more for Queensland than what the Gillard-Rudd Government had offered though Campbell expressed concern about the certainty of funding beyond the four-year agreement.

The perfect storm

The period following the federal election in the final quarter of 2013 would prove to be the most volatile of the Newman Government's term in office. At any given point, there were damaging – and in most cases justifiable – fights raging with doctors, unions, Palmer, and Jones, with criminal bikie gangs and the judiciary next in line. The Government's ability to sell its message was virtually impossible during this time. The end-of-year battle over the powerful Parliamentary Crime and Misconduct Committee (PCMC) didn't help matters.

In its first incarnation in 1989, the PCMC was known as the

Parliamentary Criminal Justice Committee, established to oversee the work of the Crime and Justice Commission (CJC) created to monitor and investigate the Queensland Police Service in the wake of the Fitzgerald Inquiry.

In 2002, the CJC was merged with the Queensland Crime Commission and rebadged the Crime and Misconduct Commission (CMC), which the PCMC now had oversight responsibilities for. The CMC had been in Campbell's sights since the 2011-12 election campaign when it appeared to have become a blatant political tool used to smear opponents. Back in 2011, Labor would simply lodge a complaint with the CMC, no matter how frivolous, and get a negative story up about it in the media.

In early 2013 the CMC was more broadly condemned over the accidental release of thousands of sensitive and confidential documents gathered during the course of the Fitzgerald Inquiry from 1987 to 1989. The "administrative oversight" resulted in the public release of files about police informants, suspects in murder cases, the identity of undercover agents and their operations, as well as police corruption. The records were intended to stay secret until 2055, long after the deaths of those who were named. The Government felt the PCMC had failed to adequately address the grave nature of the bungle, with Campbell calling for CMC chairman Ross Martin to consider his position. At the height of the controversy in March 2013, Martin revealed he had cystic fibrosis that required a lung transplant. His health problems forced him to stand down as the CMC chair.

After two replacements had been appointed and subsequently resigned in the space of a month, Dr Ken Levy was named acting chairman on May 16, 2013. The final battle between the Newman Government and the PCMC's Labor and Independent MPs began when Dr Levy wrote an opinion piece for The Courier-Mail on October 31 2013 supporting the Government's criminal bikie gang crackdown. Labor and crossbench MPs labelled him a "puppet" of the

Government and called for him to resign. When Dr Levy was accused of misleading the PCMC over the circumstances of publishing the opinion piece, Campbell and his Attorney-General Jarrod Bleijie had had enough.

The Government wanted to recalibrate the membership of the PCMC and start afresh. Late on Thursday November 21, the last Parliamentary sitting day of 2013, the Government moved a three-part motion to sack the PCMC and replace it with the Parliamentary Crime and Corruption Committee. Deputy Premier Jeff Seeney explained during the Parliamentary debate:

> The PCMC had become so biased in its approach to the issue (of Dr Levy's tenure) that it could no longer consider the matter, it could no longer be charged with the responsibility to act on behalf of this Parliament. (This motion) brings a solution to that intolerable situation.

With typically hysterical and hyperbolic rhetoric, Labor Shadow Minister Jo-Ann Miller claimed the Newman Government was motivated by a desire to "get their greedy little hands on the money again". Miller was Labor's wailing banshee in Parliament. She accused the LNP of engaging in "total payback" by sacking the committee:

> Members of this (LNP) Government and people who support this Government... want to get their greedy mitts on money, in my view, in a corrupt way. That is what this is about. In a few years' time what we are going to see is a judicial inquiry, an independent judicial inquiry, by another generation of Tony Fitzgeralds who will come through and have to clean up the mess and the corruption that this LNP Government are institutionally putting in place tonight, because that is what it is about. The interesting thing is that it does not take them long, does it, because there must be some sort of school of corruption or anti-moralism ... Or LNP membership. It must be born in them.

Independent MP for Gladstone and chair of the PCMC Liz Cunningham was more restrained and balanced in her critique of the element of the motion that sacked the Committee members:

> I would like to put on the record my appreciation for parts 1 and 2 of this motion. I believe that in terms of the pursuit of justice and a good, clear, defendable, transparent and just result that there should be an independent select Ethics Committee to consider these matters. I am obviously disappointed in the third part of this motion. I think it is disappointing that the politics of the last few weeks has led to this Parliament now considering a motion that I believe reflects poorly on what is a unicameral system reliant heavily on the committee process.

On reflection, Campbell has taken responsibility for the sacking of the PCMC. He said the Government did it for the right reasons but handled it in a "ham-fisted" way. Yet again, the pattern of taking action for the right reasons had overlooked the perception and political fall-out of that decision. The PCMC matter encapsulated the Government's image problem. The sacking of the Committee fed into the negative narrative of Campbell and his Government as arrogant, corrupt, combative and drunk on the power of a massive majority.

The war on criminal motorcycle gangs

Two months before the sacking of the PCCC, a criminal motorcycle gang sparked a melee at a Broadbeach restaurant. When that brawl broke out in September, the Newman Government was already flat out fighting fires of its own on numerous fronts, including the doctors' contracts dispute and the CMC controversy. In its early phase, the campaign to drive criminal bikie gangs out of Queensland was one of the Government's most punishing political battles.

It began with that violent brawl at Broadbeach on the night of

27 September 2013. Campbell was in Japan on a trade mission at the time. At about 8:30pm on that Friday night more than 20 members of the Bandidos bikie gang stormed into the busy Aura Restaurant to confront a rival gang member from the Finks. The Bandidos ordered the Finks member to get up from his table and "go outside". He refused, and a free-for-all punch-up began. Diners ran for cover and police swarmed in, using Tasers to break up the violent fracas. Four officers were injured, and the community was outraged. Shortly after the brawl, an estimated 50 Bandidos members assembled outside the Southport Police Station and demanded the release of their fellow gang members who were being questioned by officers inside. It was an ostentatious show of defiance that had become all too familiar on the Gold Coast. Fears of a looming bikie turf war escalated further when police were called to the scene of another violent incident involving the Bandidos at Southport later that same weekend.

With uncanny timing, left-wing columnist Madonna King became an unlikely advocate of urgent and drastic action. Before she was aware of the Broadbeach brawl, King had filed an opinion column earlier in the day titled "It's time for urgent zero tolerance on Gold Coast criminals". It was published in *The Courier-Mail* on 28 September 2013, the day after the Broadbeach incident. King wrote that Campbell had "no choice but to implement the toughest crime laws we've ever seen on the state's Gold Coast", arguing that recent acts of violent crime "should be the last straw in any argument to tinker at the edges of policing".

> The baddies are in control. Armed robbery after armed robbery. Road rage incidents where hand-guns are pulled in broad daylight. A vicious rape on a popular jogging path. Outlaw motorcycle gangs trying to recruit youngsters. And now a second police officer shot in the line of duty. What more will it take for the Government to draw a line in the sand and implement a zero-tolerance policy?

King finished her column with the prediction that "voters will applaud the Newman Government, already mid-way through its first term, for seizing this opportunity."

The Government was already planning to act on issues of crime on the Gold Coast and the Broadbeach fracas merely fast-tracked its response. Via phone from Japan, Campbell spoke to his Attorney-General Jarrod Bleijie and Police Minister Jack Dempsey. Together they would soon change the landscape of policing in Queensland with the nation's most radical overhaul of law and order legislation. They already believed existing laws weren't adequate or harsh enough. For whatever reason, police also seemed reluctant to take on the criminal bikie gangs with the force and vigilance the situation had long demanded. The final tipping point in the urgent need for action was a comment from a Gold Coast bikie who boldly declared in the media: "We own the streets". Campbell was incredulous the bikie situation had been allowed to reach this low point:

> Criminal bikies had long held the view that they were running things, that they owned the streets. That was their attitude. So the Government of Queensland needed to demonstrate that, actually no, Queenslanders owned their streets through their government. The situation required a complete change of attitude and approach. I had to push the police hard at the beginning. Police had in my view a cosy co-existence approach with criminal bikies. On the very night of the Broadbeach brawl, you had senior police calling the Sergeant at Arms of a gang saying 'you guys have to settle down'. I just said that's not on, we need to crush them, we need to put them out of business. You're not the United Nations who have to deal with all parties in a fair and equitable manner. They are organised criminal gangs and you have to shut them down. So I came down very hard on a number of senior police. I expected results or heads would roll. And to their credit, they rose to the occasion and I'm very proud of

what they did. They had 20 years of Labor Governments and they wouldn't have expected to see politicians show such resolve. They had 20 years of being told not to pursue criminals on chases, while not having helicopters to pursue them via air, so the criminals knew they could get away. That was the Labor Party and that's what police came to expect of political administrations.

On 16 October 2013, just three weeks after the Broadbeach brawl, Attorney General Bleijie introduced the Vicious Lawless Association Disestablishment Act into Parliament. In a marathon session that ended just before 3am, the package of bills was passed with bipartisan support after being declared urgent to bypass the lengthy committee process. Civil libertarians, sections of the legal fraternity, the bikies and their supporters went into a state of apoplexy, particularly over the anti-association provisions. They claimed members of Scout groups or footy clubs could be arrested under the new VLAD laws and described the Government's attempt to crush criminal bikie gangs as "unAustralian". Other provisions in the bills such as the presumption against bail for criminal gang members caused untold outrage.

Independent MP Peter Wellington staged a one-man protest outside the Maroochydore Court House by riding a sidecar motorbike containing a mock coffin displaying the sign: "Democracy killed by Newman's VLAD laws." Katter Party MP Shane Knuth – who defected to the minor party from the LNP in October 2011 – said the laws were killing off "bush pubs" that had long enjoyed the patronage of cruising gangs of criminal bikies. In its editorial of 8 January 2014, *The Age* described the VLAD laws as a "draconian and dangerous form of government overreach". Revered corruption fighter Tony Fitzgerald weighed in with his opinion that the Government's broader law and order approach was aimed at garnering "redneck support".

The wails of protests from some quarters and the clever PR

campaigns by criminal gangs – playing up their charity motorbike rides and the claims of innocent riders being targeted by police – appeared to have an impact on the Labor Opposition. First, Labor voted for the VLAD laws when the package of bills was introduced into the Parliament on 16 October. A few months later in mid-February, with pressure mounting against the VLAD laws, Annastacia Palaszczuk declared a future Labor Government would keep the laws but send the legislation to a Parliamentary committee for review. Within another three weeks, Palaszczuk changed tack again, vowing to scrap the VLAD laws altogether.

Meanwhile, Campbell and Attorney-General Bleijie received threats and were assigned extra personal security amid fears of retaliation from criminal bikie gangs. In February 2014, a 26-year-old man from Caboolture on Queensland's Sunshine Coast was arrested for threatening to kill Campbell and Lisa Newman in a message he posted via social media.

As Labor flip-flopped on its position regarding the VLAD laws, support in the broader community gained momentum. Soon after the laws were introduced, police began a series of successful raids on bikie strongholds and business confidence rebounded on the Gold Coast. The increasing support didn't stop the bikie gangs launching a challenge to the VLAD laws in the High Court in March, forcing other states such as South Australia to wait for the outcome before introducing similar legislation in their own jurisdictions. But as the months rolled on through the first half of 2014, bikies were seen packing up and moving interstate. The tide was finally turning.

Later in the year, when the High Court eventually rejected the criminal gang's challenge to the VLAD Laws and crime rates started to drop, the crackdown was legitimised in the eyes of the wider community. Beyond the ongoing cries of protest from the bikie gangs and their supporters, the VLAD laws became one of the Newman

Government's strongest selling points as it looked toward the next election, due the following year in 2015.

After advocating so stridently for urgent, zero tolerance action, columnist Madonna King never did write a follow up column with any praise or commendations for the Government's success in tackling crime, though she claimed to have supported the measures on "more than one occasion" on Brisbane radio station 4BC.[85]

The appointment of Tim Carmody

During the turbulent course of its early development and implementation, the criminal bikie gang crackdown inadvertently sparked a separate and concurrent war within the judiciary. It started shortly after Tim Carmody QC was sworn in as Queensland's new Chief Magistrate on 18 September 2013, nine days before the bikie brawl at Broadbeach. On 4 November, Carmody had issued a Practice Direction to his fellow magistrates ordering all bikie-related bail applications to be listed for hearing in a specific Brisbane courtroom. This meant bail applications would be heard by up to four Brisbane-based magistrates. Carmody's intention was to ensure the applications were heard by senior or experienced magistrates as well as allow the Office of the Director of Public Prosecutions to appear at each bail application. He believed this would improve the professionalism of the bail application process.

But the edict was interpreted as an overt and deliberate slight on his colleague's capabilities, as well as further evidence of his perceived support for the Newman Government's anti-bikie crusade. Leading judges, members of the Queensland Bar Association and others in the legal fraternity lined up to attack him over the directive, calling for his immediate resignation. The first salvo in an almighty judicial showdown between Carmody and a mob of legal elites had been fired.

As if in sync, the Newman Government was embroiled in its

own war of words with elements of the legal and judicial fraternity. Having already upset them over comments he made questioning their integrity on matters related to criminal bikie gangs, Campbell went a step further with a scathing attack on judges in a radio interview in late-October 2013. His comments reflected the views of so many in the community who lived beyond the comfortable enclaves enjoyed by the inner-city chattering classes. During the course of the past three years or so, Campbell had direct discussions with hundreds of Queenslanders who were fed up with crime on their streets. They were sick of having their homes broken into, their cars stolen and their suburbs rendered unsafe by a mellow law and order system. Campbell told 4BC Radio on 24 October:

> They [judges] are living literally in an ivory tower. They go home at night to their comfortable, well-appointed homes, they talk amongst themselves, they socialise together, they don't understand what my team and I understand, and that is Queenslanders have had enough. We had a very, very terrible thing happen in this country in the last couple of years, where a female journalist, Jill Meagher, was raped and murdered by someone who should never have been let out of jail. At the time nationally, and of course in Victoria, there was a huge to-do, people asking how could this happen, why did this happen, calling for tough penalties, calling for action. If that had happened in Queensland, we would have been absolutely distraught as a Government. With these new laws, we believe it won't happen because we will have the tools to keep people like that in jail. 'That is what this is about and those people who continue to criticise and carp, they are not offering solutions.[86]

With Penelope Wensley's term as Queensland Governor due to expire in mid-2014, the then Chief Justice Paul de Jersey was her obvious replacement. To fill the vacancy created by Justice de Jersey's preordained move to Government House, a short-list of candidates to be considered as the next Chief Justice was drawn up by Attorney-General Jarrod Bleijie and some of his top advisers in the latter part of 2013. From the very start Carmody was a strong contender, but by no means the preferred candidate. Either way he was never going to be an easy sell in certain legal circles.

The then Chief Magistrate had impressed the Government with his thorough examination of the state's child protection system as chair of the Commission of Inquiry, handed down in mid-2013. He had five years' experience as a Family Court Judge, the equivalent in status to a seat on the Supreme Court. He had been Queensland's inaugural Crime Commissioner and was a Queen's Counsel. Carmody's no-nonsense approach to the administration of justice had impressed many within the legal fraternity and the Newman Government.

Campbell and the Attorney-General also gravitated to Carmody's inspiring life story. As a former public housing kid who grew up to study law while serving as a police officer in the 1970s, Carmody came with a powerful narrative. But that type of inspiring career journey was foreign to some figures in the judicial elite. Brisbane's judicial establishment was a tight knit club Carmody didn't really belong to. For Campbell and his Attorney-General, that was part of the attraction in considering him for the appointment. The Newman Government wanted to deliver on the community's calls for an administration to be brave enough to overhaul and recalibrate the state's justice system.

Throughout the all-consuming furore from late 2013 onwards, Bleijie's rationale for supporting Carmody as the state's next Chief Justice was the LNP's tough law and order platform during the 2012 election, as well as Carmody's performance in his earlier roles, for which he had received plaudits from the legal community. In addition, Carmody's firm independence from the judicial elite and his practical approach was a telling contrast with the other candidates being considered. Above all, Carmody was a man who reflected the community he was expected to serve.

As the driver of the Newman Government's law and order agenda, including reforms to youth justice and child sex predator laws, as well as the anti-bikie crackdown, Bleijie had upset the legal apple cart early in his tenure as Attorney-General. In the face of repeated calls for his resignation by some in the legal elite, Bleijie was unyielding in his delivery of justice and legal reform, and his ability to drive change within his portfolio responsibilities was respected by the Premier (in a similar way to other Ministers in their respective portfolios such as David Crisafulli, John McVeigh, Tim Mander, Andrew Powell and Springborg). But that was part of Bleijie's problem, and that of the Government. He was delivering too much change too quickly, and was so busy defending his actions and batting away criticisms he didn't have enough clear air to sell the positive results of his reforms.

In early 2014, separate robust discussions on the pros and cons of up to five candidates went back and forth between Campbell, his Attorney-General Jarrod Bleijie, Tim Nicholls, Jeff Seeney and Campbell's chief of staff Ben Myers. Opinion was split almost down the middle. Myers made a handwritten note in early 2014 strongly advising against Carmody's appointment. Seeney had earlier said he would back Bleijie's decision, while Nicholls had long rejected Carmody. Another Minister and former lawyer Ian Walker also opposed his appointment.

On 25 February 2014, when Justice de Jersey was officially anointed as the new Queensland Governor, speculation was already rife that Carmody would be named his replacement as Chief Justice. Some in the judicial and legal elite had other ideas. Justice Margaret McMurdo, the state's second-highest ranking judge at the time, would later emerge as a key opponent to the appointment.

Earlier in her career, back in July 1998, McMurdo had been appointed to the lofty role of President of the Queensland Court of Appeal by the Beattie Government, one month after it was elected. At the time, the elevation of a relatively junior judge of the District Court to the Court of Appeal was unprecedented. Having spent most of her recent working life at the Public Defender's Office and having sat only on the District Court as a judge, McMurdo had never been a Senior or Queen's Counsel. Her elevation attracted a degree of concern at the time from within legal circles. However, in stark contrast to Carmody, she was afforded the benefit of the doubt by the judicial and legal fraternity, and given time to prove herself in the role. The irony of her conduct towards Carmody many years later was not lost on members of the legal profession. McMurdo was elevated to her role as President of the Court of Appeal while having far less experience and qualifications than Carmody at the time of his appointment. She had received so much support from the judiciary and the profession when she most needed it. But as the months rolled on after Carmody's appointment, McMurdo appeared unable to comprehend she was now sitting in a proverbial glass house throwing stones. Despite being a champion of women's rights, it is not known if McMurdo ever appreciated that the criticisms being directed at Carmody caused great personal harm to his wife and daughters.

A few years after her elevation to the Court of Appeal, the Beattie Government also appointed her husband Philip McMurdo to an important judicial role as a Supreme Court judge, an appointment that was widely acclaimed and supported.

Later that same year, in August 2003, Margaret McMurdo was one of three judges involved in the appeal hearing of Pauline Hanson, who was serving jail time for electoral fraud. When Hanson was released in a judgement led by the then Chief Justice Paul de Jersey, McMurdo leapt to national prominence with an unusual foray into the political arena. While Justice de Jersey maintained the tradition of an honourable silence, McMurdo heaped criticism on the then Prime Minister John Howard and backbencher Bronwyn Bishop, among other politicians, for their expression of concern about Hanson's jail sentence. Howard and Bishop in particular felt Hanson's original three-year sentence was too harsh. In her written judgement on the appeal case, McMurdo said those comments "could have been seen as an attempt to interfere with the independence of the judiciary for cynical political motives".

Just over a decade later in 2014, the now 59-year-old Justice McMurdo dramatically returned to the political battleground with a pointed attack on the current crop of conservative politicians. McMurdo used a speech at the Queensland Women Judicial Officers and Barristers function on 21 March to accuse the Government of having an "unconscious bias" against female judicial appointments. When her comments made it into *The Courier-Mail*, Bleijie returned fire. He highlighted what he believed was her hypocrisy by relaying details of their recent meeting in which she had privately discussed the potential for two men to be considered for promotion, including her husband. Bleijie also sought advice on the potential promotion of a sitting female judge, a candidate McMurdo rejected.

All judicial hell broke loose from this point on. Some in the legal fraternity demanded Bleijie be sacked. With a typically equal measure of eminent common sense and political recklessness, Campbell responded in an ABC Radio interview, reflecting similar comments made that day in the media by prominent barrister Tony Morris QC. On 25 March 2014, Campbell said:

> The President of the Court of Appeal Justice McMurdo ... has chosen to enter the political arena and criticise this Government, the Government I lead. Now if you want to go into the political arena, the public arena, then you have to be prepared that people will respond and defend their position.

Campbell's sentiments echoed the words of Tim Carmody, who had earlier said: "The separation of powers doctrine is a two-way street".

The spat between Bleijie and McMurdo fed into the campaign to derail Carmody's potential appointment. As rumours gathered pace that he would be the new Chief Justice, some members of the legal fraternity launched a series of extraordinarily vitriolic attacks on his suitability for the role. High-profile barrister and former Queensland Solicitor-General Walter Sofronoff QC lashed out at Carmody and the Government. As Solicitor-General, Sofronoff had earlier played a lead role in formulating the VLAD laws before quitting in a huff, accusing the Government of breaching the separation of powers doctrine. In an inflammatory opinion piece published in *The Courier-Mail* on 9 June 2014 – weeks before any announcement of the next Chief Justice was due to be made – Sofronoff wrote:

> A truly suitable Chief Justice must have long experience and successful experience in practice. And he or she must have the confidence of the profession. There are serving judges of the Supreme Court who satisfy these requirements but Judge Carmody does not. Since the Attorney-General does not have the insight to do so, Judge Carmody should himself quell this present unfortunate and unhealthy speculation about him by stating forthrightly that he would not accept an appointment to the office of Chief Justice if it were offered to him. He would, thereby, instantly gain the respect of his colleagues, including me.[87]

The petulance of the higher legal fraternity was backed by Tony Fitzgerald, the untouchable former judge and corruption buster. As part of his escalating attacks on the Newman Government, Fitzgerald joined calls for Carmody to rule himself out of contention for the top judicial job. As a young barrister, Carmody had worked on the

Fitzgerald Inquiry between 1987 and 1989. That shared history failed to temper Fitzgerald's accusation that his former junior colleague may have been on the verge of allowing his "ambition to subvert his personal integrity."

It was in the midst of this volatile climate that Campbell and Jarrod Bleijie tried to reach a decision on the next Chief Justice. During one such discussion, late into Friday night on 30 May 2014, Bleijie was sitting around the dining table at the Newman household with Campbell and Lisa Newman. At Campbell's request, Bleijie presented him with a folder full of endorsements from a range of senior legal figures backing Carmody. Given the vocal opposition to Carmody's appointment, the Premier wanted to hear from his supporters. It was an impressive list, but for the most part they were reluctant to come forward. After a lengthy discussion, no decision was made that night. Bleijie continued to consult with the legal community in the days and weeks afterwards, as did Campbell.

As the attacks on Carmody escalated, there was a keen sense of empathy in Campbell's ultimate decision to back him. The way Sofronoff and other senior legal figures were behaving in their attempts to blast Carmody out of contention for the role of Chief Justice rankled Campbell. Like the relentless media attacks the Newman family had experienced back in the election campaign of 2011-12, Carmody himself was subjected to the indignation of intense personal pressure from vested interests and a pack of journalists increasingly hungry for blood.

As the months rolled through the first half of 2014 and no decision was reached, the pressure on Carmody's family first began taking its toll, like it had on the Newman and Monsour families a few years earlier.

The behaviour of some in the legal elite during their campaign against Carmody before he was even appointed reinforced the belief within Campbell and his Attorney-General that cultural change in the judiciary was long overdue.

The turmoil engulfing Carmody was a prizefight the Premier was ready and willing to engage in. While Campbell still had reservations about the appointment, Carmody made sense to him on a practical level. Justice was delayed for too many Queenslanders and getting outcomes from the court had become so expensive it was out of reach for average citizens. The Newman Government believed administrative costs were out of control because judges refused to modernise the system. Suggestions such as video-conferencing for court mentions in remote areas were scoffed at before any debate began. And judges were never subjected to any accountability or performance measures. Official scrutiny of judges appeared to be off-limits. Campbell and the Attorney-General were convinced Tim Carmody was going to set it right by reforming the courts with common sense leadership and practical changes.

The day before Carmody was appointed, they met with him in Campbell's Ashgrove electorate office. A particularly virulent attack on Carmody that had appeared in the media that day finally pushed Campbell to reach a conclusion.

After Carmody was named Chief Justice on 12 June 2014, the judicial feud escalated into an even greater firestorm of rage and disdain. Bar Association of Queensland president Peter Davis QC resigned in protest at the alleged leaking of conversations he had earlier had with the Attorney-General, and subsequently was more than happy to appear in the media to air his critical views on Carmody's appointment. The Labor Party subsequently approached Davis to run in one of the seats it hoped to capture in the 2015 election. The attacks also continued through Carmody's tenure from both sitting and former Supreme Court Judges. Margaret McMurdo later refused to sit on any court with Carmody, while Alan Wilson, a District Court judge who had been promoted to the Supreme Court by the Bligh

Government, used his own farewell from the Bench to launch a vicious attack on Carmody. Earlier in the saga, Court of Appeal judge John Muir had also joined the fray with a critical and sarcastic speech at a North Queensland event, followed by an email to his fellow Nudgee College "old boys" outlining in rugby parlance why Carmody wasn't good enough to captain the judicial team. Muir's conduct as one of Queensland's most senior Judges created fantastic headlines in the media, naturally. However, as testament to Carmody's character, the Chief Justice later made a point of shaking Muir's hand and wishing him well in his retirement at Muir's official send off some six months after the attacks were aired.

In a collective show of disrespect, up to 25 Supreme Court Judges snubbed Carmody's public welcoming ceremony on 1 August. They had left him to "cut a lonely figure"[88] on the bench alongside new Supreme Court Justice Peter Flanagan. Their absence flew in the face of the huge turnout at the event by members of the legal profession and a conciliatory speech by the new President of the Bar Association Shane Doyle QC. Not to be outdone, Tony Fitzgerald proclaimed that Carmody's appointment would cause "irreversible" damage to the courts. The unrelenting nature of the attacks, in the end, made Carmody's position untenable.

Less than 12 months after being named Chief Justice by the Newman Government, Carmody resigned on 1 July 2015. The campaign of bullying and its impact on his wife and family were too much. Friends of Carmody believed he had the resilience to carry on, but also understood the impact the saga was having on his family. In his resignation letter published to the profession, Carmody asked his supporters to forgive him. They already had, knowing he had put his family first and the interests of the Supreme Court above his own.

For a range of reasons, Carmody's appointment became the decision Campbell regretted more than any other in his 13-year political career. With an abiding sense of regret and personal hurt, Campbell reflected on what went wrong:

> I am very upset about it. I'm upset for a whole range of reasons. I'm upset on a personal level because we've got egg all over our faces. I'm upset because we won't see the necessary reform in the court and legal system as a whole. I'm upset that in Queensland the Left now controls the legislature, the executive and the judiciary. I'm upset that we now have the precedent where the judges get to decide who the Chief Justice will be. I'm upset that one of the most public and high-level examples of bullying this country has ever seen has happened and the bullies have won. I'm very upset about it. I'm gutted.

In a most poignant twist, the preparedness of Margaret McMurdo to inject her views into the political domain may have ultimately cost her dearly when Catherine Holmes was announced as Queensland's new Chief Justice on 8 September 2015. Holmes, who maintained a dignified silence throughout the Carmody furore, had actually sworn him in as Chief Justice back in July 2014.

Indigenous land reform

Like so many of the Government's positive achievements, the move to give Indigenous people in remote communities the right to acquire freehold title was in danger of being overshadowed by ongoing controversies and fights. At the height of the Carmody imbroglio, the Indigenous land reform policy was quietly entering its final stages of development. The legislation, formulated by Minister Andrew Cripps and Assistant Minister David Kempton, granted Indigenous communities the "right to dissolve their existing tenure agreements and convert land and homes to freehold lease".

Introduced into the Parliament in May 2014, the reform was

personally important to Campbell. He believed the opportunity for home ownership was a key building block for economic development in the state's impoverished Indigenous communities. Assistant Minister for Aboriginal and Torres Strait Islander Affairs David Kempton, the MP for the vast electorate of Cook that covered Cape York, remembered discussing the idea of freehold title with Campbell during their very first meeting back in 2011. From this initial point it would take more than three years of consultation and development for the historic legislation to be included in Queensland's statute books. Kempton, a former lawyer with decades of experience in Cape York native title matters, explained:

> The Premier was very interested in the concept of freehold home ownership which would in my view go a long way to putting traditional land owners in as close a position of ownership as they held prior to white settlement. The Aboriginal and Torres Strait Islander Land (Providing Freehold) Act 2014 that we passed into law is perhaps the most significant piece of legislation for the future of Aboriginal and Torres Strait Islanders in Queensland. It provides each of the 34 discrete communities with the opportunity to opt into freehold residential ownership.

This landmark reform went largely unrecognised in the broader electorate, and the media only afforded the legislation the most cursory of glances.

By-elections and a dramatic offer

2014 was supposed to be the year the LNP Government hit the reset button. The difficult measures and reforms they had instituted since coming to office were going to bear fruit that year. They were going to sell the positive outcomes achieved in health, education, crime and the economy and put the upheaval of the past two years behind them.

But while the controversies raging at the end of 2013 – the doctor's dispute, the Carmody affair and concerns over the VLAD laws – took a brief break over the Christmas and New Year holiday period, they returned with a vengeance in 2014. Crushing by-election defeats in the seats of Redcliffe and Stafford during the first half of 2014 crystallised the Government's woes. It was during this tumultuous period Campbell offered to stand down as Premier.

The offer came in the wake of the Government's second by-election annihilation in the space of six months. First, it was the 14.4 percent swing against the LNP Government in the seat of Redcliffe on 22 February 2014. That drubbing was largely a hangover from the former LNP member, the disgraced Scott Driscoll. It was a battle Campbell and the Government knew it couldn't win, despite the strong candidacy of local nurse Kerri-Anne Dooley. In a lighter moment leading up to the Redcliffe showdown, LNP Minister and former National Rugby League referee Tim Mander spoke to Campbell about the potential to recruit Brisbane Broncos footy legend Petero Civoniceva as the LNP's candidate in the seat. As Mander animatedly described the potential star power of a household name like Civoniceva, he realised Campbell's blank look was not a reflection of his lack of interest in the potential LNP candidate. Campbell simply didn't know who this Civoniceva bloke was. He enjoyed playing sport, but never did spend much time watching it or following the on-field exploits of others. From a young age, he was always too engrossed in other pursuits.

The second by-election loss of 2014 occurred in the electorate of Stafford on 19 July, with an even bigger 19.1 percent swing against the Government. The former LNP Member Chris Davis, who had stood down over the doctor's contracts and issues related to the CMC, actively campaigned against his former Government and party.

Following a Cabinet meeting on the morning of Monday, 21 July, two days after that savage result in Stafford, Campbell offered up a mea culpa to the electorate. Flanked by his entire Cabinet on a school oval in Brisbane's south, Campbell apologised for "upsetting Queenslanders" and announced the Government was scrapping or winding back several unpopular policies. He told the assembled media:

> We will be doing a lot better in the future to try and explain our decisions and take Queenslanders with us on a bright journey into a very positive future.

That very public acknowledgement of the Government's faults preceded a private bombshell a few weeks later in early August. Knowing the public apology and reversal of some controversial decisions wasn't enough, Campbell believed the only way for the Government to draw a line in the sand and win the next election was for him to resign. The offer was made at a private meeting at Parliament House with LNP president Bruce McIver and the party's state director Brad Henderson, along with Campbell's chief of staff Ben Myers. Pollster Mark Textor was called up and put on speakerphone. Before the discussion about potential timing and logistics for the 2015 campaign began, Campbell put his future on the line. He was blunt and asked McIver, Henderson and Textor if his time was up. He knew his personal brand was a drag on the Government's chances of winning the next election and believed it would be the circuit breaker the administration needed. Those gathered at the meeting rejected the idea, preferring to wait and see what the polling showed after his public apology and the Government's new conciliatory approach, dubbed "Operation Boring" by the media. McIver suggested they hold off until September to better gauge the public mood. Campbell said on reflection:

> I should have gone then and there, I really should have. There would have been enough time, up to six months, for whoever replaced me to set their own course. I assumed I would've lost my seat so I wouldn't be around after the

election anyway. I believed that stepping down really was the best chance we had of winning.

As Campbell's team and the LNP hierarchy had hoped, the second half of the year appeared to herald a changing of the tide. The 31 July release of the final Queensland Plan, a friendlier Budget and preparations for the G20 Leader's Summit in Brisbane all added up to a more positive, attuned approach by the Government. A Newspoll published on 30 September confirmed the turnaround. The LNP was on 54 percent to Labor's 46 percent on a two-party-preferred basis, off the back of a seven point primary vote rise. Campbell's satisfaction rating didn't bounce to the same high degree but was headed in the right direction with an improvement of two percentage points.

Just a few days before that Newspoll was published, the former Labor member for Ashgrove Kate Jones confirmed what most in Brisbane's political circles had long suspected. She would stand in her old seat of Ashgrove against Campbell at the next election. As far back as late-2012, Campbell himself knew Jones would return, telling local councillor Geraldine Knapp and the area's federal MP Jane Prentice of his prediction at the time.

Strong Choices

A week after the 30 September Newspoll, Campbell and his Treasurer Tim Nicholls released the final Strong Choices plan following nearly six months of consultation and advertising. A re-elected LNP Government would reduce the state's debt by $25 billion and fund new infrastructure to the tune of $8.6 billion, as well as establish a $3.4 billion fund to relieve cost of living pressures caused by high electricity bills.

In contrast to the sales pitch on electricity privatisation in New South Wales, the multi-million dollar Strong Choices consultation and advertising drive had mixed results. Its greatest failure was in the area it actually needed to be most successful, and that was in regional Queensland, where voters were more adverse to privatisation than those in south-east Queensland. The campaign was led by Treasurer Tim Nicholls and crafted by Crosby Textor. Brisbane economist Gene Tunny, who supported the concept of asset leasing and the findings of the Commission of Audit, said:

> I think it was reasonably clear that Queensland was on an unsustainable path with respect to debt and we did need to repair the fiscal situation. But I think Strong Choices was a missed opportunity for the Government to really sell the package, to really sell the privatisation agenda. I think the Government was poorly advised on how to go about it. I would have liked to have seen a green paper and a white paper process, a more traditional public service process whereby it's communicated to the public what the issues are and the likely impacts and having that conversation. I was a bit concerned that Strong Choices didn't communicate at the right level. It was just a bit too slick and it didn't allay the public concerns.

With the final plan for Strong Choices released, there was nothing left for the Government to do except seek a mandate for it at the next election.

The G20 Summit on the weekend of 15 and 16 November provided what could have been a watershed moment for the Newman Government at the tail end of 2014. With Barack Obama, David Cameron, Angela Merkel, Xi Jinping, Shinzo Abe and Vladimir Putin among the world leaders attending, the event was on a scale never before seen in Brisbane. Campbell was everywhere during the Summit. One minute he was mixing with officers at the hi-tech police command centre, the next he was talking trade and investment at high-level talks with the Chinese President. The G20 event was flawlessly

Campbell and Lisa Newman enter the 2015 campaign launch, with Jarrod Bleijie looking on from the crowd

managed, particularly in terms of safety and security. Plaudits for the smooth running of the Summit rolled in from all quarters. The positive experience it created for Brisbane prompted Campbell to consider calling a snap election.

As fate would pan out, he was lucky he didn't. A freak storm that hit Brisbane on 27 November, two weeks after the G20, caused significant damage to buildings across the city. The LNP's headquarters at Spring Hill was one of them. The office was inundated with water and the computer network was extensively damaged. The party would not have been able to conduct the campaign if the election had been called on the date Campbell was considering.

The day before the storm, the machinations of Government were far from Campbell's thoughts. He had joined Lisa and her family at a Requiem Mass at St Brigid's Church to farewell their beloved matriarch Elizabeth Monsour, who had died unexpectedly on 20 November. In lieu of flowers, the family requested mourners pledge donations to the Home-Away from Homelessness program, an Anglicare project to help homeless women that Elizabeth was passionate about. Like Kevin and Jocelyn Newman, Lisa's parents Frank and Elizabeth Monsour had always given so much of themselves in service to the community.

Election speculation

As 2014 drew to a close, and his offer to resign put to bed, Campbell began talking with Myers and close confidants about the timing of the upcoming election, which had to be held by June 2015. Two key considerations about timing played on his mind. The first was the increasingly unhelpful behaviour of the Abbott Government. The second was the big-spending and relentlessly militant approach of the unions. With Federal Parliament sitting for the first time in 2015 on 9 February, Campbell decided it was best to hold the election before MPs flew back into Canberra. There were fears Prime Minister Tony Abbott would face a leadership challenge in the first Parliamentary week of the year, a distraction the LNP Government in Queensland couldn't afford in the midst of a re-election campaign, already fraught with enough challenges.

Most of all, Campbell and his team were concerned about the tactics of the unions. At the Redcliffe and Stafford by-elections, the Queensland Council of Unions had spent a fortune running prolonged grass roots campaigns, not to mention vile verbal assaults on Lisa Newman, her daughters and her sister Heidi. The unions had flown in volunteers from across the country to door-knock and man polling booths, vastly outnumbering the LNP's local efforts in those two by-elections. With damaging effect, the unions had also dressed up some volunteers in firefighter's uniforms. The "fake firies" were telling voters the LNP Government had closed down fire stations. The Government had done no such thing, but there was no way to counter the lies as people walked in to cast their votes at the booths in Redcliffe and Stafford.

Over the Christmas and New Year break, Campbell considered three potential dates for the upcoming election: 31 January, 7 February and 14 February. He spoke to John Howard, who favoured 7 February. LNP President Bruce McIver favoured 21 March, the same day as the NSW election. He felt it would effectively split the resources of the unions. Opinions remained divided on how the date of 31 January was eventually decided upon at a final pre-election meeting, attended by the leadership teams of both the Government and the LNP. Regardless, the rumours about a snap election surfaced in the media on 5 January. The next morning, reporters were waiting outside the Newman household as Campbell left for his morning run. He threw protocol to the wind and confirmed the rumours. He visited Queensland Governor Paul de Jersey later that morning to make it official. Queenslanders were heading to the polls on 31 January 2015.

10

A New Journey

January 2015: state election campaign

The final curtain of Campbell Newman's political career came down more than two days before the election, held on Saturday, 31 January 2015. It happened as he sat in the front passenger seat of a local MP's car, parked and idling on a tarmac at Cairns Airport on the Thursday morning of 29 January. With the early tropical heat bouncing off the bitumen and a busload of journalists waiting behind them, Campbell wasn't really sure what to do next. But having just returned to the campaign's chartered plane after a disastrous media conference, Campbell knew one thing for certain: his time as Premier was over.

At one portentous point, he turned to the driver of the car, the local backbench MP Michael Trout, and said: "That's the last press conference I'll ever have to do … that's the last time I'll ever have to talk to that pack of bastards."

The mob of reporters waiting to board the plane behind Trout's car had no idea Campbell was being torn in two directions right before their eyes. His media team wanted him to ditch the planned whistlestop visit to Townsville and return immediately to Brisbane. With their own electoral fortunes in mind, Government MPs in Townsville were imploring him to continue to their city as part of the final regional tour of the campaign. After the impasse had dragged on for more than 30 minutes, a decision was finally reached.

The reporters on the bus tweeted up a storm. At 10:25am, *Brisbane Times* reporter Amy Remeikis posted: "Seems like the LNP campaign has smelled blood in the water – in a massive change in plans, it's abandoning its seat blitz to return to Brisbane."

Campbell's Brisbane-based media team, led by Lee Anderson, had won the argument. They didn't want Campbell doing another media conference after the one he had just fronted. Just before 10am, Campbell was crowded into a small meeting room at Trout's electorate office, surrounded by the media pack.

He faced another barrage of questions about two familiar topics. Despite being in Far North Queensland to announce an important road upgrade worth $50 million, the media only wanted to know two things. Yet again, they demanded answers on who would be Premier when Campbell lost his seat. That outcome was now universally accepted as inevitable. The night before, a Seven News/Reachtel poll showed Labor's Kate Jones was ahead by 8 percentage points in Ashgrove. The reporters asked the same questions about Ashgrove they had asked for the entire campaign, and the campaign before that in 2012. They were hoping in vain for a different answer to the one they had received every other day they had asked it.

The second topic du jour was Tony Fitzgerald and his latest attack on the LNP Government. Shortly after news broke of the Ashgrove polling figures on Channel 7, Fitzgerald appeared on the ABC's *The 7:30 Report*. He accused the LNP Government of laying the "foundations" for a return to the type of corruption he had exposed in the 1980s. It was the latest in a series of grenades lobbed at the Government by Fitzgerald over the past 18 months.

The media had shown little interest in policies or costings of either side during the campaign. On this Thursday, less than 48 hours before the polls opened, they were salivating in anticipation at what Campbell's response would be to Fitzgerald's latest broadside. It was lazy journalism, the customary call and response reporting borne of convenience and habit. Instead of scrutinising the validity of Fitzgerald's hyperbolic comments, the media only had to get a response from Campbell, and their job was done. A couple of grabs here, a line or two in response there and, *voilà*, they would have their story of the day.

Campbell's media team knew the journos would only be interested in those two topics, so they briefed him via a phone hookup as he sat at the front of the bus descending the nauseatingly serpentine Kuranda Range Rd. As the reporters sat at the back of the bus tweeting and chatting, Campbell was war-gaming the upcoming media conference. He was prepped to say the line "I have the greatest respect for Tony Fitzgerald." Whether by design or by default, Campbell added the word "had" when the reporters asked for his response to Fitzgerald's claims: "I have had the greatest respect for him in the past."

Later, as he sat on the tarmac trying to figure out where to direct the plane next, Campbell almost looked relieved. He had long given up on seeing serious topics of policy and a debate about the future of Queensland in the media. Reporters were only focused on the politics of politics, on polling and personalities, and getting Campbell to respond to the latest grenade thrown his way by an opponent or critic. Michael Trout recalled:

> One minute Campbell was on the phone to (Minister) David Crisafulli, who wanted him in Townsville as planned, and the next he was on the phone to Lee Anderson who wanted him back in Brisbane. I'll never forget he turned and looked at me with those eyes that can look straight through you, and he just said 'I'm done.' He'd had enough. He knew his time was up. He said the media didn't want to know about policies and the good things we'd done in Government. All they wanted to do was pull down a good Government. The media knew they'd got what they wanted out of him at that press conference, and he was done.

The difference between the treatment and scrutiny of Campbell during this campaign compared with his Labor opponent Annastacia

Palaszczuk had been stark. Labor released a handful of policies, none of them particularly detailed. They didn't need to. The media wasn't interested in policy debate and the union's negative campaign against the Strong Choices asset program was working, particularly in regional areas. Palaszczuk just had to blurt out constant reminders about the "fights, hubris, arrogance and division" of the Newman LNP Government, and coast along for the ride.

Campbell's memory turned back to the 2011-12 campaign assault on his wife, family and integrity. He didn't wish that style of campaigning on anybody. But if Palaszczuk and her deputy Jackie Trad had their personal lives and backgrounds invaded with the same level of scrutiny and venom as the Newman family endured, the campaign might've played out differently.

Turning points

Three weeks before he was sitting on that tarmac in Far North Queensland, the campaign was humming. Campbell's shock call to go so early in January caught the unions and Labor – not to mention his own Ministers and MPs – off guard and it benefited the incumbent Government. From the outset, Campbell followed the campaign script to the letter. The strategy, written up by a team at the LNP led by state director Brad Henderson and pollsters Crosby Textor, focused on the Government's "strong team with a strong plan".

A re-elected LNP Government would use the expected $37 billion in funds raised by the Strong Choices asset leasing program to pay down debt and build a raft of new infrastructure and other projects across the state. For the first two weeks of the campaign, some minor hiccups aside, Campbell and the LNP were clearly ahead. While it was widely accepted the LNP would lose a bunch of seats in a natural correction, there was never any suggestion it would lose government.

The campaign's course took its first diversion at a people's forum featuring the two leaders on 23 January. Standing next to Palaszczuk on a stage at the Broncos Leagues Club, fielding questions from a group of about 100 so-called "undecided" voters, Campbell was asked about the Government's criminal motorcycle gang laws. Campbell answered with a claim that criminal bikie gangs were funding the unions, who in turn passed on those ill-gotten gains to the Labor Party. Campbell targeted the militant Construction, Forestry, Mining and Energy Union in particular. When asked by the media the following day to provide evidence of his claim, Campbell told the reporters to "Google it".

On the campaign trail at Toowoomba with Lisa. Pic credit: Dominika Lis

The media were taken aback at the suggestion they should do some research and fact-checking of their own, and duly ridiculed Campbell for his advice. His claim was based on a series of revelations about the unions over the past 12 months.

In July 2014, a longtime official from the CFMEU had been outed as a member of the Rebels. *The Herald Sun* newspaper had published a series of photos of Stu-e Corkran in full Rebels regalia. One photo showed he had shaved the infamous "1 percent" logo into his hair, a symbol of the bikie gang's beloved "outsider" status from 99 percent of society. Corkran was charged for his role in a demarcation dispute between the CFMEU and AWU over the construction of Melbourne's West Gate Bridge. The charges were later dropped in a plea bargain. This was the matter Campbell referred to when he told the reporters to do some research. But it wasn't the only link between the unions and criminal bikie gangs he was alluding to.

When the Government's anti-bikie crackdown in 2013 was in its infancy, the unions were helping to fund the bikie gang's High Court challenge to the VLAD laws. Union-affiliated groups had donated $15,000 to a legal fighting fund set up by the gangs. Campbell was also aware of video footage that would soon emerge showing Electrical Trades Union boss Peter Simpson speaking at a criminal bikie gang rally in protest at the VLAD laws. In the video, Simpson boasted of seeing bikie gang members handing over "wads of cash" to support union members during the 1998 Maritime Union of Australia's dispute with the then Howard Government. In his speech, Simpson said:

> Some people are a bit nervous about being associated with bikies … I'm proud to say that the Electrical Trade Union aren't. I know some guys in motorcycle clubs, some of our guys have got good relationships with guys in motorcycle clubs. The MUA dispute, I remember it well, the bikies rode up to the MUA dispute bringing wads of cash to support the guys on the picket line, I was there with them.

On cue, the Labor Party and unions accused Campbell of "gutter tactics" for making the claim at the Friday night debate. The issue ran in the media for nearly 48 hours until Sunday, 25 January, when the reporters found another line of attack.

Sick and tired of answering questions about trivial matters at media conferences, Campbell wanted to talk about the economy and job creation. The reporters weren't interested. A debate on the future of the state's economy, the Budget and infrastructure funding would have to wait. When he refused to answer the media's questions about the politics of campaigning – including his prospects in Ashgrove – they mocked him. Campbell was insistent, telling the media pack: "I'm answering the questions that Queenslanders are asking."

The media lacerated Campbell's "refusal" to answer their questions, more than 30 in total. His performance in response to the questions was always going to generate the type of wrath and condemnation it received from the reporters. Taking on the groupthink approach of a media pack trapped in its own bubble was nigh on impossible at the best of times, let alone in the heat of an election campaign. With a sense of confected outrage, the reporters went to town on Campbell. In his typically pompous style, Channel 9's Shane Doherty huffed and puffed into the camera on the news that night, sneering: "By the way Premier, I'm a Queenslander … we all are."

The contrast of images between the two leaders shown on that evening's TV news was stark. There was Campbell in a crisp white shirt and blue tie, facing a grilling in front of a dark background adorned with Australian flags. In the same news package, a smiling and relaxed Annastacia Palaszczuk was filmed playing barefoot cricket in a park.

Later that same day, Prime Minister Tony Abbott announced the awarding of a knighthood to Prince Phillip. The bizarre choice for the nation's highest honour crowded out all other issues when Campbell faced the media on Monday, 26 January, the day after the announcement. Campbell said he didn't agree with the "captain's call" by Abbott and described it as "a bolt out of the blue". Another 24-hour news cycle was lost.

At this point, Labor was skating through the campaign. They had released flimsy policies on health and education but had not yet outlined a debt reduction strategy. No-one in the media seemed to notice. They applied minimal pressure on the alternative Premier and provided no analysis of her plans for the future of Queensland. With families back from holidays and returning to work and school on Tuesday, 27 January, the LNP's campaign was at its nadir at the exact point voters were finally tuning into the election. In that final week of the campaign, the unions ramped up their asset sales propaganda and no-one in the LNP countered it. Treasurer Tim Nicholls was missing in action. Worse still, a planned all-out negative advertising assault against Labor, due to be coordinated out of LNP headquarters, never eventuated.

The planned negative advertising blitzkrieg was described by one campaign insider as "a carpet bombing of unprecedented magnitude". The TV and radio ads were supposed to dominate the airwaves right through to the media advertising blackout at midnight on Wednesday, 28 January. The attacks ads were going to remind voters of the reasons they booted Labor out of office less than three years earlier, and link Palaszczuk to the Bligh Government, including her own failures as a former Cabinet Minister. Instead, the party's campaign headquarters abandoned the plan, fearing it would be seen as too aggressive. Instead, they persisted with ads featuring surf boats and "strong" slogans. This proved to be a catastrophic error by LNP campaign director Brad Henderson and his team.

Marketing professional Toby Ralph, a veteran of more than 50 election campaigns, was astonished at the lack of negative advertising by the LNP:

> I had conversations during the election with the person making the advertising for Labor, who said the party could

not believe they were not being attacked. At the time she said, 'It's as if we're throwing stones at armed police and they are getting hit but ignoring us'. The lack of attack ads reinforced an important perception with the electorate: that Labor were not a real concern as the LNP were so confident of a win that they were not even bothering to raise the risk they might represent in a serious way. This reinforced Labor's ability to be used as a protest vote.

Another key turning point during the campaign was the confusion over the LNP's election promises. Voters were told they would only get the local projects the LNP was promising if their specific LNP member or candidate was elected. Voters and commentators viewed the move as a form of blackmail, and recoiled at the suggestion. Still, despite the LNP's horror stretch in that final week, no-one really believed Labor could win the election. A hung Parliament was only ever considered a remote possibility.

An embarrassing gaffe by Palaszczuk on 29 January, the same day as Campbell's media conference in Far North Queensland, provided a late fillip for the LNP campaign team. During a live quiz segment on Brisbane's 97.3FM, Palaszczuk was asked: "The goods and services tax is taxed at what percentage?" She replied: "Pass."

The radio hosts and listeners were stunned. For a moment the LNP thought it would be the turning point they'd been waiting for. *The Courier-Mail* ran the blunder on its front page the next day with the headline: "Annastacia Palaszczuk has one question for Queenslanders: should I be Premier? PASS."

Palaszczuk merely laughed and brushed off the gaffe: "Three radio interviews, didn't have my coffee, so, you know, these things happen."

Instead of backfiring in the style of John Hewson's notorious "birthday cake" GST blunder, the gaffe somehow made Palaszczuk appear more human. When Campbell was told of her slip-up during the bus ride back to Cairns Airport, it didn't change his view of his chances at the ballot box. His "campaign U-turn" from Cairns back to Brisbane was seen as a sign of panic, and in terms of his chances in Ashgrove, it was.

48 hours to go

On the day before the polls opened, a lunch-time debate at the Brisbane Conference and Exhibition Centre between the two leaders provided one last opportunity for a knock-out blow against Palaszczuk and Labor. To the surprise of many, Palaszczuk held her own in the debate, buoyed no doubt by tables full of union members audibly laughing and scoffing each time Campbell spoke about the Government's asset leasing plan. Palaszczuk opened her address by describing the election as a battle between "David and Goliath". According to the ABC News report on the debate, Campbell highlighted his Government's plan to lease assets "so we can get the proceeds in to deal with debt, invest in infrastructure, 25,000 jobs and $8.6 billion worth of economic building infrastructure and take Queensland forward giving them the schools, the hospitals, the roads, the bridges that Queenslanders are not just saying that they want but they need".

Palaszczuk also stuck to her script, saying time was running out for Queenslanders to prevent "the sale of our assets". Taking her lead from the unions, she ignored the difference between a lease and a sale, noting that "once our assets are gone, they are gone forever. That's it. No more. Labor makes this commitment to Queensland, we will not sell your assets."

The election

By the end of the campaign, the newspaper editorials were in sync with both public and internal party polling. They all backed the LNP for re-election. The *Australian Financial Review* wrote:

> The issues at the end of campaigning for Queensland's snap

With Lisa at Toowoomba in January 2015. Pic credit: Dominika Lis

election are the same as they were at the start: The Liberal National Party Government has a plan to boost the state economy with new infrastructure, and the wherewithal to carry it out. The Labor Party is promising little more than drift.[89]

The mood across electorates on the morning of 31 January was strangely subdued, particularly when compared with the electric mood for change at the previous Queensland election in 2012. A staggering 25 percent of eligible Queenslanders had already cast their votes at pre-poll booths this time around, one of the highest early turn out rates in Australia's history. Most people, it seemed, had made up their minds. As they filed into school halls and polling places, it was clear they wanted to send a message to the LNP Government. The punters knew the LNP would win and they were sure a kick up the Government's proverbial rear wouldn't hurt. The trouble for Campbell and his Government was that too many voters thought that way, and they all kicked in unison.

Not long after the doors of the polling places were closed at 6pm sharp, Campbell, Lisa and their closest advisers and friends were at the Brisbane Convention and Exhibition Centre waiting for the results to start rolling in on TV screens. Early in the piece, the results were already clear. The LNP had received an almighty shellacking.

Just before 8:30pm, Campbell called Kate Jones to congratulate her on winning back the seat of Ashgrove. After watching the results in a separate room with Lisa, Ben Myers and other close advisers, Campbell strode onto the platform and declared: "My political career is over, it is over". After some cries of "no, no, no" and "go for PM" from the crowd, Campbell told the gathering:

> When the history of this Government is written, people should look long and hard at a political team who did the hard yards and didn't bitch and moan, they got on with the job because they knew they were doing the right thing for Queensland. So to all those who lost their seats, I am sensationally proud of you. I just wish the community knew that you were all men and women of conviction and I wish you the very best in your future career.

Towards the end of his concession speech he turned to Lisa:

> This is the lady, the love of my life, and I thank her for supporting me for 13 years in political office. We are going to go forward together and have a great life together. I want to thank our two daughters who are not here this evening. They are far away. But thanks for their support as well. Finally, ladies and gentlemen ... to all of you, to so many people who have been terrific over the years, thank you for your support. Thank you Queensland, it has been an honour, it has been a privilege.

It would take nearly two weeks for the outcome of the election to be resolved. After a few rounds of tense negotiations and horse-trading with Independent MP Peter Wellington and the pair of Katter Party MPs, the final results showed Queenslanders had unwittingly voted in a hung Parliament. In the most shocking reversal of its fortunes just three years earlier, the LNP had lost the unlosable election. Annastacia Palaszczuk was sworn in as the 39th Premier of Queensland on 14 February 2015. Jackie Trad, one of the architects of Australia's most brutal and poisonous election campaign just a few years earlier, was appointed Deputy Premier.

Toby Ralph believed the LNP's poor handling of the asset leasing program and the failure to manage the expectations of Queenslanders put the LNP in a losing position from the start of the campaign. Ralph's analysis came to the conclusion that Queenslanders wanted a "narrow LNP win", and on the primary vote count they clearly did. When the counting was completed, the LNP had secured 1,084,060 primary votes (41.32 percent), compared to Labor's 983,054 (37.47 percent). In a first past the post system, the LNP would've won 51 of Queensland's 89 seats, compared to 35 for Labor. But Queensland's optional preferential voting system allowed Labor's second-placed candidates to leapfrog the LNP and win enough seats to form a minority Government. According to Ralph:

> Had the LNP managed the asset leasing program competently, presented Labor as a significant risk and managed expectations among voters more appropriately, the LNP would unquestionably have formed Government. It was campaign failure rather than community mood that delivered the loss.

Lisa Newman carried her mother's beloved Rosary beads with her at all times during the Saturday of the election. As they visited booths, thanked volunteers and cast their own votes for the cameras, Lisa was already at peace with the outcome long before it was officially declared:

Quite frankly I've never felt stronger than I did on the night of the 2015 election. I lost my mother in November so I remember thinking at the function afterward that losing an election is no reason to cry. I kept saying to myself and to Cam, 'don't worry, we're going to get through this, we are going to be cool'. I saw it as a great thing that had happened. We can be us again. I feel our connection back again now. This is our new journey.

Epilogue

Reform: A call to arms

Introduction

Campbell Newman is a practical person, a "doer" who had always got things done. He chose to enter state politics to improve the lot of his community, as he had done as Lord Mayor of Brisbane. But he was targeted by a malevolent brand of Labor Party politics which seeks power – not by engaging in a competition of ideas – but by attacking the reputations of those they oppose. Their tactics are legitimised by a cynical and febrile media that feeds off politics as a sport rather than as a construct for good and by a population that consumes news as entertainment.

Campbell's capacity to sell his difficult policy agenda in Government was compromised from the beginning by the mud that was slung at him during the 2011-12 campaign and which followed him into Government. It undermined his credibility and, therefore, his ability to sell difficult and complex policy. The scale of his ambitious agenda – no doubt too large for one term but consistent with the way he had always thrown himself at life – as well as the mistakes he made due to his heightened sensitivities to the tactics of the Left were, ultimately, his undoing.

In this section, the author has taken the views and actions of Campbell Newman to highlight five critical impediments and pathways to reform. The author's own observations and the comments of others are also thrown into the mix. The five topic areas for debate include the media, state-federal relations, the public service, the psyche of inner-city voters and the nature of political leadership.

It is our shared belief that if we allow the status quo of our current political and media systems to continue, the "doers" in our community will run a mile and our democracy will run aground.

The tyranny of the status quo

When Nobel-laureate economist Milton Friedman and his wife Rose coined the phrase "the tyranny of the status quo" in the early 1980s, they had no way of knowing just how entrenched that tyranny would become nearly four decades later. The systemic malaise they described involved an "iron triangle of beneficiaries, politicians, and bureaucrats" working symbiotically to stifle reform and maintain their privileged positions at the expense of the community majority.

Any attempt to disrupt this Iron Triangle – as the Newman Government did in its term – is met with fierce protest from all corners intent on maintaining the status quo. The Friedmans prescribed nothing short of changes to the United States Constitution to break up the Iron Triangle system. The Constitutional amendments they proposed aimed to dilute the power of interlinked vested interest groups, politicians and bureaucrats who mutually benefit from the administration of government subsidies and programs.

The Friedmans believed a new government had less than six months to make tough decisions and major reforms before "the tyranny of the status quo" and the Iron Triangle asserted itself and prevented further changes. By exposing the paradigm of political inertia, the Friedmans hoped they could overthrow this tyranny and facilitate its demise. But they underestimated the challenge.

More than three decades after their theory was published the status quo is stronger than ever. Benefiting from tough decisions and reforms in the 1980s and blessed with the longest period of economic growth of any nation in history, Australia has grown comfortable with its lot in life, resisting attempts by governments to herald in the next round of necessary reforms.

The Friedmans had no way of predicting how entrenched the forces of the status quo and a multitude of Iron Triangles had become. Governments are bigger, red tape is thicker, the bureaucracy is further out of touch with the public it is meant to serve and vested interest groups have more power and influence than ever before.

At the same time, service delivery is lagging behind public demand, despite increased spending. Hospital waiting lists are blowing out, education results are flat-lining and business and the broader community are ever more frustrated at the lack of responsive service, high taxes and convoluted decision-making processes of the bureaucracy. The weight of it all has made Australia's politicians more timid and reluctant to reform than at any point in the past 40 years.

While the Friedman's "tyranny" phrase has long ebbed from public discourse, United Nations Secretary-General Ban Ki-moon momentarily revived it as the centrepiece of his briefing to the General Assembly on the UN's priorities for 2013:

> My fervent hope – and our common urgent need – is that we can stop moving from crisis to crisis, from symptom to symptom, and instead address the underlying causes and inter-relationships, and recognise the flaws in many of our approaches. Issues remain in their silos; worrying trends are allowed to persist and unfold, all because 'that is the way things have been done', or because true change is seen as costly or unrealistic, or entrenched interests have a hold on the legislative machinery. This is no time for business as usual. To shape the future we want, we will have to think and act innovatively and differently. We will have to throw off another brake on our common progress: the tyranny of the status quo.[90]

While Ban Ki-moon's sentiments are admirable, it is ironic that the very institution he leads is an example of the colossal bureaucratic over-reach Milton and Rose Friedman spent their working lives railing against. The UN's constant meddling in the affairs of Australia's management of the Great Barrier Reef – fuelled by virulent misinformation campaigns by well-funded vested interest groups in the environmental movement – is in itself a neat encapsulation of the Iron Triangle at work.

The Diamond Effect

The Friedmans also had no way of foreseeing the detrimental impact on political discourse and reform caused by a declining mainstream media system and the rise of all-pervasive social media networks. So problematic to reform have these two interlinked mediums become, we may well need to update the Friedman's theory from an "Iron Triangle" to the "Diamond Effect".

The Iron Triangle of the past – the bureaucracy, vested interests and politicians who are slaves to them both – was a sufficient descriptor of the tyrannical forces of the status quo in the 1980s. Today's media system adds a fourth corner to the status quo system, creating what we might call the Diamond Effect. Operating within this new framework of quadrilateral parameters, the status quo perpetuated by the public service, special interest groups and elected officials is allowed to continue with the approbation of a shallow mainstream media and the narcissistic echo chamber of social media networks.

The tyranny of the status quo, the power of vested interests, the lack of will to reform by politicians and a spiraling media vacuum all contribute to the climate that is cruelling reform in today's political landscape. That makes the task of contemporary political leaders harder than that of reformers from Australia's modern past.

Reform: process and paradigm

As John Howard pointed out in his 2015 Sir Roland Wilson Oration titled "The Reform Challenge", political leaders of the 1980s and

1990s had the benefit of picking the "low-hanging fruit" of economic reform. The floating of the dollar, the privatisation of government enterprises and the introduction of a broad-based indirect tax took years to materialise and faced hostilities and resistance, primarily Howard's GST. But by the time those reforms were enacted, the need for change had become "self-evident", as Howard concedes.

Today's leaders face a situation much closer to the reform settings observed by Scottish philosopher and social commentator Thomas Carlyle in the mid-19th century. While the Friedmans described the tyrannical paradigm facing a reformist politician, Carlyle noted the painful process they must take their constituencies through to effect change:

> Reform is not pleasant, but grievous; no person can reform themselves without suffering and hard work, how much less a nation.

When you attempt to deliver Carlyle's "grievous" process within Friedman's "status quo" paradigm, you get the type of government and scope of change Campbell Newman tried to lead in Queensland. Campbell never was a fan of the status quo. He had witnessed so much entrenched waste and inefficiency he wasn't interested in playing politics for the sake of maintaining a position of power. Indeed, during the Brisbane floods of 2011 he had literally mopped up the mess of failed planning and mitigation policies of inept governments and bloated bureaucracies.

No government at any level had delivered the pace and breadth of reform the LNP in Queensland had engaged in over such a short period. Campbell was a crusading Premier, but Queensland wasn't sold on the urgent need for change and Budgetary repair. He was the right man for a tough job at the wrong time. During his 13-year political career, he made mistakes and his Government got the politics wrong on a range of issues. But creating change for the better was at the heart of his ambition to run for public office and it fuelled his motivation to fix what he saw as broken, inefficient systems and bad policy outcomes.

To his detriment, he sought to annihilate the status quo during his term as Premier. In the end, he paid the price at the ballot box in the most dramatic reversal of fortunes in Australia's political history. None of the stakeholders in the Diamond Effect wanted the changes the Newman Government saw fit to introduce; be it the bureaucracy, the Opposition, most of the media or special interest groups such as unions, environmental groups, doctors and judges, and even criminal motorcycle gangs.

With the volatility of a voting public willing to throw out a competent, reformist Government because they didn't particularly like the cut of its jib, Campbell Newman's career in state politics begs a critical question. If a Government with the biggest majority in Australia's political history can't deliver hard and necessary decisions without being booted out at the next available opportunity, what hope is there for the future of reform?

Open questions

Veteran political journalist Paul Kelly is adamant the days of "big bang" reform are over. In a 2015 column in *The Australian*, Kelly described Australia as the "rule out" country where policies on jobs, investment and the Budget are rejected "because of the ideological obsessions and electoral calculations of our highly destructive political and media system".

> As we watch the Greece crisis with its gobsmacking exposure of a bankrupt political model and fret endlessly about the latest corrections in China we miss the point entirely — the real problem is not Greece or China. The real problem is Australia. But the penny never seems to drop. We cannot

control events in Greece or China. We have to live with and manage what they throw up. What we do control are events in Australia where a prudent and responsible nation would prepare itself to succeed in a world riddled with multiple uncertainties and potential risks. But we refuse to make such preparation, deluded by our ongoing reprieve from economic downturn and in indulgent denial of the need for long-run economic and social policy reform. The sheer irresponsibility of much of the political class is astonishing yet we treat it with mundane acceptance.[91]

When Campbell Newman's political career came to an end on the night of 31 January 2015, he held even graver fears and concerns for the future of reform. Campbell wondered if Australia had become ungovernable. The nation is in desperate need of serious, structural reform, but more than a decade in politics has fostered doubt in Campbell's mind that any government is capable of it. While a nice personality and incrementalism now appear to be the twin precepts of reform, the scale of our country's challenges grows exponentially.

Questions of reform that Campbell attempted to answer as Premier remain open and ever more urgent.

Where is the government with a plan for reform and the political will to deliver it? Why isn't the media accountable for its actions? What role should the media play in fostering meaningful debate?

Before raising and broadening taxes like the GST, why don't we reform the Federation first? Is there a public service and bureaucracy affordable and responsive enough to facilitate and roll out reform, while meeting the demands of the community, the customers it was established to serve?

Are individual voters arming themselves with the knowledge to assess the problems facing Australia and the policies needed to address them? Do we possess the inherent selflessness to sacrifice and accept hard decisions to progress the national interest? Is social media helping to fuel a narcissistic class of inner-city voters who can't see past their own selfies to realise the hypocrisy of their political discourse and their decisions at the ballot box?

No single stakeholder group should be immune from the questions and challenges of reform facing our nation. From politicians to journalists, public servants and unions, to businesses and individuals, the complex task of reform is too important and urgent to ignore.

The media

TV news anchor Will McAvoy is having an existential crisis and it's happening live to air:

> Adults should hold themselves accountable for failure. And so tonight I'm beginning this newscast by…apologising to the American people for our failure. The failure of this program during the time I've been in charge of it to successfully inform and educate the American electorate. I was an accomplice to a slow and repeated and unacknowledged and unamended train wreck of failures that have brought us to now. The reason we failed isn't a mystery. We took a dive for the ratings.[92]

McAvoy, of course, is the lead character in TV drama series *The Newsroom*. In this episode he decides to bow out of the inexorable race for ratings and instead present news "based on the simple truth that nothing is more important to a democracy than a well-informed electorate".

Campbell Newman agrees wholeheartedly with McAvoy's brutal assessment of the media. He also wonders, like McAvoy, what might have been if early legislators were more forceful when handing over public airspace – owned by the people – to TV and radio stations. In the United States context, McAvoy wishes the networks were forced to provide their nightly hour of news without advertising. Rather than taking a dive for the ratings, they might then have been "champions of facts and the mortal enemy of innuendo, speculation, hyperbole, and nonsense".

Given the lack of self-reflection and accountability from journalists working in the profession today, perhaps it is fitting that the truth should come from a fictional character in a TV drama series.

Quality of debate

An ever increasing amount of newspaper column space and TV airtime is consumed by commentators and journalists pontificating about the poor state of politics in Australia. They lament the "policy atrophy that is the inevitable consequence of hard politics trumping genuine debate" and rail against the death of straight-talk and direct answers in favour of spin and political doublespeak. Reporters sneer and jeer from the sidelines without a skerrick of accountability or nuance, much less any experiential knowledge of what it is they are sneering at.

Ben Myers, Campbell's chief of staff during his time as Premier, points to the void of accountability and self-analysis of the media following its coverage of the 2011-12 Queensland elections campaign. For nearly 12 months, the media unscrupulously reported and broadcast a steady stream of innuendo and allegations against the Newman family, as dished up by the Labor Party. When the allegations were proven to be false, and the campaign was categorised as the dirtiest and most personal in Australia's history, the media escaped without scrutiny. Myers reflected:

> At no stage did the media ask themselves how they became part of this conspiracy Labor and Bligh were running. One thing that has changed in public life is politicians have become more accountable than ever before, but there is no accountability of what the media writes and how they

report it. They demand accountability of others, but never themselves.[93]

After more than a decade in public life and following countless discussions with government leaders across the partisan divide, Campbell is convinced the media is playing a lead role in the debasement of Australian political discourse. Campbell is in no way absolving himself of blame for his 2015 election loss. His frank and concessive assessments of his Government's political failings are featured throughout chapters 8 and 9 of this book. The media, on the other hand, has engaged in no such evaluation of its own deficiencies. Campbell said:

> I am particularly annoyed at the journalists who covered the state election campaign (in 2011-12) and our time in Parliament. Very few of them are interested in what really has to be done. They are not interested in Government or reform or the reasons behind the decisions we made. They are only interested in the tactical, the here and now, they only ever look for short-term politics and gossip. And they have got a nerve to ridicule people like me who tried to actually get things done. And they have always ridiculed and sneered. They have never actually given any benefit of the doubt or been prepared to see the big picture. Their going-in position on every story is that we are idiots, or we're corrupt, or we are doing this out of self-interest. They have no way of divorcing themselves from their inherently negative bias.
>
> Most newspaper editors get it. That's why we got great editorial support. But that doesn't count at all when on the six o'clock news every night people have been told once again the Government are idiots or we're corrupt or inept. People are told that every day and every night, and they'll believe something bad before they believe something good.

Inside the Beltway bubble

The apparent aversion to serious debate and analysis of so many journalists is only part of the disturbing trend in Australian media contributing to the ongoing decline and debasement of critical national debate. As Nick Cater explains in his book *The Lucky Culture*, press gallery journalists live in a "tertiary-educated middle class" bubble, secluded from the bigger picture and disconnected to the realities of life. Cater believes "the tyranny of distance between the Parliamentary precinct (in Canberra) and the rest of the country has become a serious impediment to the national debate":

> Within Parliament House and its satellite fiefdoms ... the endless multiple streams of news, comment and banality (feeds) a dangerous self-fascination; the political class appeared to have fallen in love with its own grandiloquence and was persuaded that it possessed even greater powers of perception.

This group "mediathink" and Beltway bubble encasing and limiting the worldview of political journalists and press galleries is seriously damaging the nation's body politic. The negative feedback loop it creates stifles reform and discourages quality candidates from ever entering political life.

Former federal Labor MP Lindsay Tanner's book *Sideshow: Dumbing Down Democracy* explores this topic at length. Tanner laments the loss of focus on outcomes by governments in favour of the "creation of appearances", resulting in "the politics of the moment" written and broadcast by gallery journalists who have limited contact with the rest of Australia:

> Policy initiatives are measured by their media impact, not by their effect. The symptoms of this shift are on full display. A dramatic growth in pork-barreling, driven by back-benchers hungry for positive local media coverage.

Growing misuse of Parliament for juvenile stunts that are designed to win momentary television coverage. Political leaders gatecrashing light-entertainment shows on radio and television. Meaningless media constructs like the concept of a government's first hundred days influencing serious decision-making. Scare campaigns about higher taxes, boat-people, and working conditions paralysing informed debate. Emotional display displacing genuine leadership as the key quality required of political leaders. Mounting distortion of facts to maximise the impact of a story.

Campbell takes particular umbrage at the myopic scope of "inside the Beltway" political reporting dominating the media's current coverage:

> The journalists I encountered were obsessed with the politics of politics, the internal machinations, the personalities. They were always treating politics like a sport, always looking for the next 'gotcha' headline or TV soundbite. The general public wouldn't have a clue what policies and outcomes were being delivered by a government because the journos are only covering what's happening inside the Beltway.
>
> There's something of a triangulation happening, where you've got the narcissism and shallowness of social media, the media themselves and the commentariat on the Left all treating government like a reality TV show. We are all being told what to do, when to do it, and people are being told 'these are the bad guys, they're idiots and they need to get voted out'. People now just accept they can vote out the 'bad guys' on a whim because of what they're seeing on social media, what they're seeing on the TV news, what the commentariat are telling them over and over again. You tell the people something often enough and they believe it.

A mirror to the media

While they won't admit it in public, journalists are at least displaying some degree of self-reflection when afforded the cloak of anonymity. A 2012 report by the Walkley Foundation titled "Journalism At The Speed Of Bytes" highlighted concerns by some journalists about the impact of today's reportage on the nation's political debate:

> 'The story gets forgotten in the search to dress it up', said one reporter, 'We need substance, not just enthusiasm for technology, it's the story that should be the foremost consideration.' Another reporter said, 'We publish a lot more now without thinking about whether it is good or not'. A more senior colleague worried aloud about the political implications of the rush to get stories up online: 'It's bad for public debate', he said, 'there's a tendency for misinformation to gather its own pace and be taken as fact when it's not'.

The flipside to this argument is the defence put forth by journalists, who blame politicians for lowering the tone of political discourse and the national debate. Countless newspaper columns and pieces to camera espouse this defence, serving to absolve the media's role in the very decline they're decrying.

In one random and stark example, a 2015 op-ed piece by Anne Hyland in the *Australian Financial Review* titled "Politics tunes in to reality TV" spends nearly 1000 words lamenting today's lack of political leadership. Hyland writes that "at a time when we need to be governed and led, we are instead riveted by how Prime Minister Tony Abbott might blow himself up with another gaffe". Not a single word of Hyland's excoriating rant against the Abbott Government is devoted to the examination of her own industry's obsession with gaffes and gotcha moments, or the role it plays in helping to create this so-called leadership vacuum.

According to Hyland's worldview – shared by so many of her

colleagues – the media is never at fault in fostering the current political malaise we find ourselves in. Many politicians do contribute to the degraded quality of public debate. The first incarnation of the Rudd Government and its relentless attempt to win the 24-hour media cycle was a disastrous tipping point in this regard. In its wake, the Kevin07 phenomena of manic media management created a generation of media advisors and their political masters who see no option but to operate in the all-consuming vortex of relentless demand for stories, tip-offs, responses, reactions and announceables.

The media blames parliamentarians for Australia's leadership woes but fails to recognise the national debate doesn't operate in a vacuum filled solely by elected officials. The media should not escape scrutiny and some responsibility for the role it plays.

In their landmark 2015 essay "The New Language Of Political Narcissism", Peter Oborne and Anne Williams eviscerate both the writing and language of today's journalists and politicians. Oborne and Williams expose the debased nature of contemporary political discourse by demonstrating how far the once serious craft of political writing has veered off course from the guidelines laid down by George Orwell in his seminal 1946 essay "Politics and the English Language". Rejecting accuracy and truth, today's political discourse places far more emphasis and importance on emotion and feelings, as opposed to the values of thought and reason so embedded in the craft's past. The essayists believe the "shrinking of language" goes hand in hand with the "shrivelling of purpose":

> The narcissism of so much public discourse makes rational debate almost impossible. All discussion becomes a parade of feelings, crowding out any analysis of effects. Political writing is collapsing into autobiography. This is turning us into smaller, trivial, selfish people. It is doing great damage to the public domain. Political writers should offer a window, not a mirror, to the world.[94]

A way forward

A new direction in our nation's journalistic culture is required to foster meaningful and rational debate that analyses policy and informs the voting public. Lasting reform of so many critical issues facing the nation will likely be out of reach until it does. Unfortunately, adequate solutions are hard to come by.

Lindsay Tanner spent an entire book exploring the issue at length, only to come up empty on the final pages:

> The need to entertain has completely taken over the media's approach to serious subjects. That's forcing those whose job revolves around communicating about serious issues with a mass audience to become entertainers. The audience might get a few laughs, but in the process the underlying issues are trivialised and distorted. No one individual, nor indeed any particular intervention from government, can solve this problem. We have no available magic wand to solve the sideshow problem ...[95]

One area of legislative reform Campbell believes is long overdue is a strengthening of defamation laws. While free speech advocates and the media will disagree with his stance, Campbell believes stronger defamation legislation is the only way to reinstate rational, factual coverage of politicians and allow for meaningful debate on the tough policy decisions they make.

> We just can't keep allowing people to go out there and say the most outrageous things and have the media broadcast it without a second thought. It's not about censorship. It's about these public figures and the media having some integrity. It's a bit like the issue of bullying and verbal abuse. We don't accept that in our schools, our workplaces, on the sporting field. But it's perfectly fine and acceptable to do that when it comes to politicians.

> I know it'd be like trying to put the genie back in the bottle, but we do need to see civility make a comeback, some politeness. We need real discourse in public life, not this trivial rubbish that goes on, or this McCarthyist style of witchhunts by the media. Since when was it right or acceptable for reporters set up camp outside the house where the Premier of the state lives, or the Attorney-General's house? Why is it OK for reporters to chase and follow the Chief Justice through the Queen Street Mall? Grow up. Stop it. If we're going to tackle bullying and abuse it needs to happen across the board, not just in the case of our kids or professional sportsmen. Every aspect of society, including Parliamentarians.

Joe Hockey expressed similar sentiments following his defamation win against Fairfax in mid-2015, saying he took the action to "stand up to malicious people intent on vilifying Australians who choose to serve in public office to make their country a better place".

With minimal prospect of legislative change to media or defamation laws, perhaps we are only left with little more than idealistic hope for a national debate about the role and responsibilities of a dysfunctional media system. Ironically we must return to the fictional drama series *The Newsroom* to capture a vision of what the future of political journalism and media organisations might look like if the nation demanded it.

In a heated discussion with news anchor Will McAvoy about the style of coverage their current affairs show is engaged in, news director Mackenzie McHale is asked what "winning" in journalism looks like. MacHale replies:

> Reclaiming the fourth estate. Reclaiming journalism as an honorable profession. A nightly newscast that informs a debate worthy of a great nation. Civility, respect and a return to what's important; the death of bitchiness; the

death of gossip and voyeurism; speaking truth to stupid. No demographic sweet spot; a place where we can all come together.⁹⁶

State-federal relations

Consumed by the persistent swirl of personalities and trivialities in the pursuit of ratings and circulation, the mainstream media displays minimal interest in the important issues facing Australia. Thankfully, there are glimmers of hope in the media landscape, but they are not as widely accessible. Pay TV channels such as Sky News feature in-depth analysis and discussions on important reform issues but their audience is still limited. Deeper analysis in articles that appear on news sites are increasingly hidden behind paywalls. For the time being at least, the wider community receives their news in bite-sized chunks on mainstream, accessible media and social media.

The mainstream media will say they are merely catering to their market, dishing out fast food journalism for a disengaged, narcissistic populace mainly interested in celebrity gossip, reality TV shows, selfies and social media status updates. Whether the mainstream media's shallow coverage of politics is a cause or a symptom of a degraded national debate remains to be seen. One thing at least is clear: they're not remotely interested in the most significant and pressing issues in need of reform in Australia today. Chief among those issues is the broken system of Australian federalism.

Campbell believes sorting out the roles and responsibilities of state and federal governments and addressing the deep-seated vertical fiscal imbalance plaguing our nation is the top reform priority for Australia. So many other reforms – service delivery, bureaucracy renewal and tax systems among them – will flow from a fundamental, full-scale overhaul of state-federal relations. Campbell explained:

> For too long in this country we've been moving towards

massive centralisation, where the Commonwealth takes over everything and tries to run it all from Canberra. We have a Constitution. It's the law. But thanks to judicial activism in the High Court and because of the taxing power of the federal government, the states have increasingly been encroached upon by the Commonwealth. Centralisation didn't work in Soviet Russia, and it won't work here.

We've got to strike a balance between regional differences and the need for regional autonomy and the broader, national issues the federal government should be dealing with. Under the Constitution, of course, the Commonwealth doesn't run hospitals and it doesn't run schools but over time they've become heavily involved in them. We need a new political compact to define what the roles and responsibilities are for the Commonwealth versus the states. I don't think it has to be taken to the Australian people and, unfortunately, there's a view that you need to reform the Federation through a green and white paper process. Federation didn't happen that way. It was a political compact, and what should happen now is for the politicians to go away on a retreat for a few days with all the support and all the necessary information there and literally sit down and hammer out a political deal. It might take a number of such meetings. But it can be as simple as saying 'right, the federal government stops dancing around education'. It gets right out of it and lets the states get on with it.

The recurrent annual savings of achieving true Federation reform is in the tens of billions of dollars. Even a low estimate of the national savings would have given Queensland between five and 10 percent extra money each year. We wouldn't have a budget deficit. If there is a single, most important responsibility right now for political leaders in this country, it's reform of the Federation.

In his book *The Sentimental Nation – The Making of the Australian Commonwealth* author and historian Dr John Hirst wrote:

> It was widely recognised that having the states rely on the Commonwealth for funds broke the central tenet of federalism: that each government should be independent in its own sphere. Largesse, begging and haggling should not characterise the relationship between the two levels of government.

As we know, that's exactly what's transpired in the post World War II-era. Many options exist to address Australia's vertical fiscal imbalance, but the lead argument raging in modern politics appears to be an increase in the rate and coverage of the GST. Campbell has always believed that was a band-aid solution:

> Government can and should deliver more services and infrastructure for the same or less money. It's not acceptable for politicians and commentators to simply call for taxes to be raised and label that 'reform'. It's not reform – it's actually the easier path.

For many years Campbell has supported the power of competitive federalism. One way to encourage that system would be to give the states and territories the power to levy a portion of income tax while reducing or removing other, less efficient taxes. This is a far from radical concept. The Constitution allows for the states to levy income tax and they did so until 1942, when the measure was forfeited to the Commonwealth to help fund the war effort. The power to levy income tax was never returned to the states, despite several attempts since. The federal Commission of Audit report of 2014 supported the move, saying "an arrangement whereby the Commonwealth would lower its personal income tax rates to allow room for the states to levy their own income tax surcharge" was necessary to address the nation's vertical fiscal imbalance. Campbell believes the benefits of such a move would be immense:

> The states should negotiate an outcome where, for example, the federal government gets out of the running of hospitals, the running of early childhood, and primary and secondary education, and the states take responsibility for those areas. But the states will need the revenue streams to do that and whatever it needs to be, whether it's 10 cents or 15 cents or 20 cents out of every income tax dollar that people are paying today, that should automatically go to the states. Then the states can stand on their own two feet and sink or swim in terms of their performance.

In his work for a 2014 CEDA report titled "A Federation for the 21st Century", Professor Terry Moran highlighted that Federation in 1901 is the middle point between the arrival of the First Fleet in 1788 and our own moment in time today:

> What we need now is a group of premiers who are interested in 'saving' the Federation that their political predecessors helped create. They would do this by being the conduit through which more power and accountability flows into the local governance structures that states and local government are best suited to build and support.
>
> For many years, the tide of funding and authorisation has flowed towards Canberra. As economic headwinds shift, this tide is turning and business as usual will increasingly struggle to make headway. As Shakespeare reminds us in Julius Caesar, his play about political leaders contemplating change, a tide 'taken at the flood, leads on to fortune. Omitted, all the voyage of their life is bound in shallows and in miseries'. We need political leadership prepared to ride with that tide.[97]

Public service renewal

The budgetary savings and increased accountability that would flow from fixing the Federation are immense. That reform could also expedite a roots and branch structural overhaul of the public service.

The Newman Government, it goes without saying, gained notoriety for reducing the size of Queensland's public service. According to government records, Queensland had 243,250 public service employees as at 30 June 2012, a few months into the Newman Government's term. By the end of 2013, the Government's drive to make the public service more affordable reduced that figure to 227,836 public service employees, a drop of 15,414 people. In full-time equivalent positions, it was a drop of 14,135.[98]

Reducing the public service was just one of many reforms the Government introduced in this realm. But the extreme and sustained backlash against its downsizing measures meant its work in the area of public service "renewal" went unnoticed. Technological upgrades aside, the hierarchical, centralised, process-driven bureaucracy has operated much the same way it has for more than a century, so the renewal framework of the Newman Government involved looking at the public service in entirely new, creative ways. Campbell told the Queensland Parliament of the Government's "renewal" mission in April 2013:

> There are Queenslanders who need services and are not receiving them because the way we deliver them has not changed for decades. There are public servants who want to do more for their fellow Queenslanders but have not been provided with the tools to help them to do it. There are private sector operators and non-government organisations that have new ideas and ways of approaching problems that are not being heard. This has to change. The Government… is about ensuring the Queensland public sector is the best public service in Australia, delivering services to all Queenslanders.[99]

To achieve its stated goal of transforming the Queensland public service into "the best in the nation", the Newman Government tried to think differently about the bureaucracy. With voters increasingly seeing themselves as 'customers', do departments need a customer service strategy? What organisational and structural lessons could the government and bureaucracy learn from companies like Apple and Google? Should there be a leadership and talent academy to identify stand out performers in the public service and help them progress their careers? Could a great teacher become an even better workplace trainer in an entirely different department, and how easily could they make the transition? Do public service managers need to be paid more to attract talent from the private sector?

After fixing the Federation, Campbell believes remodeling the public service is a priority reform task facing Australia:

> The quill pens and ledger books may have been replaced by computers and other technology, but the fundamental modus operandi has not changed at all. In fact we have really only computerised the status quo and computerised the inefficiencies. The community today expects a far more agile and responsive Government. People want more and they want it more quickly. When you're a politician, people send you an email at 8am and expect their problem to be sorted out by 5pm. Local Government is about direct delivery so there you have the best opportunity of any level of government to give people that sort of responsiveness.
>
> But there is no hope at this stage for state and federal governments to do anything to meet people's current needs and demands. We tried to do something very different with the public service, and that was to create a bureaucracy that knew exactly what it had to do for the community. We wanted the public service to be set up and resourced to the required levels, using modern technology very efficiently, to respond more directly to the community's needs.

The Newman Government pursued the concept of "contestability" during its term, borne out of its political philosophy and crystallised in the work of the Commission of Audit led by Peter Costello. Primarily, contestability compares and assesses the productivity and cost of government service delivery, particularly in monopolistic or non-contested conditions.

In the Queensland contestability experiment, Labor and the unions refused to engage in the debate. They dismissed and sloganeered it away as a 'backdoor to privatisation' and successfully broadcast their opposition through mainstream and social media channels in another example of the Diamond Effect at work. Under the theoretical laws of the Diamond Effect system, it is clear Labor is incapable of reforming the public service so long as it is indelibly tied to the unions and the media chooses to report emotion over reason and entertainment over meaningful debate and analysis. Recall Kevin Rudd's "dead serious"[100] 2007 election promise to take a meat axe to the Commonwealth public service. The punters loved the sound bite, but the unions kicked up a stink. By the time he was dumped as Prime Minister, the bureaucracy had grown by around six percent, with no discernible improvements in frontline service delivery.

The job of bureaucratic change and service delivery reform, it would seem, is up to conservative governments. But reducing the top-heavy, bloated bureaucracy is but one part of the reform task; efficiency, contestability and responsive, localised decision-making are other necessary goals.

In the case of contestability, the largest and most courageous example has occurred in the UK's Justice Department under the Cameron Government. For more than 100 years, the Justice Department had delivered all probationary services, costing around $1.6 billion (£800 million) and administered by nearly 20,000 public servants. In 2013, the department began a process of opening up around 70 percent of probation services to the private and non-government sectors to look after low to medium risk offenders. The department offered incentives for reductions in re-offending rates and supported public sector staff to start their own businesses or find joint venture partners already working in the field overseas. The probation service initiative is part of the UK Department of Justice's aim to save $4.2 billion (£2 billion), with much of it set to be reinvested in rehabilitation services for repeat offenders.[101] While the relevant unions have gone out on strike over the initiative, the UK Government is confident the safeguards and management mechanisms it has put in place will produce better outcomes at a much-reduced cost to taxpayers. So far, none of the dire consequences predicted by the unions and the Left have eventuated.

In Queensland, the unions threatened strike action over decisions made by the Newman Government. They simply weren't willing to accept the state's budgetary woes or participate in its repair. And one wouldn't have known it listening to the union's rhetoric at the time, but the Newman Government actually kept a range of services in-house after opening them up to the contestability process. Contestability is not a one size fits all, blanket solution for managing state budgets but where it does identify efficiencies and innovative models of delivery it should be pursued as part of a broader vision of public service reform. Campbell said:

> The Left keeps carrying on like contestability is a spin-off of class warfare, which is their typical type of rubbish. The fact is services are being paid for by taxpayers, there's a limited bucket of money, and at all times things should be delivered in a competitive way.
>
> We wanted to test whether the most competitive way of delivery was by government departments or firms that, because of competition, were able to do things better. Yes you must have checks and balances, and you will get problems if you don't set the contracts up correctly or have

good people and processes managing and monitoring those contracts.

But there is massive potential for services to be delivered a hell of a lot better than the stodgy way we are doing things now. The thing that really bothers me about it all is this disconnect in people's minds between the delivery of services and the taxes they pay. They don't seem to get that it's their money. It's not the Government's money – it's their money. And everything we were doing was always about trying to give them the best deal for their money.

The Labor Party rarely talks about spending restraint and practices it even less, preferring instead to increase taxes and raise revenue to pay for ever-increasing services. Now some conservative leaders appear to have joined them, abandoning the heavy-lifting of reform in favour of an increase to the rate of the GST. This is the lazy, short-sighted option. According to law professor and writer James Allan, state premiers have been turned into "mendicants"; and we know "beggars always want more of someone else's money."[102] Allan, a fierce advocate of competitive federalism and a return of income taxing powers to the states, believes any lift to the GST would only fast-track more government spending "under the same dysfunctional set-up". Jeff Kennett agrees, telling the ABC:

> We're hearing about increasing taxes, be it the GST or Medicare levy, to be applied to either health and/or education. That to me is profoundly wrong. We shouldn't be changing tax structures without reviewing the entire tax structure of this country. This should happen for two reasons. Firstly, if either of these measures were put into place and the money was returned to the states for health or education, that immediately removes from the states any pressure to continue with the necessary reforms that should be in place. And secondly, can I say to you that if you simply

lift taxes without understanding the importance of the needs of the country as a whole, you set in process a motion which I think in three years will have us back in the same place. So you remove the incentive to continue reform and you put in a bastardised form of tax reform which in three years' time will already be seen to be obsolete.

A lot of this discussion is also now just based on the cost of health delivery, not reforming delivery, but the reality is in Australia, health is just one component. It may be a large component but just dealing with health does not deal with the fundamental issues that require major reform and changes in the way in which we operate.[103]

University of Western Sydney chancellor and long-term federal public service leader Peter Shergold believes "vision and courage" are missing in the realm of bureaucratic reform, leaving pockets of change to operate in silos rather than feeding into broader systemic transformation:

A burden of red-tape micro-management is too often imposed on front-line staff and contracted service providers in order to avoid any risk. This stifles the creativity that might come from diversity, program flexibility and customer choice.

Too many good ideas remain at the margin of public administration. Opportunities are only half seized; new modes of service delivery begin and end their working lives as "demonstration projects" or "pilots"; and creative solutions are progressively undermined by a plethora of bureaucratic guidelines. Hierarchical controls, intended to ensure quality standards, can often end up deterring local initiative. The limited resources of public administration need to be allocated and deployed to maximum effect. Working smarter, or doing more with less, is a worthy goal. It can't be pursued half-heartedly.[104]

Rather than pursuing public sector reform half-heartedly, few governments are pursuing it at all. In the same way the Howard Government's WorkChoices policy scared off any talk of industrial relations reform, the Newman Government's attempt to reshape the public service has made any overhaul of the bureaucracy an unspoken taboo for the conservative side of politics. There is no shortage of ideas, plans and reviews on the future of public service reform. World's best practice in service delivery is achieving results today and can be implemented in Australia tomorrow. A combination of militant union opposition to any change, a lack of political will on the conservative side of politics and the media's reportage of any such changes remain the forces preventing it.

The mindset of voters

If anyone is going to know what makes voters tick, it's advertising and marketing expert Toby Ralph. A regular guest on *The Gruen Transfer* and a veteran of more than 50 election campaigns across three continents, Ralph contends the public will accept reform on two conditions: the reasons for it are communicated and understood; and the scale of reform must walk a tightrope between "too much and too little".

> There's a common misconception that the public is politically naïve. They are not; but they are often cynical, disinterested or disengaged. They often have a strong sense of what needs to be done, and even if they don't like it if it's not delivered, they'll punish the underperforming politician. The trick of leadership is not to develop great strategy or cunning tactics; it is to get people to understand what must be done and why, then walk in lockstep toward that reform.[105]

While we may not be politically naïve, we are becoming more selfish in the search for instant gratification. The gradual shift from the "we" of the national interest to the "me" of self-interest has been happening for decades, super-charged in recent years by social media.

Demographer Bernard Salt points to "fewer kids, more household income, continuous economic growth, and unabashed and unashamed parental indulgence" as drivers and symptoms.

As political commentator and academic Ross Fitzgerald notes, the incentives for governments to pursue reform today are few and far between because our attention spans are shorter and tolerance for long-term gains is dwindling. With the pay-offs for reform arriving many years into the future, the burning of political capital is no longer seen as being worth it for politicians:

> All we are concerned about are our individual circumstances and our material and emotional wellbeing in the next minute or hour or two. I question whether Australians have the same appetite and patience for reforms of the past if reforms of that scale were proposed today. Maybe, just maybe, the next time we vote, we should think more clearly about Australia's future before we take our short memories and even shorter memory spans back to the ballot box.

One demographic group, in particular, exemplifies this descent into social narcissism.

Inner-city aristocracy

The "self-appointed ruling class of sophisticates", as Nick Cater describes them, have an undue influence on political discourse because they dominate so many of the nation's key positions in media, the public service, the arts, law and universities. They are not necessarily engaged in a culture war or struggle for power. Rather, as Cater explains, "it is a dispute about the opinions that should be listened to, and those, if any, that should be considered beyond the pale".

The chattering class of inner-city intellectuals rejects rational debate and practical measures on the big issues facing Australia in favour of emotional, so-called progressive causes. Looking down at their fellow Australians from their privileged positions, they support the Greens Party in record numbers and update their social media statuses with calls to action on gay marriage, climate change, Indigenous disadvantage and "equality". According to Cater:

> The decadence of wrist-band politics, in which a plastic bracelet denotes not only a point of view but the moral worth of the bearer, has had a destructive effect on civic debate, turning the battle of ideas into a contest of personal integrity. Compromise, the saving grace of democratic civil debate, is simply not on the table.

In trademark style, Campbell is rather more blunt.

> I'm afraid we've got a bunch of kids in the media and a bunch of kids as political staffers. We've got a bunch of kids as politicians and all of that is helping to create a bunch of kids in the electorate. The national debate is dominated by silly, time-wasting nonsense rather than the big issues. We are not debating how we create jobs and a real future for the country. As a community, we're not really engaged with and debating Government spending or debt or the Federation. We are instead distracted by the 'causes' propagated by the commentariat.

The leafy, upper middle-class electorate of Ashgrove in Brisbane, Campbell's seat during his term as Premier, is one example of the shift in priorities for voters in the inner-cities of Australia's capitals. Nearly 90 percent of Ashgrove residents were born of Anglo-Saxon descent in Australia, the United Kingdom, New Zealand, or the United States, around 10 percent higher than the national population average. Compared to the national average, they are also more educated, higher paid and nearly twice as likely to work in white-collar jobs. Similar patterns are repeated across the nation's metropolises.

Their wrist-band, Facebook profile photo style of activism skews rational debate. An example out of Queensland is the chattering and fretting on social media about the apparent death of the Great Barrier Reef and the destruction of rainforest in Cape York. None of that occurred, of course, but social media and the Greens told them it was happening.

And as Bernard Salt has written, there can "only be less, not more, public testing of ideas" in our post social-media world. Evidence to the contrary presented to them – practical solutions and the actual nature of affairs in rural and regional areas – was rejected in the pursuit of their self-righteousness.

With the echo chamber of social media and certain journalists telling them how 'bad' Campbell Newman and his Government were, they voted against a state leader who had delivered tangible benefits for their community and more funding for local services and infrastructure than any other electorate during the LNP Government's term. In a similar way to Jackie Trad's victory in the nearby South Brisbane electorate, Labor's candidate Kate Jones won the seat of Ashgrove on the back of Greens preferences.

Professional elites

Many of those inner-city voters increasingly turning to the Greens at the expense of the common good – and common sense – are among the clique of professional elites who've arisen over the past three decades, most of them off the back of the largesse of state and territory Labor governments across the nation.

In the early 1980s, Milton Friedman identified this intellectual class of the United States as hypocritical elites who failed to practice what they preached. Key offenders listed by Friedman included government bureaucrats, academics, the staff of vested interested groups, and journalists (who today flit back and forth between news reporting and PR work in ministerial offices). Friedman argued they were "among the most ardent preachers of the doctrine of equality, yet they remind us very much of the old, if unfair, saw about the Quakers: they came to the New World to do good, and ended up doing well".

If we take Friedman's added observations on the British elite's post-World War II search for greater equality and transpose it with the actions of the Greens-voting sophisticates of today, their "word-deep" movement has only created:

> ... new classes of privileged to replace or supplement the old: the bureaucrats, secure in their jobs...the trade unions that profess to represent the most down-trodden workers but in fact consist of the highest paid laborers in the land – the aristocrats of the labour movement; and the new millionaires, people who have been cleverest at finding ways to avoid paying taxes on their income. A vast reshuffling of income and wealth, yes; greater equity, hardly.[106]

Take the industry thriving around Indigenous disadvantage, or the myriad green groups who accept public grants and tax breaks only to use that money on falsified campaigns to attack and scuttle private sector projects and government policies. The new breed of union bosses like Queensland's Alex Scott and Beth Mohle are another fine example. They led protests against pay rises to politicians and vehemently opposed any attempts to introduce temporary wage restraints on public servants. At the same time, they were entirely comfortable in their elite positions. In 2013, they received annual salary packages in excess of $205,000 each,[107] around triple the average amount paid to the public servants and nurses they represent.

Rise of the Greens

Gerard Henderson has observed and worked in the nation's body politic for more than 50 years, including a four-year stint in the Ministerial office of Campbell's father Kevin Newman in the late 1970s. Henderson predicts the increasing support for the Greens

Party among inner-city voters has the potential to stifle economic reforms in the future:

> What has changed since the reforming era of Hawke, Keating and Howard is the emergence of the Greens and the tendency of the Labor Party, in order to preserve parts of its own inner-city base, to go with the Greens on policies that restrict the economic reform process. The Greens already hold Melbourne and in Sydney they're after the seats of key Labor people like Anthony Albanese and Tanya Plibersek, so you can see how that changes the reform agenda.
>
> The political situation is a lot more difficult today and the problem is that Greens voters in the cities are a well-educated, articulate and vocal group and they project their ideological agenda much farther than any other group in the country because of their largely professional and well-off background. They have the ability and the time to engage. For those working in the suburbs and bringing up a couple of kids, they don't really have a lot of spare time to engage in the same level of political activity.[108]

The Greens candidate for Ashgrove in 2015 Robert Hogg is the quintessential symbol of the emerging divide between inner-city elites and the rest of us. Hogg was something of a triple whammy; a Commonwealth public servant for more than 17 years before becoming an academic historian and lecturer at the University of Queensland and a Greens candidate. The flow of preferences from his 10.1 percent of the primary vote handed victory to Labor's Kate Jones at the election.

As Cater argues, the Greens long ago discovered that a "cause is mightier than ideology", allowing it to avoid having to "confront the impracticality" of its own agenda:

> Causes bestowed virtue upon those who supported them and vice upon those who did not. Morality replaced pragmatism

as the framework of politics; governments were no longer bound to govern in the interests of the country but in the interests of what was right.[109]

Paradoxically, the threat to reform posed by the rise of the Greens and their inner-city supporters may, in fact, represent an opportunity to conservative politicians and parties. Families, tradespeople, small business owners and retirees must all live within their means, and they generally believe a government should too. They support, as former Senator Richard Alston noted in the wake of the 2015 UK election, "hand ups rather than handouts, and the pursuit of pro-growth policies".[110] When the "progressive social impulses of comfortable urban activists"[111] are seen to be triumphing over economic growth and the reforms needed to facilitate it, causing Australia's standard of living to decline, the changes opposed by the Greens and in turn Labor will become self-evident. A Government with the vision to propose and explain tough reforms and stick to its guns may find itself the champion of a new breed of aspirational voters in the suburbs.

Political leadership

As noted earlier, politicians must also shoulder part of the blame for the national malaise and lack of reform in Australia. Toby Ralph says reform is something "politicians want to do when they are not in power, but tend to find reasons to avoid when they are".

> Change means disadvantage and pain to someone, somewhere, who is then motivated to vote against you while the people who are advantaged tend to be thankless. Thus reform is electoral poison, and the more reform there is, the deadlier the response.[112]

The short-termism and reform avoidance afflicting most politicians in this country can be attributed to a range of factors. Commentator and academic Peter Van Onselen blames the "patronage of power" for the risk averse nature of our nation's politicians, a notion that they are only in it to win it, and keep on winning it:

> The trappings of office – the cars, the travel, the extra staff and the salaries – matter as much, if not more so, than do the opportunities for reform that incumbency affords. Indeed the pursuit of reform becomes something functionaries who feel strongly about retaining power are cautious about because 'doing stuff', as one shadow minister put it to me, entails risks.[113]

Jeff Kennett is among many former political leaders highly critical of the lack of clear communication and enunciation of a vision by contemporary political leaders. Kennett told the ABC in July 2015:

> I will lay you London to a brick: the public of Australia will support leadership. They want to be able to buy into part of the narrative, but with due respect there is no narrative now. There is no narrative. If I was to ask you or any of your listeners, 'Where do you think the politicians of today want to take Australia by 2050?' do any of us have any idea at all?
>
> There is no vision. The media keep looking for simple solutions because it's today and their cycle is 24 hours and the political class have, more obviously than any time I can remember, simply given in themselves to that 24 hour cycle. I think the leaders of the last 10 years have failed the national interest. It's across all parties. We are a country without a vision. We are a country at the moment that is terribly complacent. We are a country that in my opinion has wasted 10 years, and I'm fearful we may waste the next 10.[114]

Business leaders Catherine Livingstone and Kate Carnell apportion blame for the lack of reform to bickering and point-scoring across party lines. While John Howard was credited with supporting the bulk of Hawke-Keating reforms in the 1980s from the Opposition benches, such bipartisan cooperation in the national interest is long gone. Livingstone said politicians had a responsibility to "ensure that there is a constructive, well-informed debate, leading to implementable outcomes", rather than undermining the debate "in the cause of party political positioning"[115]. Carnell too despairs at the nation's reform inertia, saying policy options are "ruled out almost before morning tea on the day of discussion".[116]

The protection of patronage and risk aversion, muddied visions and poor communication with the electorate, as well as party political warfare are all valid explanations for today's lack of political leadership and will for reform.

But as the Newman Government demonstrated so vividly, political leadership and vision is only part of the equation. Without a likeable personality or the skills of soft politics, reform is fraught with electoral danger. The hopes for the future of reform are often pinned on current New South Wales Premier Mike Baird, who won the 2015 state election in the face of strident opposition from Labor and the unions over electricity privatisation. There can be no doubt Baird's likeability and strong communication and media skills made the privatisation push much easier than it did in Queensland. But apart from electricity privatisation, New South Wales has not undergone any meaningful or systemic reform for at least a decade, or more. Baird could afford to take the privatisation of electricity assets to an election because he hadn't burnt political capital on any other reforms or tough decisions, and neither had his predecessor Barry O'Farrell.

Dr Mark Triffitt, a public policy lecturer at the University of Melbourne and former adviser to the Kennett Government, eschews talk of personalities and the typical finger-pointing of blame directed at politicians. He points instead to the urgent need for systemic change to "better align our political system with the new realities of today". Writing in the *Australian Financial Review* in February 2015, Dr Triffitt says the political arena is now dominated by "increasingly truncated media cycles, together with a non-stop avalanche of social media-driven opinion" that make our political leaders increasingly retreat into short-termism and reactive responses:

> This is an arena where the complexity of policy problems have become so great, and the time to decide on them so small, that politicians struggle to grasp what will occur next week, let alone anticipate or shape what might happen next year. This is an arena where Parliament – the seat of policy decision-making – is locked into the languid rhythms of 19th-century debate and deliberation that are increasingly left behind by the hyper-speed 21st century. This is a system where the major parties can no longer count on stable blocs of voter support – otherwise known as a mandate – for any policy change for any lasting period of time into the future.
>
> So, even if our leaders come up with good policy, they are no longer guaranteed long-term public support for it. In short, nearly every aspect of our current system now works to dismantle the building blocks of effective political and policy leadership.[117]

Dr Triffitt's scenarios for change are worth pursuing though it's unclear which stakeholder group or combination of institutions would be responsible for enacting his suggested reforms. He believes new ways of better engaging citizens in government and policy decisions are required, giving leaders a "stronger base to generate public buy-in for hard policy decisions". Secondly, "new decision-making spaces" must be carved out to provide political leaders with the room and scope to think on and formulate future-focused policy. According to Dr Triffitt:

> Many will say major change to our political system is impossible. I say we have no choice. Failure to do so will amount to a collective failure of imagination to address the key issue of our time – the corroding state of our political system and the failure of leaders who are now held hostage to it.[118]

The challenge ahead

To finish where we began in this epilogue, Milton Friedman summed up the cyclical challenge of reform back in 1982 when he said:

> There is enormous inertia – a tyranny of the status quo – in private and especially governmental arrangements. Only a crisis – actual or perceived – produces real change. When that crisis occurs, the actions that are taken depend on the ideas that are lying around. That, I believe, is our basic function: to develop alternatives to existing policies, to keep them alive and available until the politically impossible becomes politically inevitable.[119]

Campbell Newman was a conviction politician who served the community for 13 years. Like his parents before him, he gave more of himself than he ever received. His fierce determination to challenge the status quo underpinned that service, and his experiences and insights provide some valuable lessons for our nation's shared future.

Campbell lived and breathed the frustration of a cumbersome, confused system of Federation. He saw the inefficiencies and centralised approach of an outmoded bureaucracy. He grappled with the shortfall in state revenue and advocated for income taxing powers to be returned to the states and territories. Stung by the loss of reason and respect in public discourse, he has called for a return to civil debate. Through it all, Campbell holds out hope we can all do better and rise to the challenge of reform:

> The extensive number of reforms introduced during our time in government stretched across all portfolios. We really did give reform a red hot go in a state that desperately needed it. Some of the changes were for the long term, others were more urgent. I think we got most of those reforms and policies right and got the politics wrong on some of them. On others we did a poor job of both selling

the initial problem and then the benefits of the changes as they emerged later on.

Everything we did, every single day we were in office, was about creating a Queensland where we could all be optimistic about the future of the state. We wanted to get out of the way businesses and help them build a stronger economy and create more jobs. We wanted our hospitals to be the best in the nation. We wanted our kids to get the very highest standard of education our schools could offer. We wanted the Government and public service of Queensland to be the most responsive, flexible and dynamic in Australia. To do all of that, we also needed to be disciplined and careful with how we spent taxpayer's money. We had to do more with less. Reform can only be truly successful when all those who seek public office want that for our nation too. Australia's bright future won't be served up on a silver platter. Some things will have to give. Tinkering around the edges won't be enough.

As a nation, our shared future can be a prosperous, safe and dynamic place to live and work but we have to be brave and bold and mature about it. I think all of us need to do better. Politicians, journalists, the unions, the bureaucracy and, perhaps most importantly, the rest of us, the community of private citizens whose lives will be impacted the most if we don't engage in meaningful reform. The nation's future is at a crossroads. It's not good enough to take the easy path or let short term political expediency override decision-making in the best interests of the majority. We must have the courage to disrupt the status quo. Australia has a proud history of making difficult decisions that reap benefits over the long term. We need to update that history with a new round of reforms. It's too important not to take up the challenge of reform today.

Author's Acknowledgements

When Campbell Newman invited me to breakfast one week after the 2015 Queensland election loss, I had no idea what I was getting myself into. Over several cups of coffee and a hearty breakfast at the wonderful Pearl Café in Brisbane, Campbell gauged my interest in writing his life story and capturing his thoughts and views on reform. After nearly 15 years in journalism and politics, it seemed like a good idea at the time.

In the ensuing six months, Campbell and I conducted countless hours of interviews, exchanged innumerable phone calls, text messages and emails and spent many days rifling through boxes of his personal archives at his Brisbane home. Throughout, he didn't shy away from a single topic – personal, family or professional – of his varied and accomplished life. He was frank and forthright about his successes and failures. Lisa was equally forthcoming and open about her life and experiences, and her vibrancy and strength of spirit is a wonder to behold. They are a remarkable couple who have given so much of themselves to the community over many years. I thank both of them for the opportunity to explore and delve into every aspect of their lives. Their departure from politics is a great loss to the Queensland and Australian community, and I have tried my very best to ensure their public service is remembered with a factual and honest account of their lives and work.

In terms of writing the book, I am indebted to the editing services and feedback of Nicky Horstmann and Robert Cavallucci, who both dedicated hours of their time to help me craft and finalise this book. The input and fact-checking of Campbell's sister Kate Roff was incredibly important to the finished product. Similarly, the anecdotes and insights provided by Lisa's father Frank Monsour and her sister

Heidi were enormously valuable. In addition, the writing was shaped by dozens of conversations with friends, colleagues and staff who have known and worked with Campbell in the different phases of his career over the past 35 years. The book wouldn't be complete without the extensive quotes reproduced with the kind permission of Anne Henderson and Ross Fitzgerald from their book *Partners*. I thank Gerard Henderson for his early encouragement and advice and send a huge thank you to Aaron Coshaw from cre8 design for his stunning work on the book cover and to Dominika Lis from Photography by Dominika for her generosity and skill as a photographer. For their patience and support I owe Anthony Cappello at Connor Court Publishing and layout guru Michael Gilchrist a large debt of gratitude. Peter Kao has also been a tremendous source of support and encouragement as have our legal advisors.

The book certainly could not have been written without the support of my parents-in-law Nicky and Paul Horstmann, who among many other things took care of their grandchildren Saskia and Percy on so many occasions during the writing process we gave up counting. Gratefully, we don't have to pay them by the hour.

Most of all, I thank my wife Leah for keeping the family afloat while I undertook such a large project in such a short period of time. We were looking forward to a return to normal life after politics but quickly discovered writing a book is not anything remotely like normal life, especially a manuscript about politics. Leah has given up so much during the past four years while I sat in Parliament and then wrote this book. There are no words to fully express my gratitude for the love and support she has provided for so long.

Appendix

Campbell Newman's Key Achievements in Public Office

Lord Mayor of Brisbane

Conceived and delivered the TransApex road infrastructure project which saw the construction of:

- Clem 7 Tunnel
- Airport Link Tunnel
- Legacy Way Tunnel
- Go Between Bridge

Constructed the Eleanor Schonell Bridge (Green Bridge)

Conceived and delivered the $1 billion Road Action Plan for Brisbane in the period 2008 to 2011

Put 740 new air-conditioned buses on the road in seven-year period

Took the air-conditioning of the Brisbane City Council bus fleet from 25 percent in 2005 to 100 percent by 2011

Built two new bus depots

Commissioned seven new City Cat ferries and built three new terminals

Introduced the CityCycle bike hire scheme

Undertook comprehensive city-wide community engagement and planning for the future of Brisbane for the period 2004 to 2024

Introduced a program to plant two million trees

Renovation of Brisbane City Hall (including the saving of the historic Shingle Inn) at a cost of $210 million

Delivered seven consecutive balanced or surplus city budgets

Led south-east Queensland councils in the response to the drought of 2005 to 2008

Led Brisbane through the January 2011 Brisbane floods and the clean-up response

Initiated the building of Frew Park in Milton

Upgraded the bayside parks at Wynnum/Manly and Shorncliffe/Sandgate

Initiated the purchase of 100 percent green energy for Brisbane City Council operations

Signed three new Sister City Agreements for Brisbane with Chongqing in China, Abu Dhabi in the UAE and Hyderabad in India

Introduced Homeless Connect event as a bi-annual city council activity – reaching out to homeless people to provide focused support services and help people get off the street

Premier of Queensland

Balanced the $48 billion state budget by cutting wasteful expenditure and downsizing the workforce, achieving an Australian first since World War II as a government that spent less in one financial year than it did the previous year

Reforms to the public hospitals system that saw them deliver the best emergency department performance and surgery waiting times in the nation. Long wait lists for dental and ophthalmology services were reduced to zero

Introduced Independent Public Schools to Queensland providing for school autonomy and local decision making

Eliminated the $150 million maintenance backlog in Queensland public schools

Took on the Criminal Motorcycle Gangs and oversaw significant drop in reported crime of 15 to 20 percent

Recruited, trained and deployed an extra 1100 police in a three-year period

Developed the Queensland Plan – a comprehensive blueprint for the next 30 years of the state's growth

Developed industry sector plans for each of the state's economic pillars (mining/resources, agriculture, tourism and construction)

Reformed the building construction industry watchdog

Reforms to workers' compensation laws that saw an average 15 percent reduction to business WorkCover insurance premiums

Introduced land tenure reforms to enable Indigenous people to acquire freehold title and purchase their own homes

Host state for a highly successful G20 conference

Commissioned former Governor-General Quentin Bryce to undertake a comprehensive review into domestic and family violence in Queensland

Delivered apology to victims of forced adoptions

Committed Queensland to the implementation of the National Disability Insurance Scheme

Developed and commenced implementation of a 10-year, $10 billion Action Plan to upgrade the Bruce Highway from Brisbane to Cairns

Developed the Business Plan and achieved Federal Government support for the Toowoomba Second Range Crossing and initiated the tender process

Cut payroll tax and property stamp duty

Cut public transport fare increases

Appointed Tim Carmody QC to run the Commission of Inquiry into Queensland's child protection system and allocated $406 million over five years to overhaul the system based on the Inquiry's recommendations

Allocated an additional $868 million in funding over five years for disability services in Queensland

REFERENCES

1. *The Daily Telegraph*, 14 January 2011
2. *The Australian*, 22 January 2011
3. *The Sydney Morning Herald*, 14 January 2011
4. Queensland Parliament, Hansard, 30 October 2007
5. Interview with the author
6. *The Courier-Mail*, 23 December 2013
7. Interview with the author
8. All quotes in the book from Lisa Newman are from interviews with the author unless otherwise stated
9. Interview with the author
10. *Brisbane Times*, 22 March 2011
11. Ibid.
12. Antony Green's election blog, ABC, 22 March 2011
13. *Inside Story*, Swinburne University of Technology, 29 November 2012
14. Newman family archives
15. Audio recording, Newman family archive
16. University of Melbourne website
17. *Sydney's Century: A History*, Peter Spearritt, UNSW Press, 1999
18. All quotes in the book from Campbell Newman are from interviews with the author unless otherwise stated
19. Australian War Memorial records
20. Unless stated otherwise, quotes from Jocelyn Newman in this book are from *Partners*, edited by Anne Henderson and Ross Fitzgerald, HarperCollins, 1999
21. Unless stated otherwise, quotes from Kevin Newman in this book are from *Partners*, edited by Anne Henderson and Ross Fitzgerald, HarperCollins, 1999
22. *The Courier-Mail*, 2 March 2013
23. *The Courier-Mail*, 12 January 2015

24 *The Advocate*, 23 March 2012
25 *The Courier-Mail*, 11 July 1976
26 "The military, masculinity and the media: the 1983 Duntroon bastardisation scandal", Andrews J; Connor JM, 2013
27 Interview with the author
28 *The Age*, 18 March 2000
29 *The Australian*, 4 August 2012
30 *The Courier-Mail*, "Vital Interest Blog", 20 April 2007
31 *Australian Journal of Politics and History*, Volume 50, 2004
32 *Australian Financial Review*, 9 February 2004
33 *The Australian, 23* March 2011
34 *Benchmarking Brisbane* document, Brisbane City Council, 2013
35 *Australian Financial Review*, 1 November 2005
36 Campbell Newman personal archives
37 *The Courier-Mail*, 30 April 2006
38 ABC News, 14 June 2006
39 *The Australian*, 16 August 2006
40 *Australian Financial Review*, 16 June 2006
41 *The Courier*-Mail, 5 November 2006
42 Ibid.
43 Ibid.
44 *The Monthly*, December 2011
45 Queensland Parliament, Hansard, 30 October 2007
46 *Brisbane Times*, 7 March 2008
47 Campbell Newman personal archives
48 Australian Bureau of Statistics, Regional Population Growth, Australia, 2008-09
49 *Queensland Review* 18, University of Queensland Press, 2011
50 *Gold Coast Bulletin*, 28 July 2008
51 *Foundations for a New Era: The Road to Amalgamation*, Compiled by Ken Crooke for the Liberal National Party
52 Ibid.

53 "Severe Thunderstorms in Southeast Queensland 16- 20 November 2008", Bureau of Meteorology
54 ABC Radio, 17 November 2008
55 *Sydney Morning Herald*, 16 February 2009
56 *Sunshine Coast Daily*, 6 January 2010
57 Nick Bryant, *The Monthly*, December 2011
58 *The Courier-Mail*, 13 October 2010
59 ABC Radio, 14 October 2010
60 *The Courier-Mail*, 14 October 2010
61 ABC Radio, 13 January 2011
62 *The Australian*, 28 September 2011
63 Brisbane City Council media release, 23 November 2010
64 *The Courier-Mail*, 27 April 2012
65 Interview with the author
66 *The Monthly*, December 2011
67 *The Australian*, 26 March 2011
68 *The Courier-Mail*, 30 April 2014
69 *The Monthly*, December 2011
70 *The Courier-Mail*, 24 March 2012
71 Queensland Parliament, Hansard, 15 February 2012
72 Ibid.
73 Ibid.
74 *Sydney Morning Herald*, 13 March 2012
75 Queensland Parliament, Hansard, 15 February 2012
76 *The Courier-Mail*, 5 April 2012
77 Interview with the author
78 *The Courier-Mail*, 26 March 2012
79 Ministerial media release, 14 February 2010
80 *Australian Financial Review*, 29 April 2013
81 *Queensland Economy Watch* blog, 30 April 2013
82 Interview with the author

83 Interview with the author
84 ABC News, 12 August 2013
85 Interview with the author
86 4BC Radio, 24 October 2013
87 *The Courier-Mail*, 9 June 2014
88 ABC News, 1 August 2014
89 *Australian Financial Review*, 29 January 2015
90 Address to the UN General Assembly, 22 January 2013
91 *The Australian*, 18 July 2015
92 *The Newsroom*, HBO, Season 1, Episode 3, 2012
93 Interview with the author
94 *Standpoint Magazine*, 13 March 2015
95 *Sideshow: Dumbing Down Democracy*, Lindsay Tanner, Scribe, 2012
96 *The Newsroom*, HBO, Season 1, Episode 1, 2012
97 *The Drum*, ABC, 26 October 2014
98 *Queensland Public Service Workforce quick facts*, Public Service Commission, Queensland Government
99 Queensland Parliament, Hansard, 30 April 2013
100 *Sydney Morning Herald*, 22 November 2007
101 Policy paper: 2010 to 2015 Government policy: reoffending and rehabilitation, UK Department of Justice
102 *The Spectator*, 25 July 2015
103 *Lateline*, ABC, 22 July 2015
104 *The Mandarin*, 20 July 2014
105 Interview with the author
106 *Free To Choose*, Milton and Rose Friedman, 1980
107 *The Courier-Mail*, 8 April 2013
108 Interview with the author
109 *The Lucky Culture and the rise of an Australian ruling class*, Nick Cater, HarperCollins, 2013
110 *The Australian*, 26 May 2015

111 Ibid.
112 Interview with the author
113 *The Monthly*, May 2011
114 *The World Today*, ABC Radio, 22 July 2015
115 *Sydney Morning Herald*, 16 June 2015
116 *AM*, ABC Radio, 15 July 2015
117 *The Age*, 9 February 2015
118 Ibid.
119 *Capitalism and Freedom*, Milton Friedman, 1982

www.ingramcontent.com/pod-product-compliance
Lightning Source LLC
Chambersburg PA
CBHW052050230426
43671CB00011B/1861